Animating the Uncon

Animating the Unconscious
Desire, Sexuality and Animation

edited by Jayne Pilling

WALLFLOWER PRESS
LONDON & NEW YORK

A Wallflower Book
Published by
Columbia University Press
Publishers Since 1893
New York • Chichester, West Sussex
cup.columbia.edu

A complete CIP record is available from the Library of Congress

ISBN 978-0-231-16198-5 (cloth : alk. paper)
ISBN 978-0-231-16199-2 (pbk. : alk. paper)
ISBN 978-0-231-85014-8 (e-book)

Design by Elsa Mathern

Columbia University Press books are printed on permanent
and durable acid-free paper.
This book is printed on paper with recycled content.

Printed in the United States of America

c 10 9 8 7 6 5 4 3 2 1
p 10 9 8 7 6 5 4 3 2 1

Contents

MODES OF REALITY

Notes on Contributors

Karen Beckman is the Elliot and Roslyn Jaffe Associate Professor of Film Studies in the Department of the History of Art at the University of Pennsylvania. She is the author of *Vanishing Women: Magic, Film and Feminism* (2003) and *Crash: Cinema and the Politics of Speed and Stasis* (2010), the co-editor of *Still Moving: Between Cinema and Photography (2008)*, and is an editor of the journal *Grey Room*.

Olivier Cotte has worked in film and animation as a director, Flame artist and special effects director, and as a teacher. His publications include technical manuals, an international animation encyclopaedia *Il était une fois le dessin animé* (2001), *Georges Schwizgebel, animated paintings* (2004), *Secrets of Oscar-winning Animation* (2007), and the graphic novel, *Le futuriste* (drawings by Jules Stromboni) (2008).

Leslie Felperin is a film critic and independent international film editor for *Variety* and often appears on broadcast media. Previously, she was the editor of *Moving Pictures*, film critic for *The Big Issue*, deputy editor of *Sight and Sound*, and a part-time lecturer at Middlesex University in Film Studies.

Clare Kitson was commissioning editor for Animation for Channel 4 in the UK from 1989–99. She is the author of the acclaimed book *Yuri Norstein and Tale of Tales: An Animator's Journey* (2005) and recently published *British Animation: The Channel 4 Factor* (2008). She has also translated two animation books and a crime thriller.

Ruth Hayes is an award-winning animator producing in analog and digital media as well as flipbooks and other pre-cinema formats. She teaches at

Evergreen State College in Olympia, Washington. Her films *Reign of the Dog: A Re-Visionist History* (1994) and *Wanda* (1990) have screened and toured internationally. Her flipbooks are in the collections of the libraries of the Museum of Modern Art, UCLA and the University of Washington, among others. She earned her MFA in Experimental Animation from California Institute of the Arts in 1992.

Ruth Lingford is an award-winning filmmaker who is currently Professor of the Practice of Animation at Harvard University. She previously taught at the Royal College of Art, London and the National Film and Television School, UK. She is the recipient of a 2008–09 Harvard Film Study Center Fellowship for *Orgasm Project*, a short animated film using recorded interviews. Her filmography includes *What She Wants* (1994), *Death and the Mother* (1997), *Pleasures of War* (1998), U.N.K.L.E: *An Eye for an Eye* (2002) and *The Old Fools* (2002). Her latest film is a documentary about orgasm, *Little Deaths* (2010).

Michael O'Pray is Professor of Film in the School of Architecture and Visual Arts, University of East London. He has published widely on animation, avant-garde film and film aesthetics. He is the editor of *Andy Warhol: Film Factory* (1989), *Inside the Pleasure Dome: The Films of Kenneth Anger* (1990), *The British Avant-Garde Film: 1926–1995: An Anthology of Writings* (1996) and the author of *Avant-Garde Film: Forms, Themes and Passions* (2003), *Film, Form and Phantasy: Adrian Stokes and Film Aesthetics* (2004).

Simon Pummell has created more than a dozen animated and special effects films for television, winning numerous international awards, and film festival career retrospectives. He received a UK National Endowment for Science, Technology & Art Dream Time Fellowship 2005/06. He was a 2007–08 visiting lecturer at Dept. of VES Harvard University and a Harvard Film Study Center Fellow 2008–09. He is currently Course Director of the Lens-Based Digital Media Programme at the Willem de Kooning Academy, Rotterdam. His filmography includes *Surface Tension, The Secret Joy of Falling Angels* (1992), *The Temptation of Sainthood* (1993), *Rose Red* (1984), *Violent Blue; Butcher's Hook* (1995), *Queen: Made in Heaven* (1997), *Ray Gun Fun* (1998), *Blinded by Light* (2000), and *Bodysong* (2003), winner of a British Academy Award and a British Independent Film Award. He has also recently completed the feature-length film *Shock Head Soul* (2011).

Julie Roy is a film graduate of Montreal University and the author of several texts on women in animation. She has been a producer at the National Film

Board of Canada since April 2007. She produced *Hungu* by Nicolas Brault (2008) and *The Necktie* by Jean-François Lévesque (2008). Working closely with emerging filmmakers, she also co-produced *Rosa Rosa* by Félix Dufour-Laperrière and *Rains* by David Coquard-Dassault (both 2008). She is currently working on Patrick Bouchard's and Michèle Lemieux's upcoming films.

Introduction *by Jayne Pilling*

This book springs from a desire both to explore animation's unique ability to portray aspects of human experience and relationships that affect us all – desire and sexuality – in relation to a specific set of films that are significant in this respect, and to prompt further reflection on what this might tell us about the specificities of the medium of animation itself. As this is a rather large field of enquiry, it seems useful to first explain the book's genesis, and indicate its scope and focus.

Thinking around this topic was prompted, in part, from working on an international animation symposium, entitled 'Textures of Reality'[1] which set out to explore a range of inter-connected issues, as outlined in its programme introduction:

> Say 'texture' and 'animation' to many people and they'll probably assume you mean developments in new technologies, such as 'texture mapping'. But, as animation filmmaker Joan Ashworth asks: 'What is texture? What does it make us feel or communicate in a film? Mind and senses need to be stimulated to be able to feel a feeling as well as see it.' This event offers an exploration of aspects of the unique contribution that ani+mation can make to film. The textures of animated fantasy, conveying unconscious feelings, desires and sexuality. The texture of memory, as explored in Norstein's *Tale of Tales*, or the textural materiality of alternative universes, as in the films of the Brothers Quay. The texture of empathy, which animation can so mysteriously make us feel. The textures of bodily experience, from raw visceral sensation to highly mediated analysis. Textures of reality, from 'pure' drawn animation to fascinating hybrids of live-action and animation. Animation can make a unique contribution to the exploration and expression of states of mind, unconscious impulses, sexuality and sensory

experience. Unrestricted by the dictates of photographic realism and traditional narrative, animation can make such experience palpable via visual imagination, metaphor, metamorphosis and highly creative use of sound.'[2]

Some of these issues, particularly those around desire and sexuality, in turn arose from reflecting upon a number of developments in animation over the past twenty five years or so, and a felt need to revisit observations made much earlier, specifically about animation made by women filmmakers:

> The animated short film in particular can offer, quite literally, a blank page on which to draw forth an imaginative vision, and can also do so without words. Transcending the boundaries of language can also give voice to that which is hard to articulate, because so bound up with unconscious feelings, e.g. to desire and fantasy. Sex – as in sexuality, as well as in stereotyping – is also approached with an audacity, and authenticity, rarely found in animation made by men. (Pilling 1992: 6)

Curating film programmes about sexuality and desire for a women's animation festival, and a consequent frustration at being unable to include a number of important films made by men in this regard, prompted thoughts about how much has changed in animation since that paragraph was written. Although it seems clear that it was primarily women animation directors who opened up new terrain in terms of the subject matter animation could explore, sometimes from a specifically feminist or gender perspective, and often unafraid to explore personal experience, the emergence of a number of male filmmakers whose work deals with issues around desire and sexuality, and particularly in relation to masculinity, has shown that what had previously been considered very much the preserve of women filmmakers is now no longer necessarily so. And to that extent, it might be considered that animation can be said to have finally come of age.

This book does not essay any over-arching theoretical paradigm, nor an historical overview, of representations of desire and sexuality in animation generally, which is a much wider topic, but rather seeks to explore, in a variety of ways, why and how animation is so appropriate a medium for such subject matter, and how such films may work with viewers.

The focus is on short films, particularly those that are variously termed independent/personal/art/auteur animation. (Each of these terms is problematic,[3] but for the sake of brevity I will opt here for the use of 'auteur' or 'art' animation[4]). This is because such films can be much more adventurous, original and provocative in their approach, as they are made outside mainstream commercial production,[5] and because they are made for adult audiences. In relation to animation, the comparison between prose – or the novel – and poetry has often been made to point out how the short form animation film can allow for ellipsis, condensation, multiple associations and so on;[6] the format also allows for narratives that are neither linear nor rational – just as desire is rarely rational in how it plays out in human relationships – but which can communicate to powerful effect. It is surprising just how much of the complexities of human experience a short animation film can convey in the space of five, ten or fifteen minutes. Such length also makes such films very useful for discussion of these and related issues in the classroom.

The introduction to *A Reader in Animation Studies* (Pilling 1997: iv-xviii) pointed to a lack of widely-shared viewing experience around much auteur animation and the relative inaccessibility of many films, outside of very specialist circles, as an impediment to the development of analytical and theoretical work about it. It also argued for more sustained textual analysis of individual films as part of this project. Since then, distribution problems have all but disappeared, with DVD making both historically important and contemporary short films widely available, as well as the fact that so many animated shorts now find their way (legally or not), onto the Internet.[7] Since then, the field of animation studies has expanded enormously: both in terms of the number and scope of scholarly and more accessibly written publications available, and the number of degree courses, either purely academic or as a critical studies component in practice-based study, where students are required to engage with critical thinking about animation. Paul Wells, as one of the most prolific and influential of such scholars, has played a key role in developing theoretical and analytical approaches to animation, in both its multiple manifestations in the commercial mainstream *and* in the auteur short film, as has Maureen Furniss.[8] And whilst the problematics of inter-disciplinarity may continue to perpetuate a Babel-like configuration of discourses, it is an energising and exciting Babel's Tower to explore.

It therefore seems legitimate and, I hope, useful to explore in some detail a collection of key animation films that relate, both directly and more tangentially, to the subject of this book. Here, it is worth stressing that desire is taken not as necessarily or only ever sexual in meaning, but as it speaks to a more general human desire for connection, for relationship, for the push and pull of the urge to feel at one with another, yet retain a sense of identity. From humour to provocation, realism to surrealism, the intimate confessional to cutting-edge social comment, via fable, myth and metaphor, as well as acute and comic observation of human behaviour, the films discussed offer a range of varying perspectives on desire and sexuality in human relationships.

It is a commonplace to observe that animation can take far greater liberties than live-action, in form and subject matter, via its capacity to express the unfettered imagination. Indeed, Paul Wells has commented that 'animation has become a vehicle by which inarticulable emotions and experiences may be expressed' (1998: 184). It is worth considering, in the present context, albeit briefly and tentatively, some aspects of why and how this 'has become' the case.

A number of factors seem to have contributed to this development: a general shift in auteur animation culture that has seen a move from the universal to the more particular; the influence of feminism; the emergence of a specific form of animated documentary film; and much more frequent use of the human, rather than 'cartoony' or anthropomorphic, voice, i.e. one that confers a sense of a real person speaking of their own experience. With all due caution as to the dangers of making large generalisations (since more detailed analysis would require another book altogether) these developments are briefly outlined below.

First, there seems to have been an observable shift away from a long-standing and hitherto dominant tradition of 'universality' in the subject matter of short art animations to a focus on depictions of more individualised, specific and subjective experiences. However individual by virtue of a recognisable authorial signature (in visual style, thematic preoccupation or approach), however personal in terms of inspiration, and in some cases to whatever extent exhibiting a distinctive 'national' imprint, for a long time a great many of what are considered classics of art or auteur animation seemed predicated on a belief that animation was a universal language, able to convey universal truths; tall tales, parables and allegories, or observations of human behaviour often cast as such that used stories to point up more general conclusions. More recent approaches have begun to embrace the complexities and contradictions of the individual's lived experience. Or perhaps, to be more accurate, since such a 'universal' model continues to flourish – evidence of the vitality and appeal of that tradition – this shift might be attributed to the development of a generally much broader conception of what animation films can deal with, and the forms in which they might do so.

Historical context is important here, especially in regard to the experience of World War II and its effects on short film animation in the post-war era. In part because the period saw a relatively widespread development, primarily in Canada, Western Europe and the Eastern-bloc Communist countries,[9] of institutions that enabled the production of animation as an art form for adult audiences (in addition to cartoons made for children);[10] in part, and not unrelated to that production context, because animation was seen as an accessible and effective conduit for 'messages'.[11] This seemed all the more imperative after the horrors of World War II, and the continuing anxieties of the Cold War.[12] Of course, the reasons for state support for such forms of animation, and in particular the way it operated, has differed from country to country, and specific national contexts will impact upon the nature of films produced.

A proliferation of films about man's inhumanity to man, man's stupidity, the folly and futility of war, the grand existential dilemma, the alienations of modern and bureaucratic society, and the apparently endless comedy to be had from observations of the battle between the sexes seem characteristic of many animated shorts produced from that time. As Wells has observed, in a discussion of gender representation, 'if masculinity is not coded through role and function, it is often played out through the universalising concept of "everyman", in which male figures, or figures which are assumed to be male, become the symbolic embodiment of humankind' (1998: 196).

For a long time it was also more usual than not for such animated shorts to have no dialogue: again, for reasons of universality of address (and, in practical terms, facilitating exhibition at international festivals, and foreign sales). Indeed, the debate as to whether the use of voice somehow undermines animation's claims to being a distinctively different cinematic form, of universal address, one that is at its purest without the need for the spoken word, continues to this day.[13] Gianalberto Bendazzi, in an essay on the human voice in animation written in 1995, was still able to comment that voice-over or dialogue in animated auteur shorts was relatively unusual, and the films he cites as having such are clearly indicated as exceptions (1995: 309).

The influence of feminism, and a consequential opening up of opportunities in the 1970s and 1980s for women to emerge as animation filmmakers in their own right, and in increasing number, also had its impact on the subject matter of, and approach to, auteur animation. As this development has been discussed in detail elsewhere (see Pilling 1992: 5–7; Wells 1998:184–99), suffice it to reiterate here that in addition to a desire on the part of (some) women animators to challenge a male-dominated tradition of stereotypical gender representation, the films produced by women went far beyond what might be seen as merely 'women's issues', opening up a space for more personal stories and often more innovative formal approaches.

In this respect it is worth noting animation historian Richard Taylor's comment on the film *The Black Dog* (1987) by Alison de Vere, one of the first wave of women animators to break through to international prominence in the 1970s. '*The Black Dog* represents the same sort of advance in animation that *The Marriage of Figaro* was in opera... Just as the characters in *The Marriage of Figaro* were portrayed as more rounded, more subtle, more real than those in operas up to that time', so, he feels, at the time it was made this film represented 'the most complete rendering of a human being ever seen in animation' (cited in Kitson 2009: 86).

Whilst some might challenge this assertion, it points to the impact the film made through the way it drew upon the filmmaker's own experiences and dreams to combine them with mythological source material, in what was felt to be a very new approach.

The development of a particular form of animated documentary, based on recorded interviews with real people, may also have played a role in this shift to depictions of individual, specific experience. This type of film is now so relatively familiar it may be difficult to imagine how groundbreaking works such as Aardman Studio's *Animated Conversations* (1978), or more formally experimental work such as Marjut Rimmenin's *Some Protection* (1987) and Tim Webb's *A is for Autism* (1992), appeared at the time they were first seen. The animated documentary format, and audiences for it, have since spread worldwide; recent high-profile examples being Chris Landreth's Academy Award-winning short *Ryan* (2004) and the Israeli feature film, Ari Folman's *Waltz with Bashir* (2008), with the latter achieving international cinema release. However different all these films might be from one another – ranging from social realism to explorations of social issues, through psychological investigations to quirky and comedic interpretation – the format offers viewers opportunities to feel something of the lived experience of the films' protagonists in ways that differ significantly from those of live-action.[14] Critical work on this development has enabled a much wider platform for new thinking to emerge around the specificity of animation's contribution to the documentary format,[15] and in particular as to how it can depict subjective experience.

Most animated documentary is based on recordings of real people, the human voice, as opposed to voice-actors making 'cartoony' voices. As Michel Chion (1994) has observed, we process voice more quickly than we do images, and, in terms of films that employ complex formal strategies to explore equally complex aspects of experience, hearing the human voice offers viewers a handle with which to process imagery that may not be uniform or which may combine different techniques, that is, images we need time to make sense of. An unfolding narrative may employ non-linear sequences of images but the linearity of a voice-over can provide an anchor for the viewer.[16] Equally, the interplay between a human voice recounting recognisably human experiences and an animated *mise-en-scène* allows for the filmmaker's interpretative strategies.

To return to issues around desire and sexuality, more generally, it is clear that in the wider culture, at least in much of the Western hemisphere, the changing climate in both sexual politics and sexual mores has put discussion of such matters firmly in the public domain. Whether in the fine arts, or in such barometers of contemporary pop culture as TV reality and chat shows and YouTube, the confessional culture seems to have become all pervasive.[17]

What once may have seemed purely private and personal matters, hardly to be discussed outside the psychotherapeutic space or the academic arena, are now out there in the public domain.

How can animation really represent and make the viewer *feel* the complexities of human experience, in anything but a necessarily abstracted, because stylised, way? Bendazzi has pointed out that much animation is a form of pantomime (1995: 309). The broad gesture, exaggeration, caricature, abstraction remain the predominant stock in trade of animated depictions of the human figure. The astonishing variety of forms this can take is indeed often part of its appeal to the viewer. It is also often remarked that the one thing that animation cannot do, in comparison to live-action, is convey the extraordinary subtlety of facial expression (as testified by the endless discussion on the 'uncanny valley' effect in CGI and mo-cap animation, and the 'synthespian' debates).

Marcel Jean suggests the importance of physical presence in live-action films 'as a factor in audience identification with a film's protagonists'. He continues:

> More often than not, it is the actor's body that the camera films ... I'd even go so far as to say that the body is the main vehicle of emotion. I'm thinking here of the body as an object of sexual desire ... from Marilyn Monroe to Sharon Stone ... but also of the body as emblematic of illness, Tom Hanks as the AIDS sufferer in *Philadephia*, or of failure, Robert de Niro as Jake la Motta in *Raging Bull*... (1995: 77; author's translation)

Jean refers to how the physical tension that results when we observe a protagonist in peril can make viewers grip the edge of their seats, react physically to the impact of violence, remarking that such intensely felt gestures

> bear witness to a relationship to the film that goes beyond the emotional and intellectual to a more physical order ... The viewer's identification with characters that appear on screen, a crucial phenomenon in live-action cinema, happens very rarely in animation. It is as if this form of cinema lacks something with which to anchor the viewer's feelings. And that something is the body, the weight of the body, which acts precisely as an anchor, guaranteeing the stability of the means of emotional communication (1995: 80; author's translation).

He goes on to suggest this as a reason for animation often being considered, and undervalued, as merely a vehicle for amusement and harmless fantasy.[18]

The intent here is to explore a number of films that *do* affect and empathetically engage viewers in ways that live-action does not. To do so, this volume offers a combination of approaches. A selection of filmmakers who have produced some of the most significant work in this area are explored in monographic essays, and some of their films are also discussed, along with those of other filmmakers, in a set of more thematic essays, to provide a range of intersecting perspectives. To expand on these critical perspectives, some of those filmmakers were also invited to reflect on their own and on others' practice, via interview and/or in written form.

While some may feel one should observe D. H. Lawrence's admonition to 'Never trust the teller. Trust the tale', it is nonetheless revealing and instructive to know more about individual filmmakers' working processes, including retrospective thoughts on their films. It is also interesting to see to what extent a filmmakers' view or focus might differ from that of a critic who is a non-practitioner: particularly in terms of engagement with the formal strategies of the films. Interviews with filmmakers have been edited to offer, as far as is possible, a more structured and legible account than a full transcript of what are long and sometimes discursive discussions. In most cases, the interviews emphasise process, intention and meaning, rather than technical aspects, since there are already many books that cover such issues far more comprehensively. The few exceptions regarding technique have been largely dictated by my experience of teaching such films, when questions have been asked where material is not so easily available.

In much conventional live-action narrative, and animated features, sound and music are used to underscore drama, emotion and sometimes comedy, to cue viewer response, but usually in respect of the action and dialogue. In many of the animated films discussed here (and arguably in most art animations) sound has a far more creative role to play. The usual distinctions made between diegetic and non-diegetic sound seem far less clear cut.[19] As Daniel Goldmark has observed, whilst recent developments in musicology and film studies have begun exploring sound in far more detail,

> the application of film music terminology to cartoons, such dichotomies as source/underscore, diegetic/non-diegetic ... fail to take into account that music is far more integral to the construction of cartoons than of live-action films because the two forms are created in completely different ways. (2005: 4)

This speaks to the fact that the sound in animation is created from scratch (with the obvious exception of those films that use voice-over narration).[20] Sound can function as a narrative device in itself; hence the section on sound, music and voice, as it relates to the films under discussion.

The issues raised around bodily presence and audience response to a film's protagonists seem germane to these issues, and more generally to depictions of desire, and inform a number of the essays and interviews, in conjunction with detailed consideration of the role of voice and sound in viewer identification. Simon Pummell's film *The Secret Joy of Falling Angels* (1992) provides a useful focus for these, and other intersecting concerns. It is totally unlike a traditional cartoon, lacks a conventional narrative, and consequently presents difficulties of comprehension for some viewers, which may be clarified through discussion. At the same time, its self-conscious referencing of bodily representation in both Western art traditions and Disney cartoons opens up further perspectives on representations of the body in animation. The film's extraordinarily powerful soundtrack combines music with voice, the latter as both an instrument and an embodiment of its female character, to shape the emotional trajectory of a visual narrative that oscillates between figuration and abstraction. This is discussed and illustrated in detail, via an interview with its composer and a reproduction of the annotated 'film log' she kept during the process, providing a rare insight into a composer's thinking and developmental process.

Most art is produced through a combination, or negotiation, of unconscious impulses and conscious reflection, and filmmakers display differing degrees along this continuum of conscious design. In animation, much of the development process is more likely to be visual, hence the inclusion of such material. Extracts from notebooks and storyboards are one format. But in the case of a film such as *guy101* (2006), which has provoked many contradictory interpretations, and where storyboarding only began once the final script for voice-over was completed, an annotated draft, from around midway through the writing process, is included for comparison with the final version.

In paying close attention to the interaction of form and content, and exploring possible readings of films that are sometimes both formally and thematically dense and complex works, the aim is to provide both a 'way in' for the viewer, and a springboard for further reflection. Although it is more usual for a book about animation to be either purely critical/theoretical or much more practically oriented, i.e. for aspiring animators, I hope that this more kaleidoscopically explorative approach will prove useful.

Notes on the films discussed

It seemed to make sense for this discussion to opt for a range of films that have made an impact on the international scene over the last twenty years or so, as testified by the fact that most have won multiple international awards; that the films should be both interesting in themselves yet seem to speak to one another; are easily available on DVD;[21] and demonstrate a diversity of thematic and aesthetic approaches, styles and techniques. It is hoped that the reader/viewer will make comparisons with other films from their own view-ing experience. Although each film stands on its own, viewed together, or in thematic groupings, their concerns intersect in ways that are briefly outlined below.

Fairy-tale, myth and fable have been perennial sources for literature and the visual arts, and animated cartoons are no exception, both for family audi-ences (from Disney's feature film adaptations to 3D spoofs of such, as in the on-going *Shrek* series, and for adults (e.g. the overt sexualisation of many Tex Avery cartoons that play on familiar fairy-tale narratives). They also prove fruitful critical terrain for gender studies.[22] Independent filmmaker Vera Neubauer – a pioneer of feminist filmmaking (notwithstanding her refusal of the attribution), has often drawn on fairy-tale but also on myth as in her *Wheel of Life* (1999). This film and Alison de Vere's *The Black Dog* both draw on Biblical stories, mythology and fable; one in more literally earthy mode, being made in the sand on the beach and playing on notions of the 'natural order', the other in more fabular style, yet both examine the social construction of femininity.[23] While de Vere's film concentrates on the indi-vidual journey of an 'everywoman', Neubauer squares up to patriarchal and authoritarian Judeo-Christian traditions, with specific reference to the Old Testament stories in Genesis.

Masculinity is explored by Andreas Hykade in his trilogy of films *We Lived in Grass* (1995), *Ring of Fire* (2000) and *The Runt* (2006); the first two in particular dramatise how pressures to conform to ideas of what it is to 'be a man' can impact on a youth's capacity for both sexual and emotional connection with the opposite sex. Both films are also resonant with religious imagery, a reminder of the Judeo-Christian tradition's associations of sex with sin. *Ring of Fire* also draws upon the mythology and iconography of the cowboy figure, another powerful construct of masculinity.

Desire is sometimes characterised by ambivalence and ambiguity, and such emotions are conveyed, in very different ways, in the films of Michèle Cournoyer. Her film *The Hat* (2000) is shocking, for some, in its explora-tion of these issues, rather than simple condemnation: as Chris Robinson has noted, it is 'not just a film about sexual abuse. It is a film about addiction, love, seduction and emotional manipulation' (2005: 91). Ambivalence also seems to characterise many of the relationships depicted in Igor Kovalyov's films, which are fraught with unspoken tensions between men and women. Although rooted in deeply personal memories, they also speak more gener-ally of a sense of the essential unknowability of other people, and how this plays out against the desire for connection, partnership and family – a simul-taneous attraction to, and repulsion for, the ensnarements of domesticity and intimacy. The men and women in his films seem destined to experience intense emotions whose power ultimately isolates them from one another. The prevalence of characters who continually watch one another, through doors and windows in domestic spaces that both contain and exclude, builds a sense of a constantly frustrated desire to see so as to understand. Family secrets, the hidden erotic undercurrents that are sensed by the child in Igor Kovalyov's *Milch* (2005), are explored to very different purpose in Marjut Rimmenin and Christine Roche's *The Stain* (1991); in one respect, more directly, from a clearly socio-political and feminist perspective, yet in formal terms, via a complex and looping narrative structure. (The film also provides an interesting contrast to Cournoyer's *The Hat* in terms of its exploration of incest: the one raw and from inside subjectivity, the other more coolly analytical amidst its family melodrama.)

Pummell's *The Secret Joy of Falling Angels* plays out the co-existence of coercion, compulsion, complicity and violence in its vivid depiction of the sexual act, although to ultimately more celebratory effect, whilst Cournoyer's *A Feather Tale* (1992), which has provoked both metaphorical and allegorical interpretations, is particularly interesting for its interrogation of the ambiguities of submission and seduction, and the way sexual game-play enacts power relationships between individuals. The latter is taken to further extremes of sexual 'edgeplay' and the eroticism of anonymous sexual encounters in Ian Gouldstone's *guy101*, in a story that is recounted through the virtual world of a gay internet chatroom.

The mediated 'confessional' format of *guy101* is in marked contrast to that of Ruth Lingford's *What She Wants* (1994), where the filmmaker unflinchingly puts herself in the picture in a rawly immediate depiction of a woman's frustrations in the face of the omnipresent sexual imagery of consumer culture. First-person voice-over features, in confessional mode, in both Alys Hawkins' *Crying and Wanking* (2002), about the consequences of sexual honesty, and Ruth Hayes' *Wanda* (1981), a diary account of a woman's developing jealousy of her cat's more active sex-life. Startlingly frank first-person narrative is also a feature of *Never Like the First Time!* (2006), based on recorded interviews with four individuals of differing ages about their loss of virginity.

Desire and sex are often experienced as problematic simply because of the implications of surrendering the self to another, loss of control and vulnerability (again also explored in *guy101*). Marie Paccou's *Un Jour* (1997) is a poignant and deceptively simple account of a relationship that uses bodily metaphor to explore such emotions. In Kojiro Shishido's wordless *Naked Youth* (2006), the admission of homosexual desire for another, the risk and excitement of the act, is conveyed purely through the gaze of its main character. The structure of the film reflects an obsessive reworking of emotionally charged moments, and its protagonist's growing awareness of the nature of his desire, a tension that climaxes, literally, in the laying bare of the self.

Fear of female sexuality, and attempts to control it, are addressed in both Alys Hawkins' *Hysteria* (2001) and Craig Welch's *How Wings are Attached to the Backs of Angels* (1996). The former, via a very short and witty take on contradictions in the history of the medical establishment's attempt to understand women's bodies; the latter, via a complex narrative on which Tom Sorley comments 'the film re-examines the Icarus myth as a search not for freedom but for control. The film is an icy gothic sliver of masculinity in crisis. Unable to control the world beyond his doors, and confused by his own desires, the protagonist constructs his own prison' (1999: 48).

Humour is a traditional remedy for soul-searching and anxieties around sex. The 'battle of the sexes' is a subject that has informed a long tradition of animated short films, be they tired and misogynistic, didactic and feminist, or post-feminist (as in the films of Signe Baumane) or various points in between.

In this respect it is even-handedness that characterises the work of Michaela Pavlátová, an acute and extremely witty observer of human behaviour, whose films play on missed connections, and mutually frustrated romantic expectations between the sexes. The delusions engendered by seductive notions of the 'happy ever after' romance are wittily dissected in her film *Forever and Forever* (1998), whilst in *Repete* (1995) the characters' ultimate inability to free themselves from the ingrained patterns of behaviour in which they imprison themselves and their partners is driven by the furious energy of frustration. Disappointed desires and (literally) deflated expectations are explored with wry humour in Alison Snowden's *Second Class Mail* (1984), about a lonely middle-aged woman who sends away for a male blow-up doll: here the humour arises from traditional cartoon tropes of visual puns, incongruity and reversal of expectations. Almost as a commentary on the (very) short film format, its capacity for condensation and temporal ellipse, Monica Fosberg's *His Passionate Bride* (2004) both replicates and spoofs the depiction of desire as an emotional rollercoaster of excess, as in soap-opera, where lust for money, power and sex become inextricably linked.

Finally, although most of the films discussed hereafter are more focused on the dynamics of desire and sexuality in terms of how people relate to one another, animation's freedom to depict genitalia in ways neither live-action, including porn, could possibly achieve may result in films that are both humorous and fascinating in terms of different gender approaches. Does the gender of the filmmaker or the viewer make a difference? Is it in fact immediately clear whether the filmmaker is male or female? Reactions to the film may vary according to whether the film is seen by a mixed or same-sex audience. Do these questions matter? The baldly entitled *Penises* (2007) by Mario Addis, a series of anatomically probing mini-analyses of male sexuality, could also be said to be calculated to dispel all traces of penis envy, while Emily Mantell's *To Have and to Hold* (2003) offers a female perspective on the male organ that makes toyboys seem positively redundant. The film *Pink Komkommer* (1980) is an unsettlingly comic cartoon cornucopia of sexual fantasies, whose explicit depiction of sexual acts would simply be impossible to show in live-action, for two very obvious reasons: firstly, censorship, and secondly, because much of the sexual behaviours in it are fantastic in the sense of not being physically possible. Animator-director Marv Newland invited a number of his peers – internationally renowned animation filmmakers, both male and female – to create a visual interpretation of the exact same soundtrack – a sound 'performance' suggestive of sexual acts (moans, groans, gasps, bouncing, slurping, suction and accessories, such as whipcracks). Whilst most of the filmmakers opted to take this literally, some play against expectations of the sexually explicit. For a detailed examination of the way the film conjugates issues of transgression, gender and comedic animation tropes, plus a psychoanalytical reading, the reader is directed to Paul Wells' rigorous – and entertaining – analysis (1998: 174–8). The film is also an almost text-book example of how the same sounds can be put to different images, and still 'fit', though to radically different effect.[24]

Since the initial preparations for this volume, there have been significant developments in the critical thinking on this area of animation, including the 'Animating Realities' conference held in Edinburgh in June 2011. In addition, new publications are being prepared, including Thomas Martinelli's volume *Il Docomentario animato*, scheduled for release in 2012. It is hoped, therefore, that this collection assists in the exploration of this critical subject.

Work on this book was supported by Norwich University College of the Arts and Digital Media Exchange, and special thanks are due to Tom Simmons and Suzie Hanna there. I am also grateful to the students at the University of Pennsylvania for their lively and thought-provoking views, and to those teachers in both animation and gender studies who have provided useful feedback on using some of these films in the classroom. And I would like to thank all the filmmakers and other contributors for their time, patience and engagement with this project, and the wonderfully efficient, ever-supportive Gulsen Yanik for her practical help on this project.

Notes

1   This was organised by the present author, Joan Ashworth and Ruth Lingford in collaboration with the Royal College of Art, and held at the National Film Theatre, London on February 10-12

2004, and was accompanied by a series of film programmes.

2 National Film Theatre programme, February 2004.

3 'Independent' is often used to signal a film made outside of the commercial mainstream, but such films often depend on institutional or public funding for at least part of their production costs; 'personal' may suggest a narrowness of focus, or subject matter that is not in fact the case.

4 See Paul Wells' summary of definitions of auteurism (1998: 245–6).

5 Although, as Ruth Lingford, has pointed out in a communication to the author, 'cheaper production techniques and more flexible distribution methods mean that the world of feature films is now opening up to individual voices'.

6 See Wells' discussion of condensation, synecdoche, symbolism and metaphor (1998: 76–4).

7 Even if this may pose problems in terms of aesthetic analysis due to poor image and sound quality.

8 For examples see Wells 1998 and 2002, and Furniss 1998.

9 This is not to deny movements in the USA, the UPA Studios being a case in point, for its innovative aesthetic and determination to speak to adult audiences, and the 'limited animation' style they developed was highly influential internationally, particularly on the studio that became known as the 'Zagreb school' in the former Yugoslavia (see Amidi 2006: 182–7) and has continued to inspire successive generations of animators around the world. It should also be noted that although this book specifically focuses on short films largely made outside the commercial mainstream, this is not because the latter is without importance and interest, generally or to the topic at hand, nor that there is any implied hierarchy of artistic talent involved. Both the history of animation, and the practice of contemporary animation, clearly demonstrates the fruitful interaction, reciprocal influences of art/auteur animation and the mainstream, and reflects the working realities of many animators in both domains.

10 The emphasis here is on institutions; of course there had, been particularly in Europe, a great deal of art animation produced from the 1920s onward, as is well documented in most histories of animation, but these were often one-off films, dependent on grants, private money, small studios, whereas in what was then the USSR, and Eastern-bloc countries, it was state-funded studios that ensured continuity of production; in Canada, the National Film Board; on a lesser scale, in France, television, government funding and the Institut National de l'Audiovisuel; in the UK, the British Film Institute.

11 The National Film Board was initially established in order to produce films that contributed to government policies such as propaganda for the war effort and forging a national identity in a nation full of immigrants.

12 Although such 'support' was subject to censorship, it is still the case that in comparison to most other countries, this continuity of funding did enable a remarkable amount of freedom and innovation. The censorship problems encountered, for example by Yuri Norstein (see Kitson 2005) or Estonian filmmaker Priit Pärn (see Robinson 2006), did not finally prevent the films being made.

13 See also comments by Priit Pärn (Pilling 2001: 115).

14 For a dissenting view on this point, at least of the earlier Aardman series of Animated Conversations, see Jean 1995: 161–70.

15 See, in particular Ward 2008.

16 It is also sadly the case that the vogue for using recorded conversations may also result in films that are merely illustrated voicetracks, where voice is used to prop up or substitute for actual mise-en-scène.

17 See the discussions on 'confessional culture' at http://www.culturewars.org.uk/204-02/dec04.

htm.

18 However, Jean does then discuss the work of animation filmmakers he feels have succeeded in making meaningful representations of the human body, such as Norman McLaren and Pierre Hébert.

19 Similarly, traditional shot-by-shot analysis in live-action films becomes rather more problematic with many animation films, since it is often impossible to determine where 'a shot' starts and ends. For a more general consideration of the diegetic/non-diegetic use of sound, see the highly influential and provocative article, Stilwell 2007.

20 But even here, narration is not always recorded first; for example, Andreas Hykade's films *We Lived in Grass* (1995) and *Ring of Fire* (2000) where it was added after the picture and sound-effects film were completed.

21 Specifically and primarily, the three-volume collection *Desire & Sexuality: Animating the Unconscious* (2007) available from www.britishanimationawards.com.

22 See www.answers.com/topic/feminism-and-fairy-tales

23 For more detailed discussion, particularly relating to the use of mythology in de Vere's film, see Law 1997 and Kitson 2009: 83–6.

24 See also Michel Chion's account and comments on filmmaker and composer Marizio Kagel's experiments in playing fifteen different soundtracks to the same sequence of images, then playing the same soundtrack to fifteen different film sequences (1985: 117).

References

Amidi, A. (2006) *Cartoon Modern*. San Francisco: Chronicle.

Bendazzi, G. (1995) 'Alla ricerca della parola umana', in G. Bendazzi & G. Michelone (eds) *Coloriture: Voici, rumorii, musiche nel cinema d'animazine*. Bologna: Pendragon, 209–314.

Chion, M. (1985) *Le Son et le Cinéma*. Paris: Editions Cahiers du Cinéma.

_____ (1994) *Audio-Vision: Sound on Screen*, trans. C. Gorbman. New York: Columbia University Press.

Furniss, M. (1998) *Art in Motion: Animation Aesthetics*. London: John Libbey.

Goldmark, D. (2005) *Tunes for 'Toons: Music and the Hollywood Cartoon*. Berkeley: University of California Press.

Jean, M. (1995) *Le Langage des signes*. Montreal: Cinema Les 400 Coups.

Kitson, C. (2005) Yuri Norstein's *Tale of Tales: An Animator's Journey*. London, John Libbey.

_____ (2009) *British Animation: The Channel Four Factor*. London: Parliament Hill Publishing.

Law, S. (1997) 'Putting Themselves in the Pictures: Images of Women in the Work of Joanna Quinn, Candy Guard and Alison de Vere' in J. Pilling (ed.) *A Reader in Animation Studies*. London: John Libbey, 48–70.

Pilling, J. (1992) *Women in Animation: A Compendium*. London: British Film Institute.

_____ (ed.) (1997) *A Reader in Animation Studies*. London: John Libbey.

_____ (2001) *Animation: 2D and Beyond*. Crans-Près-Céligny: Rotovision.

Robinson, C. (2005) *Unsung Heroes of Animation*. London: John Libbey.

_____ (2006) *Estonian Animation: Between Genius and Utter Illiteracy*. London: John Libbey.

Stilwell, R. (2007) 'The Fantastical Gap Between Diegetic and Non-Diegetic Music', in D. Goldmark, L. Kramer and R. Leppert (eds) *Beyond the Soundtrack: Representing Music in Cinema*. Berkeley: University of California Press.

Sorley, T. (1999) '*How Wings are Attached to the Backs of Angels* (review)', in *Take One*, Summer, 48.

Stilwell, R., (2007) 'The Fantastical Gap between Diegetic and non-diegetic music' in Goldmark, D., Kramer, L., Leppert, R., (eds) *Beyond the Soundtrack: Representing Music in Cinema* (2007) Berkeley: University of California Press.

Ward, P. (2003) 'Animation Studies: Disciplinarity and Discursivity', in *Reconstruction*, 3, 2; online: http://.reconstruction.eserver.org/032/ward.htm

_____ (2008) 'Animated Realities: The Animated Film, Documentary, Realism', in *Reconstruction*, 8, 2; online: http://reconstruction.eserver.org/082/contents082.shtml

Wells, P. (1998) *Understanding Animation*. London & New York: Routledge.

_____ (2002) *Animation: Genre and Authorship*, London: Wallflower Press

Women:
From Outside In
and Inside Out

The Body and the Unconscious as Creative Elements in the Work of Michèle Cournoyer
by Julie Roy

For Michèle Cournoyer, a leading figure in contemporary animation cinema, the body is central to the aesthetic and thematic concerns of her work. Her films are characterised by their powers of evocation and surrealistic use of metamorphoses and collages. The films derive from a highly personal vision, marked by a quest for a female form of cinematic writing as part of an enterprise in autofiction. Thus she deals with male/female relationships, incest, ageing, and so on from a resolutely female point-of-view. Her work clearly reflects the influence of several modern art movements, especially surrealism, from which she draws certain practices (notably automatic writing), black humour and dreams.

Initially working as an experimental filmmaker (perceived by specialist critics as a neo-Dadaist), she made, on very low-budgets, *The Man and the Child/L'homme et l'enfant* (1969), *Alfredo* (1971), *Spaghettata* (1976, co-directed with Jacques Drouin), *La toccata* (1977), *Old Orchard Beach, P.Q.* (1982) and *Dolorosa* (1988). In 1988 she joined the National Film Board of Canada (NFB) where she made *A Feathered Tale/La Basse Cour* (1992) which attracted attention on the animation festival circuit. In 2000, her hard-hitting film *The Hat/Le Chapeau* was selected for the Cannes Film Festival's Critics' Week, and in 2004 *Accordion* was screened in competition there. She completed her most recent film, *Robes of War/Robe de Guerre*[1] in 2008.

In thematic terms, Michèle Cournoyer's filmography constitutes a pen-etrating meditation on women, their sexuality, fantasies, desires and anxieties. Her work speaks in a female voice, in turn strong, gentle, vulnerable, rebellious: the difficult emotional situation of being an occasional lover/mistress in *A Feathered Tale*, anxiety at witnessing the self ageing in *Dolorosa*, a female victim of incest in *The Hat*, the difficult process of grappling with and disengaging from an invasive virtual relationship in *Accordion*, a mother's despair in *Robes of War*. Young or ageing, lovers or warriors, dreamers or pro-active agents, coming to terms with romantic disenchantment and dependency, Cournoyer's women courageously move towards a growing sense of awareness (*Dolorosa*; *A Feathered Tale*), sharing a desire for emancipation (*La toccata*; *Old Orchard Beach, P.Q.*), for affirmation (*An Artist/Une artiste*, 1994) and a decision to abandon victimhood (*The Hat*; *Accordion*; *Robes of War*.)

Sexuality and desire

The dimensions of sexual desire, so important to Cournoyer, merit more detailed analysis. In fact, her filmography shows a clear development in the expression of aspects of sexual desire. The early films rely more on surrealistic symbolism whereas the more recent work displays increasingly explicit sexual imagery. In her last three films, *The Hat*, *Accordion* and *Robes of War*, the images are increasingly raw and crude, with more naked bodies and phallic symbols and hence a much more direct address.

In *The Hat*, for example, the protagonist is a naked erotic dancer who offers herself to male spectators. Several scenes in the film, such as that of the young girl astride a penis, are highly disturbing. Cournoyer pushes this audacity further, in terms of the simulated camera moves, notably when she practically draws the viewer into the sex of the dancer, who is supine and legs splayed, positioning the viewer as a captive voyeur.

In *Accordion*, a keyboard key is an erect penis. Elsewhere in the film, sex takes place between humanoid boxes endowed with sexual organs. From this progressively more explicit treatment of dimensions of desire, it can be inferred that for Cournoyer there is indeed a real correlation between the technique of animation and the fleeting, dazzling attack of shocking imagery. In her earlier films, Cournoyer used photographs (until *Old Orchard Beach, P.Q.*)

Images from *The Hat* (2000)
© National Film Board of Canada

then rotoscope (particularly in *A Feathered Tale*) before opting to draw in ink on paper from *The Hat* onwards. It is as if this choice of a more simple and direct technique offers her greater freedom and intensity. 'To achieve greater emotional intensity, there is a process that is like an exclusive relationship between myself, paper and ink, and the characters. That's how I get to the drawn line. Stripping it down to the bare line, to depict the nakedness of the dancer, her childhood and the hat in her body' (quoted in Roy 2006: 56).

But this move to drawn animation was not an entirely painless transition. Cournoyer had been working on *The Hat* for two years, using digital rotoscoping before taking on board a suggestion from her producer, Pierre Hébert, that she change media. 'She had been a painter. I suggested she should rediscover the paintbrush, and trust her savoir-faire and skills', comments Hébert in an interview.[2] He continues: 'She was happy with the results, but worried her animation was poor in comparison with that of other filmmakers at the studio. But given the nature of the film and the kind of drawings she was doing, there

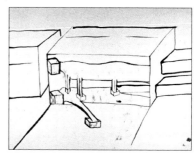

Images from *Accordion* (2004)
© National Film Board of Canada

was no way she was going to embark on fluid, Disney-style animation, it would not have been appropriate. Whether it was well or badly animated was simply a non-issue! She just had to shake off those fixed, traditional, ideas about animation.' In respect to Hébert, Cournoyer comments: 'He removed all my crutches. I had been working for two years. It was like a divorce. I had to start again. It was like a religion. It was in my mind all the time. I was raping my brushes and staining my drawings. It became more and more liberating. I worked in a primitive, direct communication with my devils and found the story in the execution' (quoted in Robinson 2005: 95). An astute analyst of Cournoyer's working methods, Hébert sums up her process since *The Hat*: 'After watching her make several films, I realised that she's seeking a kind of welling up of material, when she gives expression to something that is beyond her control. She is looking to create conditions in which this will happen. That's how I interpret her hesitations, the obsession with details which, objectively-speaking, don't seem that important, but are useful to her as a way of sorting things out, getting things right. What then emerges seems natural, obvious.'[3]

To further this reflection on the theme of desire, I asked Québecois psychiatrist Dr. Pierre Drapeau to offer an analytical reading of some of Cournoyer's works. He found the films *Old Orchard Beach, P.Q., A Feathered*

Tale and *Robes of War* particularly interesting. *Old Orchard Beach, P.Q.* takes a clearly ludic approach to its portrayal of desire. Sexuality is everywhere, and the message is easy to understand, since everything is illustrated literally. The setting is the seaside, where holidaymakers frolic on the beach. The protagonists' erotic fantasies are illustrated by amusing surrealist collages, with the hostage body as a recurrent motif. Sardine-women, two young mermaids, a beach umbrella-man, a lobster-seducer and so on. Using the analytical term 'object relation',[4] Drapeau points out the 'object' nature of the woman, who becomes, here, something to be consumed. The image of the sardine-women, packed into their tin container, is a good illustration of this concept. Here the female is displayed as passive and manipulated. At the end, we see an ambiguous sex scene between a woman and a lifeguard who turns into a lobster: although this graphic collage might be superficially amusing, it leaves the viewer with an uneasy aftertaste. One could see it as the expression of emotionally cold sexuality, animal and primitive, which seems to give the woman pleasure. Drapeau remarks: 'One may take pleasure in a sado-masochist relationship. This is far removed from a healthy "object relation" where pleasure is more transparent. Here the animalistic predominates.'[5]

In *A Feathered Tale*, the theme of dependency is confronted directly, and here desire is both unhealthy and disturbing. In response to a phone call in the middle of the night, a woman takes a taxi to go and see her lover. The car

Image from *Old Orchard Beach, P.Q.* (1982) © Michèle Cournoyer

Image from *A Feathered Tale* (1992) © National Film Board of Canada

rides over the same woman's naked, supine body. She is delivered to the man in a box, from which she emerges in the form of a woman-chicken, ready for plucking. With body language that suggests domination and voracious passion, the man removes his lover's plumage and feeds on her flesh. In filmed interviews, Cournoyer talks of the autobiographical nature of this dependent relationship, describing it as 'toxic'.[6] She summarises the film as follows: 'She becomes a taxi. She closes her eyes but turns on the headlights to see what's going to happen. She knows what's going to happen. And she is determined to play it out to the end, in order to be able to finish it. This is the last time she's going to get hurt.'[7]

Drapeau sees in the film the tragedy of a couple playing out a particular form of human relationship that is essentially sado-masochistic. Again, with recourse to the term 'object relation', he emphasises the notion of control that characterises this kind of relationship. The woman is not considered as a subject, but rather as an object whose needs are secondary: she is an animal (here, a chicken) whom the man dominates, controls, keeps to hand and eats (literally crunching the plucked bird). The psychoanalyst reads this image as an expression of the oral and anal phases as defined by Freud, with orality illustrated by the man who devours his chick and anality in the control he exercises over the woman.

Cournoyer's most recent work, *Robes of War*, is also extremely interesting from a psychoanalytical point-of-view and in relation to Cournoyer's

Image from *Robes of War* (2008)
© National Film Board of Canada

previous work. The film takes the standpoint of a veiled female suicide bomber. In mourning for her dead son, a mother takes up arms and goes to war. One particularly hard-hitting scene encapsulates the spirit of the film well. The mother, heading an army of veiled women, gradually turns into a woman-tank. The veiled women metamorphose into the vehicle's caterpillar tyres. A phallus rises in the centre, the tank tyres seem to become the knees of the woman-tank. Bandages appear on her legs whilst the phallic canon spits out its fire. In *Robes of War* desire takes the form of archaic fantasies. Pierre Drapeau associates the female character with the image of the primitive mother who he describes as follows:

> In the film there is a truly striking image: an archaic, phallic mother with an omnipotent penis, in total control. She has a deadly aspect.[8] We recall that at the beginning of the film, the child has two images of his mother: the good mother, arousing pleasant memories, and the terrifying mother, to whom he attributes his suffering and grief. When he has colic, the image he has of his mother is that of a bad mother, who makes him suffer. One often encounters psychotics who produce images of primitive mothers that are not dissimilar to this totally destructive woman. It is as if Michèle Cournoyer is dramatising certain primitive fantasies that occur in early development.[9]

This primitive mother is thus the dominating, deadly and persecuting female. From Drapeau's perspective, Cournoyer has delved deeper into her unconscious than in the preceding films to arrive at these primitive images. And in this he sees an interesting trajectory, with Michèle Cournoyer offering an increasingly in-depth analysis of human nature.

> In Cournoyer's films, the female is usually treated as an object. It is as if, in the development of her body of work, she has delved more deeply into her unconscious, to uncover this destructive, phallic image. It is a trajectory that appears as an analysis of human nature in its fundamental components. If one takes *Old Orchard Beach, P.Q.*, we are at an Oedipal level, we see seductive women, women who are objects to be consumed. But we are in the realm of a simplistic conception of sexuality. With *A Feathered Tale*, it is a more primitive sexual realm, dominated by orality (eating) and anality (the control of the Other). Then, with *Robes of War*, we are no longer in the sexual, but in the realm of archaic anxieties of persecution, of destruction. It's very interesting. This is something that occurs in the trajectory of several artists: the more they delve into their

unconscious, without necessarily intending to, the closer they get to primitive organising fantasies.[10]

Cournoyer compares the female characters in *The Hat* and *Robes of War* as follows:

> In both films the women have been damaged and this leads to self-destruction. The dancer in *The Hat* is a victim of incest, the veiled woman weeps for the dead child in her arms. Yet there is a difference in the fact that the woman in *Robes of War* never opens her eyes. She prays. The war is happening inside her, within her body and her heart.[11]

The ambiguity of desire and pleasure

Michèle Cournoyer's use of metamorphosis is the basis for powerfully effective ellipses that concertina different places, temporalities and levels of reality. But it is equally clear that these metamorphoses might also be at the root of the ambiguity of her films, confronting the viewer with a dilemma of interpretation: what is the meaning of what I have just seen? What exactly did I see? As if Cournoyer was juggling different ideas, prioritising some but leaving others on the table, relativising, complicating her position to an extreme, reinterpreting each image, each assertion through a new image, a new assertion, as if she was leaving within the film diverse hypotheses of representation, and hence of interpretation. In *The Hat*, for example, the dancer is naked, on all fours, in front of the customers at the bar. In the brief moment of a single image, Cournoyer reverses the position of the dancer, draws her breasts and sex in the very same place where her back and buttocks had been a moment before, as if to graphically inscribe within the film an option, a possible idea, discarded along the way. Similarly, the rapid succession of metamorphoses conjugates a series of sometimes contradictory or generally considered incompatible emotions in a single flood of images. Thus the denunciation of incest, central to *The Hat*, does not exclude the presence of several levels of guilty and unacceptable pleasures: pleasure on the part of the victim of sexual abuse, Cournoyer's pleasure in creating these images, the viewer's pleasure in these same images.

However disturbing this idea might be, the victim's pleasure is a locus of ambivalence experienced by some victims of sexual abuse. Child psychiatrist Drapeau explains this notion of pleasure through the confusion that exists between the adult's perspective and that of a child. A little girl may take pleasure in her father's caresses, or in displaying herself to attract the attention of a father or other male figure. Such contact may be enjoyable for the child who does not realise any apparently sexual connotation; which is different from the adult perspective. In the film, the girl seems to have moments of happiness, as when she dances in her ballet dress. And the music that accompanies these images has nothing threatening about it. However, as the film demonstrates so well, the situation turns to nightmare.

The second source of the film's pleasure is that experienced by Cournoyer in drawing. It is clear that an artist derives satisfaction from the actual execution of her art, in which she finds self-expression and fulfilment. Finally, there is the viewer, who, despite the rebarbative nature of the subject-matter, experiences a certain pleasure at the beauty of these moving images, at the virtuosity of the series of metamorphoses. But that is precisely wherein lies the ambiguity and sense of discomfort. How can one admit to the enjoyment of images that are so raw and explicit, however beautiful they might be, as they articulate a message that is so harsh and disturbing, especially if one believes that through or behind the denunciation one has perceived fleeting pleasure on the part of the victim?

The influence of surrealism

> ... in the beginning, in my head, it's realistic, then it becomes surrealistic. I draw the movement and the transformations happen. The images develop through intuition. (Cournoyer, in Grugeau 2000: 39)

Very early on, while still a student, Cournoyer was strongly drawn to surrealist artists such as René Magritte, Salvador Dalí, Marcel Duchamp, Man Ray, amongst others, and became fascinated by the films of Luis Buñuel and Jean Cocteau. She felt a natural sense of identification with this creative spirit, as wild as it was free, and this influence is apparent in various ways in her films. Thus she works through free association, be that in the use of collage or a form of automatic writing, or of metaphor and metamorphosis. She attributes real significance to the dreams and visions that are very often the source of her films. Finally, as is often the case in surrealist art, her short films are characterised by the predominance of desire and the presence of black humour.

Observing Cournoyer's creative process, it is clear that it constitutes a form of writing. Indeed, it is during the writing process, i.e. the actual act of drawing, that the subject and narrative develop and metamorphoses appear. This desire to prioritise a form of automatic writing influenced, to some extent, Cournoyer's use of ink-drawing on paper since *The Hat.* As we have seen, this simple and direct technique allows her to eliminate any substantive technological mediation, any artifice, in order to concentrate on her own emotions and to let them emerge spontaneously.

Thus Cournoyer's working methods are quite unique in comparison with animation's usual procedures. It is noticeable that most of the films she has made at the NFB since 1989 were made without a storyboard. On the making of *The Hat*, she has said: 'I never knew what was going to happen. I was communicating with my unconscious, the demons, angels and everything else inside me. I was in a state of need. It was utterly compulsive.'[12]

This importance accorded to the raw material of the unconscious is expressed in her process. She animates an initial fragment, then a second, a third, and so on. These fragments are then stuck on the wall in her studio. A storyboard gradually develops. A few months later, she meets with the editor of the film. From a picture-scenario pinned on the board, Cournoyer and the editor move the fragments around, threading the series of metamorphoses together. It is in the process of taking these fragments, each of which has its own meaning, and linking them together that an emotion, a guiding line, maybe even a narrative, emerges. Cournoyer then returns to her drawing board to fill in gaps between sequences of metamorphoses. At that point the narrative might take on a completely different direction. So a large part of the editing of the film happens along the way, without the editor actually having to make any cuts: in the end, the sequence of metamorphoses gives the impression that the film is a long, unbroken single shot.

The body

For Michèle Cournoyer, the body is the central pivot around which all artistic decisions are articulated. The choice of *mise-en-scène* (the body is the stage on which all the action takes place), the sensuality of her films (in both picture and soundtrack), the choice of animation techniques, the physical implication of the artist in the creative process are all elements that allow for a real, literal inscribing of the body into her work.

In *A Feathered Tale*, the taxi travels, literally, over the woman's body to take her to her lover. It is also the woman's body that undergoes the transformation into a chicken, and it is in this form that the power game between her and the man plays out. In *The Hat* the body is the source of all the metamorphoses, it is through the body that these visceral and powerful sensations are heightened, and are experienced both by the dancer and the viewer. Underscoring the film's theme, the protagonist's body is the object of distortion: stained, dislocated, deformed, smeared, dismembered, pummelled. Cournoyer expresses clearly how she felt as she was drawing this body: 'I needed to dirty the drawings, spatter them, make them suffer, to reflect the experience of the character of the little girl' (quoted Grugeau 2000: 39).

A sensory cinema

Picture, sound and music in Michèle Cournoyer's films all constantly reference the senses (particularly sight, hearing and touch), underscoring the visceral nature of her work. One might even see this as a form of 'tactilism', an expression associated with the work of the Czech filmmaker Jan Švankmajer (see Jodoin-Keaton 2000: 35). We know the latter has worked with a wide range of tactile materials (clay, marionettes, objects showing the wearing effect of time, crumpled paper, cartons) and his tactile sensibility is manifest in the continual foregrounding of textures.

With Cournoyer, this 'tactilism' manifests itself in several ways, from the marked presence of smudges in the execution of the drawings to the use of non-diegetic sound that foregrounds its materiality; in the number of elements, both plastic (feathers and eggshells in *A Feathered Tale*) and thematic (eyes, hands) that relate to the senses and to materiality. The presence of eyes is highly significant. It is striking that in over half her films, right from the opening shots, Cournoyer shows us a face – and thus a gaze – or just the eyes.[13] Sometimes the eyes are closed, which then open as if looking directly at the viewer (*A Feathered Tale*), sometimes they remain closed (*Accordion*, *Robes of War*) and in other cases they are open but close an instant later (*The Hat*, *An Artist*). There are several possible interpretations to the significance attributed to the eyes: it may reflect Cournoyer's desire to engage the viewer's scopic drive, by offering indecent images that penetrate the private selves of its characters. It may also be a clear signal on Cournoyer's part, a conscious projection of her project of autofiction. In a way, it is she herself who gazes out, and engages the viewer, as if to say: look, this is my story.

The Hat foregrounds those parts of the body related to the senses: hands, eyes, ears, mouth, genitals, and so on. The film opens with a close-up of the dancer's hands on her belly.[14] Seconds later, the camera moves into the woman's ear, a portal into her memories. Further on, in front of the bar's customers, the dancer's body assumes a kind of Cubist form when a large mouth replaces the buttocks, and eyes appear in her back around the shoulders. This is immediately followed by images of several eyes that invade the body's outline before entering the woman's sex; then several hands, followed by arms grab at the naked body. Facing these men, the woman is the object of desire, they watch her, touch her, lick her. Just a few drawings later, an enormous tongue caresses the young girl between her legs.

This constant recourse to sensory imagery combined with a *musique concrète* soundtrack that also plays on the senses – particularly in the *The Hat* and *Accordion* – contribute a tactile dimension to what appears on screen by evoking its materiality. Québecois musician Jean Derome, who worked on both these films, used wrenchingly painful sounds and broken glass to accompany the soiled and sullied body of the young girl. Just as he chose to include gasping and moaning during the hat-phallus masturbation scene (the man's hand holding the child's hand).

A filmmaker working with auto-fiction, the unconscious, the body... Over a forty-year period, Michèle Cournoyer has developed a significant body of work and moved forward in her artistic project with astonishing coherence. Drawing from personal experience, she embarks on the making of her films in an intuitive manner, not knowing in advance where the adventure will take her. Her personal quest affects her films, in the same way that her creative process is part of her work of psychic investigation. An impassioned, honest, tormented woman, we cannot but admire the audacity she has demonstrated in confronting her own demons and sharing them on the big screen.

(Translation by Jayne Pilling)

Notes

1   As the National Film Board of Canada is officially bi-lingual, films produced there usually have both a French and English title: subsequently in this article the English titles are used.
2   Interview by the author with Pierre Hébert, the film's producer, April 20, 2008.
3   Ibid.
4   The term 'object relation' is often used in contemporary psychoanalysis to designate 'the subject's mode of relation to his world; this relationship which is the complex and total outcome of a particular organisation of the personality, of an apprehension of objects that is to some extent or other phantasised, and of certain special types of defence (Laplanche & Pontalis 1988: 277).
5   Dr. Pierre Drapeau, interviewed by Julie Roy, Spring 2008.
6   *Love in the Cold* (1994); documentary directed by Donald McWilliams and Isabelle Turcotte, produced by the National Film Board of Canada.
7   Ibid.
8   In psychoanalytical terminology, the 'deathly mother'.
9   Dr. Pierre Drapeau, interviewed by Julie Roy, Spring 2008.
10 Ibid.
11 Press book for *Robes of War*.
12 Filmed interview with Michèle Cournoyer, made at the NFB in 2001 and shown as part of a P.A.U. Education (a private organisation providing training and education about children's rights) event in Barcelona, to which Cournoyer was invited to participate in a discussion about sexual abuse.
13 This is the case in seven of the twelve films: *Alfredo*, *A Feathered Tale*, *An Artist*, *The Hat*, *Accordion*, the title sequence for the Festival du Nouveau Cinéma and *Robes of War*.
14 The film *Accordion* also opens with an image of hands.

References

Grugeau, G. (2000) 'La mise à nu', in *24 images*, 102, 38–42.

Jodoin-Keaton, C. (2000) *Le cinéma de Jan Švankmajer: un surréalisme animé*, Montréal: Les 400 coups.

Laplanche, J. and J. B. Pontalis (1988) *The Language of Psychoanlysis*, trans. D. Nicholson-Smith. London: H. Karna.

Robinson, C. (2005) 'Where Memories Breathe: Underneath le Chapeau of Michèle Cournoyer', in C. Robinson, *Unsung Heroes of Animation*. London: John Libbey.

Roy, J. (2006) 'Entretien avec Michèle Cournoyer, "De la représentation à l'évocation du vivant"', in Jean, M. (ed.) *Quand l'animation rencontre le vivant*. Montréal: Les 400 coups.

Michèle Cournoyer:
Comments on making *The Hat*[1]

Research and development: I went to see exotic dancers, I took photos, and photos of people in bars. I had all these images, backgrounds. I had other research: I interviewed a lot of girls, and an adult, who had been abused. And then... what do I do with all this material? Someone who encouraged me told me not to censor myself; so I just started drawing in bed by myself. I have to go inside myself just to do the essential; because it is an intimate story. I suddenly just put all that information aside, and everything I knew, and started anew, working with just what's left in my subconscious and just start to draw, just draw and draw and see what comes. With the pen, I made my drawings suffer, with the character, I was breaking my pens. When there was violence, I was very hard with my brushes, I was wearing them out. With the drawings: it's a little bit like gathering children together and saying 'now play together'. They start organically linking up with each other. I photocopy and put them on the wall and move them around, that's how I find the story.

There are images that come from my own memories: a female cousin who became an exotic dancer... I had taken photos of her when she was little as a ballet dancer – that's how it is with me, things that have remained with me. For example, with the staircase and the hat: when I started, the man is going upstairs. In a sense, as a visual image it relates to a memory of my father. I was in a convent, my father was often away, we never saw him. Once he came in the evening to see me, with lots of presents, but the nuns didn't want him to come up, but they couldn't stop him, they said he was jumping up the stairs, so that's where the staircase came from. When I woke up in the morning I found he had left me a book, a storybook, I know he had been there, he was wearing a hat, so that's where that comes from.

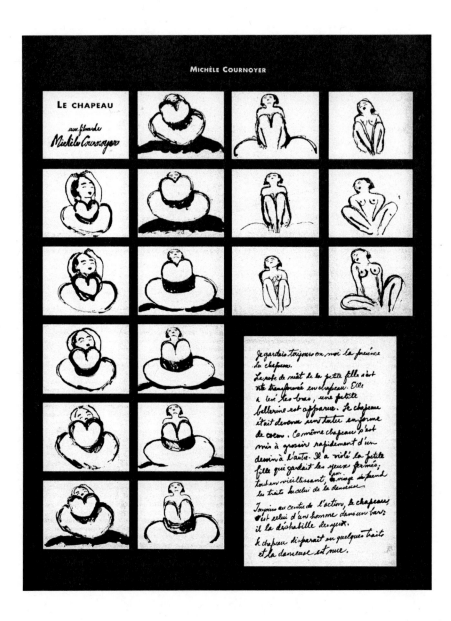

I started drawing a man going up the stairs, I had taken photos, so then I thought I would turn it around, it would be better if the hat comes this way so then I could use it ... so I did about thirty versions of the staircases, and the producer was coming in and telling me 'I've seen that already' and I'd reply, 'but I have a new version'. I was obsessed, it was so difficult a subject, I kept repeating the staircase. It was too difficult to arrive at the top of the stairs. My analyst was always telling me you are afraid, telling me to stop being afraid. I had to find a way to get up to the top of the stairs and open the door. Finally it is the hat that is coming up the stairs. Once it was done and shot, and I threw it out; it had been so important for me, then afterwards I didn't want to see – as though it was a crutch I needed then I could throw it away. I wanted to get rid of it. I threw away the sequence and Martin picked it out of the garbage. Once I'd got it OK I said it was not good and if Martin had not picked it up it would not be in the film.

Metamorphoses: It's about getting to know your shapes to do transitions ... do the ones that recur. Before going to bed, just prepare drawings for the next morning, just doing little drawings ... then getting up in the morning, I didn't use them ... sometimes I was just checking if there were other options. I was repeating myself, sometimes it just works: I'd do two hundred drawings and it just works.

Music: When the film was finished Jean Derome had two months to do it. I bought a CD of Bernard Herrmann music, I wanted something like the violin in *The Birds*; in *A Feathered Tale* there is also a violin. He suggested rock 'n' roll for the exotic dancer. When the little girl becomes a dancer in a vase, there's almost the sound of a rape, abuse. He broke up childrens' toys, he had a table full of toys, the sound of them. Some are animal sounds, his wife did the voice of the little girl. And at the beginning he also sang a lullaby, as he goes up the stairs and undresses the girl, peels back the cover, the father seems a very nice father, we feel a sense of closeness with him, singing such a nice lullaby; then there's the scream when the woman is de-structured. The scream is not a human sound, more like a sound from an object in a tunnel. It was a very strong sound, far more realistic than a real female sound.

Note

1   Compiled from an interview with the editor, Montreal, April 19, 2008.

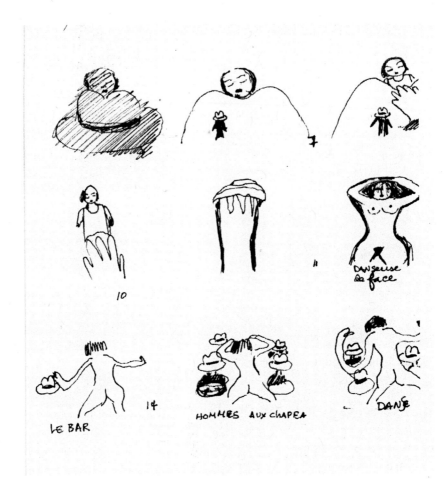

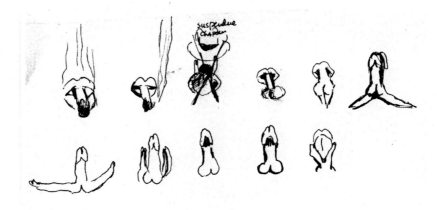

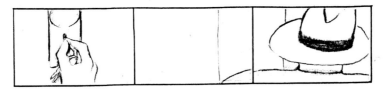

0. **LE PÈRE.** Tard dans la nuit, une main cherche maladroitement à mettre une clef dans une serrure. Un homme, vêtu d'un habit et d'un chapeau, entre chez lui,

1. **ESCALIER.** Il monte les marches d'un escalier. Il s'appuie en glissant une main sur la rampe. Il titube légèrement. L'homme longe le corridor en frôlant le mur.

2. **LA MÈRE.** L'homme s'arrête devant une porte entr'ouverte. Il voit sa femme qui dort paisiblement. Il ferme la porte, doucement.

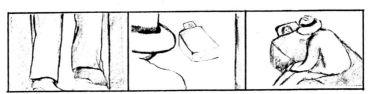

3. **SA PETITE FILLE.** Sur la pointe des pieds, papa entre dans la chambre de sa petite fille de 5 ans. Il s'approche. Il reste immobile un moment devant l'enfant qui dort. Il s'asseoit sur le bord du petit lit.

4. **SANS VISAGE.** Le souffle court, le père se penche sur le beau visage plongé dans le sommeil. La petite fille plisse des yeux et les ouvre avec surprise. Le père lui met la main sur la bouche. Il lui chuchotte dans l'oreille. La peur efface le petit visage. Un signe de plastre se dessine à la place du visage, puis disparaît.

5. **LE CORPS DE SA FILLE.** Le père descend la couverture. La robe de nuit disparaît. Il regarde le corps de sa fille.

6. **LE VIOL..** La main viole. Le chapeau se penche et cache le viol.

7. **LA BLESSURE.** Le plis du chapeau devient la blessure. La blessure saigne entre les deux jambes écartées. Le corps de la petite fille nue gît, inerte.

8. **LA DOUCHE.** Les gouttes de sang deviennent des gouttes d'eau d'une pomme de douche, qui coule à grands jets. L'eau pleure comme des larmes sur les cheveux rouges d'une jeune fille de 16 ans. L'eau veut nettoyer. Mais le chapeau revient.

9. **LE CHAPEAU.** La fille se touche le cou. Elle ressent le chapeau de son père, près de son cou. Elle réentend ses chuchottements dans son oreille. Le chapeau la couvre comme un vêtement et la déshabille.

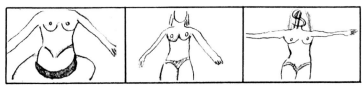

10. LE BAR. Elle est nue, sans visage, Sa tête devient un signe de piastre qui disparaît.
Les phares s'allument. Elle danse comme un automate sur la scène d'un bar.

11. LES HOMMES. Elle regarde les hommes qui la regardent. Pour un moment, elle les
imagine tous avec le chapeau de son père. Bruits de verres, murmures et musique.

Spit

12. UN CLIENT. Un homme est assis à une table, il boit et regarde le corps de la
danseuse. Il balance une jambe.

13. FLASH BACK. La danseuse se voit petite fille assise à cheval sur la jambe de son
père. Il la fait monter et descendre. La main de papa devient la main du client, une
cigarette entre ses doigts. L'épaisse fumée cache la scène.

14. CIGARETTE. Le client fume une cigarette. Il baisse sa main. La cigarette grille.

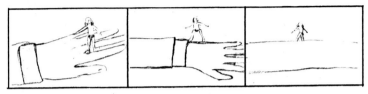

15. **FLASH BACK.** Droite entre les deux gros doigts du père, la cigarette prend la forme de la petite fille. Elle s'avance en dansant avec innocence sur la grosse main, tout au long du bras de papa.

16. **LA SCÈNE.** Le bras du père devient la scène du bar. La petite fille redevient danseuse. Elle danse et pense. Sa culotte noire devient le ruban puis le chapeau de son père.

17 **FLASH BACK.** La petite fille s'agrippe sur le rebord du grand chapeau. Elle est suspendue devant le visage de son père.

18. **FLASH BACK.** Elle tombe dans le vide en glissant sur la cravatte rayée, puis assise sur la cuisse de papa. La grosse main s'avance vers elle.

19. **LE SOUVENIR.** La main du client posée sur la danseuse lui rappelle le toucher de son père. La tête du client se couvre d'un chapeau. Le chapeau grossit. Elle le repousse.

20. **LE CRI**. Elle se met à crier avec sa bouche qui réapparaît. (chant). Elle bascule.

21. **LE CHAPEAU**. Elle tombe à l'intérieur de l'immense chapeau vide. L'image du père a disparu.

22. **L'AIDE**. Des mains de femmes en blanc la raniment. Ses yeux réapparaissent. Ses larmes coulent comme une fontaine.

23. **LE COEUR, LE CORPS, LA TÊTE**. Son coeur reprend sa place. Il bat. Les traits de son visage se complètent. Elle se réapproprie son corps.

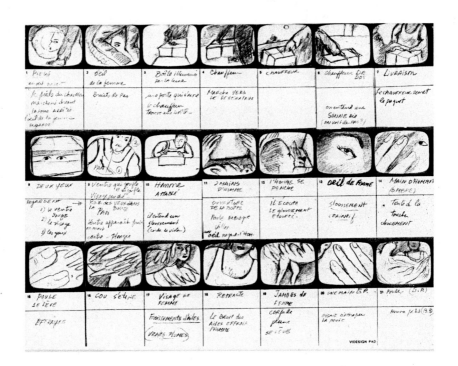

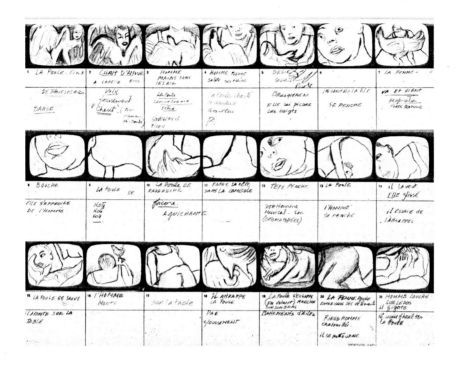

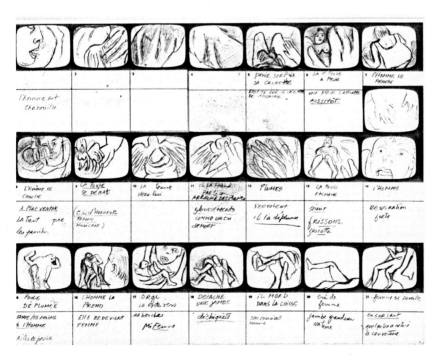

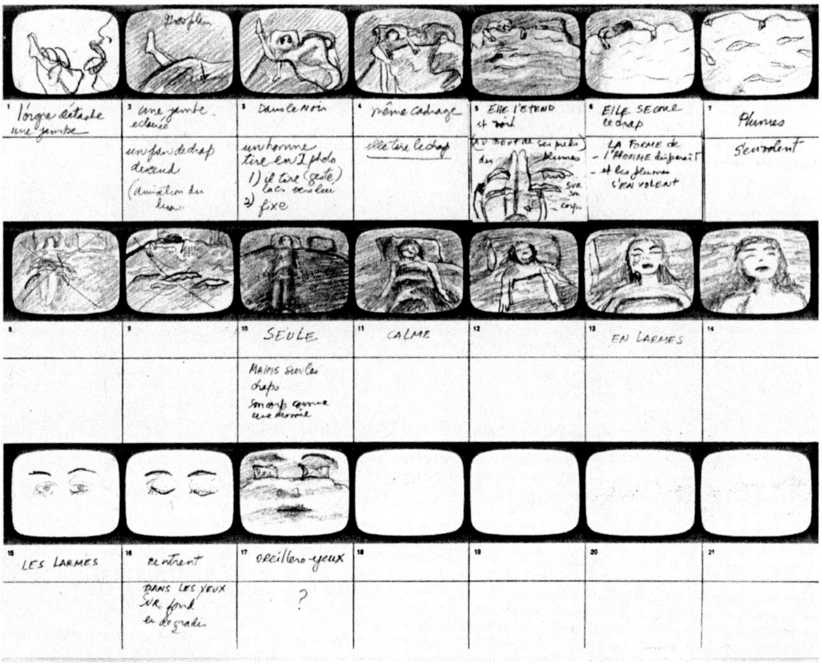
SEULE
CALME
EN LARMES
LES LARMES
DANS LES YEUX
?

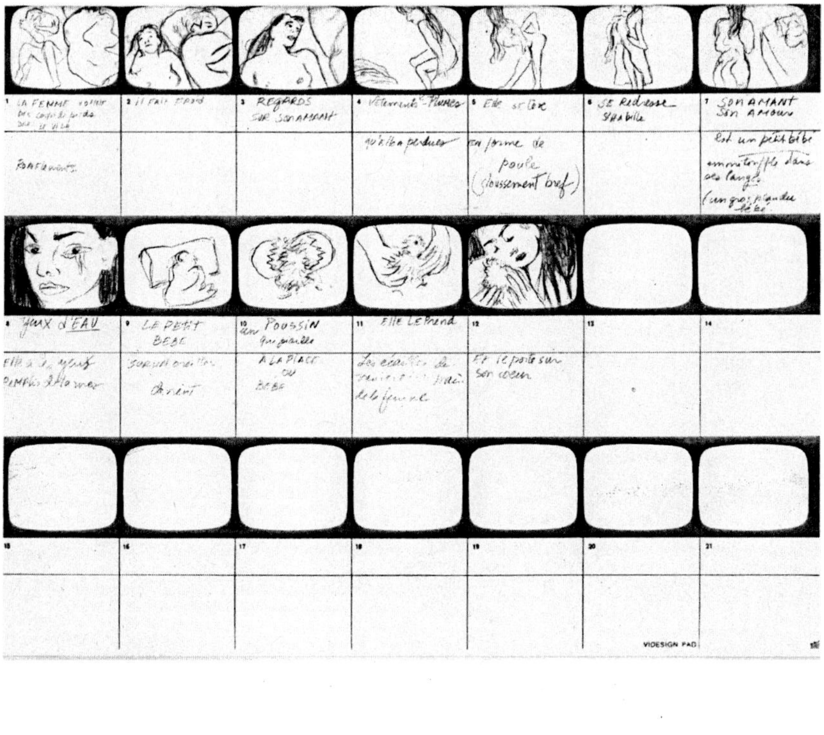
REGARDS
SUR SON AMANT
SE Redresse
SON AMANT
SON AMOUR
yeux d'EAU
LE PETIT
BEBE
POUSSIN
VIDESIGN PAD

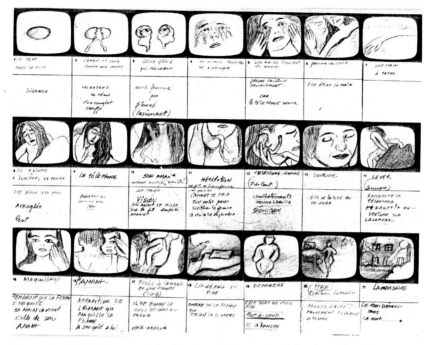

Extracts from Michèle Cournoyer's sketchbooks and early storyboards for *The Hat* (1999)
© National Film Board of Canada

Michaela Pavlátová: Frustrated Coupling
by Olivier Cotte

Desire and sensuality are abiding preoccupations for Michaela Pavlátová, and her animation films exploit these enduring themes to the full. But although the filmmaker often plays games with the bodies of her characters and the pleasures of their flesh, she remains focused above all on the depiction of social behaviour and the psychology of relationships, of which she offers an acerbic critique.

Although in some of her films, such as *Carnival of the Animals* (2006), Pavlátová employs sensuality as the stuff of dreams (the woman whose skirt rises and falls of its own accord, a moment of pure poetry) or of humour (the orgy in the same film which pairs women and birds), in *Words, Words, Words* (1991). *Repete* (1995) and *Forever & Forever* (1998) she offers a far less rosy view of the relations between men and women.

For the filmmaker, sexuality could be a subject for playfulness, erotic games an endless source of amusement if human beings weren't so prone to complicate things. In other words, this inward-looking animal (more so than other species at any rate) ought to put its ego aside more often and think about its 'significant other', should live more and dream less and ought, in short, to enjoy life instead of tying itself in knots.

The representation of eroticism

Talking about eroticism is one thing – depicting it visually is quite another, as it is more a matter of suggesting than showing. This can often prove tricky.

Repete offers a fine demonstration of the principle of the unspoken. The film opens on a close-up (thus concealing the surroundings), revealing

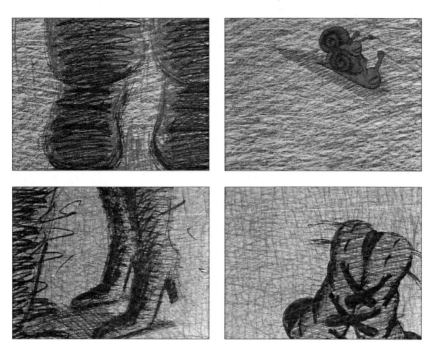

Images from *Repete* (1995) © KF a.s. – Studio Bratri v triku

physical contact based on a mechanical to-ing and fro-ing, the soundtrack marking the rhythm: it is a swing. A man pushes a woman (they are identified by their shoes, a highly symbolic, if not fetishistic, indicator of gender). This swinging movement is followed, using the same arcing camera move, by a more explicit image – of two snails having sex. The same camera move continues and we see another human couple come together, introduced as such by a discreet shot of their feet (for the story of love and sex is universal and thus requires no individual identification). In the final frames of this sequence, the woman stands on tip-toe in order, we imagine, to kiss her partner, followed by a long shot of two caterpillars kissing (this time, full-frontal). The squelching sound effect accentuates the act. The camera, still sweeping through space, then reveals another pairing: ants, making love 'human style', the two-backed beast: face to face, in other words. Pavlátová follows up with a human couple similarly engaged, again in close-up, in contrast to the framing of the insects. There is a progression in these acts – games on the swing, kiss, coitus – which is conveyed by the parallel montage of animal and human scenes. This information is offered parsimoniously, leaving the viewer to fill in the blanks in some scenes, while others are shown very explicitly. The use of animal characters also allows for unambiguous depiction of the sexual act, more difficult to achieve with human characters, especially in animation.

This scene is idyllic, with a bucolic soundtrack – composed of natural sounds – and the buoyant mood of the protagonists creating an atmosphere of uncomplicated happiness. It is paradise. But, as we know, man has broken with nature, eaten of forbidden fruit. This becomes clear as the film goes on to reveal more realistic aspects of relationships between couples in a contemporary context – relationships rather less exuberant than those seen earlier. To start with, the filmmaker completes the roving camera movement to show the bond between human and animal with a dog begging his master for some attention, a bit of petting.

In fact, the bit of stroking the dog receives so gratefully is only given to compensate for the restraint of the leash. The leash anticipates the scene to come, an enactment of the power play underpinning the relationship of the couple, where one partner is often dominant, the other submissive. The dog-owner fixing the broken leash is thereby also taking control of his own animal nature: instinct is subjugated. The corollary to this act of repression is the loss of his true nature: behaviours become fixed, codified by civilisation. Desire thus extinguished, routine sets in, irrevocably. It is, incidentally, from this scene between the man and his dog that the camera ceases its balletic circling movement to assume a fixed position from which to record. The man's short-stepped, military gait then signals the start of mechanical behaviours

Images from *Repete*

– so mechanical that they can be looped and repeated to the point of absurdity. The film's title is very eloquent in this respect.

Repetition, an expression of existential absurdity

Repete, as its title suggests, is a superb example of a play on repetition. The storyline supports this stylistic device, for Pavlátová's films are often organised around an assemblage of short sketches which she can revisit via parallel editing.

What emerges from this masterpiece is not so much a display of desire and sensuality (once past the rather explicit opening sequence described above), as that of its basic idea: communication. In a good many of Pavlátová's films this primordial need, so characteristic of the human species, is doomed to inevitable failure. The woman feeding her husband, for example, continually needs to raise the lamp he has positioned not so much in order to illuminate the book he reads in solitary enjoyment but to hide his face from view. The woman who removes this protective barrier in order to feed him, using food to penetrate his defences, is offering a sensual invitation (to his sense of taste), which the man declines. He, once the food is eaten, puts the lamp back in place and carries on reading, totally unmoved by his partner's ministrations. The repetitive structure allows, and even encourages, Pavlátová to re-frame her shots, via incremental forward movements, to close in on and surround the couple. This same stylistic device, this gradual approach, is also used in the film's second scene, in which a suicidal man is cut down from his noose by a woman who then, rebuffing his gesture of gratitude, gives him reason to start hanging himself again. This interaction is all the more effective because we are given no clue as to how it might all have begun. The man cannot express his gratitude, nor even justify his desperate act. As for the woman, we cannot tell whether she is trying to save the man from making a terrible mistake, is acting from pure love or moral duty, or whether she wields her scissors in a symbolic castration (thus precluding the possibility of any relationship with the opposite sex). Thus the suicidal man has to suffer in perpetuity for no reason other than the quest for a possible love which, one might wonder, perhaps never existed. The final scene, showing a couple whose kiss is constantly interrupted by the phone ringing, obliging the woman to break off her amorous caresses, uses the same structural *leitmotiv* to the point of absurdity.

Fortunately, this repeat mechanism finally brings us to an endgame, an ultimate paroxysm introducing a different way of experiencing these events. It is the dog, restrained by its leash and echoing the force-feeding of the man, stuffed to the point of nausea, that sounds the death knell for these

Images from *Repete*

mechanical behaviours, doomed to fail for their lack of soul. And until his master makes him set off again the whole world is brought to a standstill, right down to the cyclist balanced on his bicycle, waiting to pick up his life again, a life considered right and proper: an existence without communication. It is the desire, or rather nostalgia, for a physical, carnal relationship that makes the dog refuse to continue: via a zoom into its eyes, we return to the beginning of the film, back to the insect couple, but they are no longer in love. Everything is contaminated: even the hope of finding paradise is definitively lost.

Thus the machine is irreparably jammed. Via a reframing that is typical of Pavlátová's work, allied to a run-through of the routines previously observed, the flex of the pendant light suddenly breaks the flow, bisecting the image and separating the couple. Once this breakdown is reached, the woman can go back and fantasise another kind of life. This proves, however, to be impossible. The scene she imagines is blank: there is no one waiting for her. She will have to return and accept a situation she is unhappy with because there is no love. The same thing happens with the woman who saves the man from hanging. After a weary yawn, she dreams of being caressed by loving hands, whose colour – red – signifies life. The man wanting to be saved from the noose kindles an anger within her that has been too long repressed. But we should not infer that the women in this film get the best roles, those of the victims. The one who was kissing her husband on the bed is now waiting, even hoping, for the phone to ring: her escape route has disappeared and, contrary to what one might have hoped, she cannot assume her role as lover. This woman can only love when safe in the knowledge that she will not have to go all the way. The mechanical behaviour patterns are altered to such an extent that the couples now swap partners, repeating their now-meaningless gestures, until the moment the dog – symbol, do not forget, of humankind's animal nature – finally escapes by breaking his leash. Love can now reassert its rights. The couples change partners and their desires are now in sync; even the colours that had previously characterised each couple are now interspersed, visually establishing a new set of relationships. With the liberation of instinct, there is no obstacle to real life reclaiming dominion. Even the would-be suicide has the cord removed from his neck, just as the dog had broken free of its leash. It is not only the external elements that change, but the individual ego as well, which now steps aside to allow real life in. Until, once the leash is repaired, the film begins again. The moment of freedom has been brief.

Frustration(s)

Which brings us to the recurrent theme of frustration. One of the characters embodying this theme in *Repete* is the man sitting on the bed, whose phone rings every time his wife kisses him. His expression clearly conveys both helplessness and unsatisfied desire.

One method of investigating this theme of frustration, leaving no way out of the conclusions drawn, is to break down the established models – the symbols of desire fulfilled – such as marriage. In the case of *Forever & Forever* the title, once again, is clear as to the content. Moreover, the juxtaposition of live-action and animation scenes (each using a different technique) enables a parallel to be drawn between the world we hope for (the live-action wedding) and the world as it risks turning out (animation).

The film's live-action scenes are hardly likely to inspire desire in the viewer. For the characters, apart from one very beautiful and sensual young brunette, symbolise the cultural straitjacket of tradition rather than the dream of a fairy-tale life. In contrast, the animated sequences let us see ourselves in various possible and probable futures. They show us the many possible outcomes of any union between a man and a woman: this is marriage seen from backstage, from behind the razzmatazz of wedding, family party and joyful celebration. Most of these scenes express a pessimism that only the filmmaker's offbeat humour (sometimes) alleviates.

Image from *Forever & Forever* (1998)
© KF a.s. – Studio Bratri v triku

Some of them make explicit reference to the classic situations with which any couple is, has been, or will be, familiar. Such as that of the second sequence, in which the couple's attempts to make love are constantly interrupted by the sudden arrival of the sleepless child, who must be taken care of.

The couple's passion is extinguished, as seen in the switch of colour, from the blue rendering of their frolics, shot in extreme close-up (for the sake of

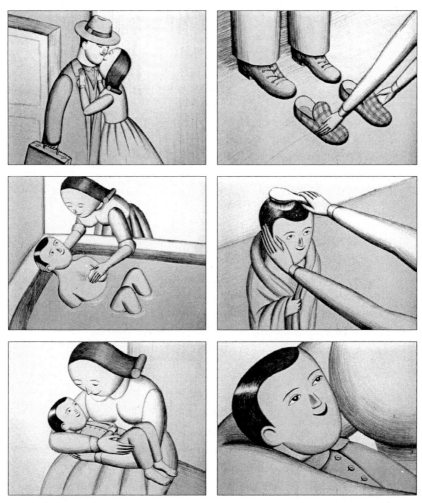

Images from *Forever & Forever*

discretion), becoming an abstract play of line and texture, to the monochrome used to depict the child's appearance, the dramatic impact of which is accentuated by the symmetry of the framing, with the infant's silhouette in the doorway implacably centre-screen. In the end, the man falls asleep before the umpteenth reprise: the couple must yield to the family, a situation which the woman, incidentally, deals with better than her partner.

Another sequence is a direct attack on the traditional image of the couple and the old-fashioned household, i.e. the housewife awaiting the husband's return from work. Yet, contrary to what we might expect, the perspective is not feminist – the focus here is on the infantilisation of the man. Thanks to his wife's cosseting and coddling, the male finds himself an infant again. Over the course of the scene he gradually decreases in size, until the pair assume the respective proportions of a mother and her little boy. Sexuality is clearly no longer possible, since the adult male/female relationship is destroyed. But might this not have its compensations? After all, the couple are exchanging blissful smiles, their eyes full of love. The almost nauseatingly saccharine music underscores the fact that some kind of happiness has been achieved. And is the man not getting masses of affection? Yes, a kind of equilibrium seems to have been reached – until the final shot, which reveals a more unequivocal message. In live-action we see the man, reduced to a tiny paper cut-out, end up in a handbag which is snapped firmly shut. A prison, in which he is jumbled up with lipstick, hankies, tampons and other feminine accessories. Marriage may thus lead to the diminishing of one of the partners; paradoxically, however, with no suffering involved.

This theme of the subjugation of one character by another is developed in the scene which is animated on slips of paper placed on a table cloth. In the first section, women are seen meeting, talking, and then the camera pulls back to reveal their husbands, held on a leash, like animals. In the second, it is the women who are literally clinging on to their partners' legs. These two short sketches make the same point: the lack of respect and an absolute lack of desire on the part of the dominant partner. The only communication that

Images from *Forever & Forever*

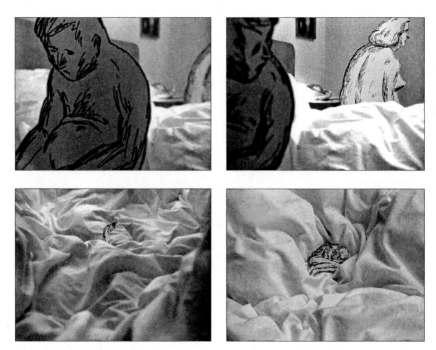

Images from *Forever & Forever*

occurs is that between the masters, first the women, then the men. We are witness to the gulf that can separate human beings, making desire and sensual pleasure impossible.

The latter theme is particularly well expressed in the following sequence. Here, a couple sit, on either edge of a bed with their backs turned, able to observe one another only via covert glances, expressing guilt and embarrassment. The man, who attempts a physical *rapprochement*, has to traverse inhospitable terrain, a cold, deserted no-man's-land. It is the absolute converse of any notion of human relationship: the bedsheets have become an

Images from *Forever & Forever*

icefield. Inevitably, he will lose his way in the quest to reach his partner, and will end up asleep, or dead, curled into a fœtal position, while the woman tries to forget her loneliness by gorging on fatty and sugary food.

As for the couple at the kitchen table, there is no fellowship in the meal they eat together: communication is reduced to a few glances fraught with memories and long extinguished desires. Here again, the combination of animation and live-action, by referencing our own world, makes it easy for any viewer to identify. The soundtrack, consisting solely of clinking cutlery and noisy chewing, underscores the only physical act they can still share: ingestion – that of sex being long past.

The only scene with a strong sexual connotation is that in which the partners are in separate rooms, watching an erotic or pornographic film. Their

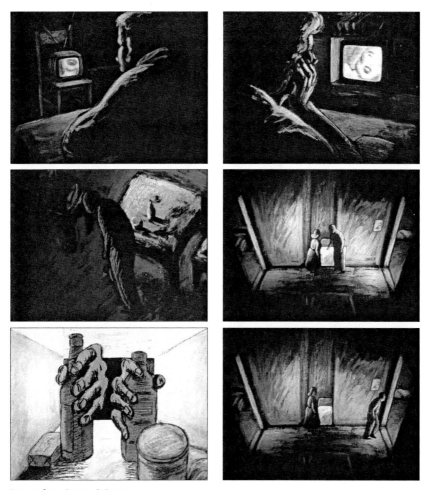

Images from *Forever & Forever*

facial expressions are empty, devoid of passion or desire. Sex, or rather its virtualised image, is reduced to a TV show that cannot be shared. Marital libido is dead or forgotten. Their urges are experienced separately, although a glance between them, as they meet at the refrigerator on the landing between the two rooms, suggests that with just a little effort on both sides a shared life together, might still be possible. If only they could dare to rethink the whole relationship: but they will not try it. Coupledom, contrary to the ideal and the hope we invest in marriage, is not about living as a pair, but about living alone together.

When the models no longer function

Words, words, words is another highly apposite film title since words are everywhere in this film, represented by the balloons and blobs that emerge from the mouths of the characters and (literally) enter the ears of others, form a thought or get lost, get mis-shapen, and so on. There is one couple in the film, however, who manage perfectly without these cloud-shaped blobs that are too ill-defined to afford communication. We realise these two are destined for love because love does not need words. For love is a communion of souls.

It all begins with an attraction at first sight, represented by an arc of electricity shooting between the two characters. Simmering desire, a fiery physical magnetism, is the basis on which a couple is formed. Indeed, in their excitement there's nothing more for them to do than verify that they have chosen the right body. The two lovers thus do as lovers do the world over: they enjoy their perfect match and, we can assume, praise the destiny that brought them together. The film, as is often the case with animation, and in particular with Pavlátová, has no dialogue, so their words are depicted as physical embodiments: domino pieces that join together to form a bridge, the creation of ever more complex two-piece jigsaw puzzles. The couple's perfect accord gives Pavlátová leave to zoom in bit by bit until closing in on just their two faces. It is an idyllic, perfect love, of the kind celebrated in song since time immemorial, the quest for which might consume an entire lifetime. It is based, as we have seen, on the idea of each completing the other. And it can only develop when this long-awaited and desired perfection has been authenticated, when both partners have confirmed the validity of a cultural model: that of perfect love, the encounter with one's soul-mate. It is clear that the slightest deviation, the tiniest bit of grit in the works, could easily destroy the dream, since such perfect love is nothing but a mental construct created to fit a cultural chimera. This is, fatally, what happens when the Masterwork, that ultimate validation, the giant jigsaw they are building together, convinced that their love transcends all, cannot be completed because of the

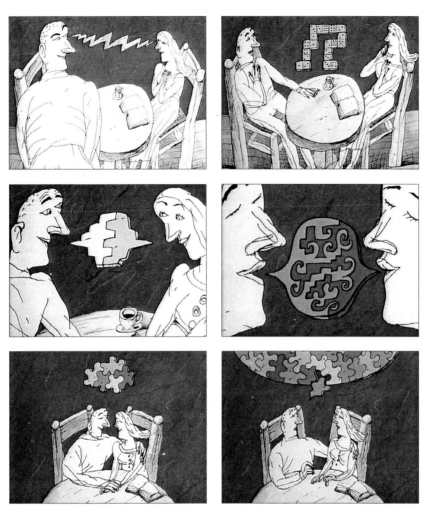

Images from *Words, Words, Words* (1991) © KF a.s. – Studio Bratri v triku

last, misshapen piece that just won't fit. The entire edifice collapses because perfection cannot tolerate the slightest flaw. The couple hurl insults at one another, each holding the other responsible for this failure. This phase is always illustrated by a symbolic object: here words are pairs of jaws, each devouring the other's words. The rupture is complete. The man leaves. But the icon of this perfect love is powerful enough to make the woman swallow her anger and try to hold on to the object of desire, despite his imperfections... but in vain. From the very beginning of this story – which is strongly critical of overly uncompromising desires – we had noticed a waiter pledging a sincere love for the woman. It is he who finally completes the jigsaw with just a single 'word'. This brightly coloured jigsaw stands out, against a

Images from *Words, Words, Words*

particularly monochrome world. Does this mean love will blossom between the the woman and the pure-hearted waiter? No. She, now beaming with happiness, seizes the jigsaw and rushes off in pursuit of the man who has left her. She will, no doubt, spend the rest of her life pursuing him. And we know what happens then: as seen in the later films.

Reading the foregoing analysis, one might well assume that Michaela Pavlátová's short films are depressing, if not unbearably bleak. This is not the case however. These acutely observed films offer a reflection of our world, our fears and failings. All under the cover of humour, which stops the content getting too heavy. This is the very principle of a certain kind of comedy, such as

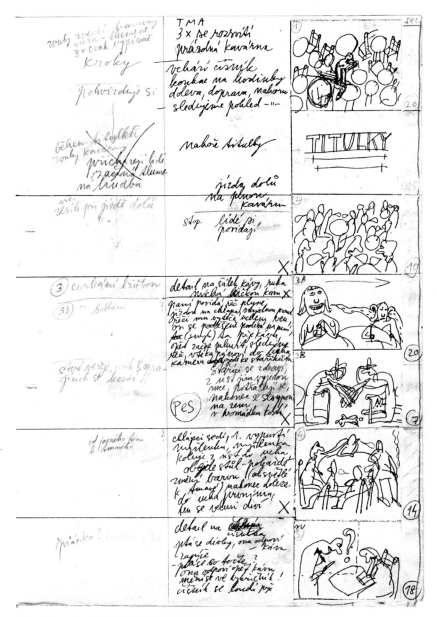

Extract from storyboard for *Words, Words, Words*

that practised by the great Hollywood directors, such as Frank Capra or Howard Hawks. To succeed in such a delicate enterprise, combining a critique of social and individual behaviours with such lightness of touch, is a far from easy task.

(Translation by Clare Kitson)

On Vera Neubauer *by Leslie Felperin*

If, as some academic theorists like to insist, animation can be/is the most subversive form of filmmaking and if the work of most independent female animators represents a dissenting faction from mainstream normative narratives, then Vera Neubauer's films are the terrorist branch of the art form, the Red Brigade of the animated film.

Thematically and aesthetically, they are resonant with a heritage of female filmmakers that starts with Maya Deren and leads to Yvonne Rainer, Cecelia Condit or Leslie Thornton, experimental filmmakers and video artists whose employment of *bricolage* and Brechtian mannerisms, radical feminism and repetition, avant-garde montage techniques and monstrous Mother figures make them the darlings of feminist film theory.

But Neubauer's work has never received commensurate attention, although she is probably the most prolific independent animator, male or female, in the UK, and has directed a strikingly diverse body of challenging work. One might conjecture that it is precisely her innovative use of live-action experimentalism and animation that have contributed to her neglect.

She has said in interviews that she prefers her art to 'provoke rather than entertain', and the films hold good to this aim, provocative to the last frame. Brazenly unpretty, mischievously playful, they bring to mind the drawings of a wilful but clever child who when asked to draw a house depicts the primal scene in the upstairs bedroom, the dog eating the baby in the downstairs one, and the garden on fire, and then crumples it all up to throw at the teacher.

And yet, her films do entertain the mind, with their rapid-fire stream of ideas, but also by their savage wit, irony and humour.

Born in Czechoslovakia in the mid-1940s, she moved to Britain in 1968, and specialised in print-making at art school. After graduation, she became interested in film, and began to make short films using animation, which she perceived as a medium not unlike printmaking, both using techniques that generated limited series of images and requiring a high degree of repetitious work. She soon developed a unique style, one which uses seemingly crude, thick wobbly lines to create simply-drawn characters that move through a sparse background, formally somewhat reminiscent of the work of Emile Cohl.

Neubauer's work strikes the viewer as *faux-naif* with the accent on the *faux*, for the simple drawing style belies and contrasts with the complexity and sophistication of her subject matter, which uses strong, even occasionally shocking, images to illustrate her concerns. Thus, her films have a raw, spontaneous quality that enhances and underscores the sketchy narratives that they illustrate, which often draw on the imagery and elliptical qualities of fairy-tales. The tension which Neubauer's draughtmanship maintains, managing to appear fresh and direct rather than merely clumsy and badly drawn, is symptomatic of the tension she maintains throughout the body of her work on a more thematic level.

Some of these are difficult films, sometimes inaccesible after only one viewing. They require the viewer to think critically and watch closely. This intransigence is both her oeuvre's greatest virtue, in terms of artistic quality, and its greatest vice, in terms of securing wider recognition, for Neubauer's films resist categorisation and refuse to take predictable stands on political issues such as feminism.

Like some of the woman filmmakers cited above, Neubauer's films attempt to tell stories through montages of striking images and fragmentary scenes which refuse to pull the wool of linearity over the spectators eyes. Instead, the time of her narratives is fractured, the 'plots' cut up and reassembled on the editing table, evoking the feel of stories half-remembered, narrated by someone perhaps with the digressive tendencies of Laurence Sterne's Tristram Shandy, or perhaps with an unreliable memory, or perhaps just someone trying to say not 'this and then this' but everything at once.

The animation's graphic style, which gives a sense of swift and urgent execution, does not fetishise technical perfection. Neubauer's films consciously swerve away from a tradition in animation which has elevated fluidity of movement and solidity of figure above all other artistic virtues. Moreover, in their consistent use of collage-like montage, in which fragments of animation and live-action are edited together to create ironic juxtaposition instead of narrative cohesion and closure, Neubauer's films are more consistent with what Peter Burger describes as the project of the 'historical avant-garde' (1984: 90).

Like the work of Frida Khalo, Max Ernst or John Heartfield, Neubauer's films work through negation, deny the organic unity to the art object and use shock 'as a stimulus to change one's conduct of life; [because] it is the means to break through aesthetic immanence and to usher in (initiate) a change in the recipient's life praxis' (Burger 1984: 42). The project of the avant-garde is thus an inherently radical one politically, and while Burger pessimistically insists that the 'true' historical avant-garde has been and gone, current artists still employ its strategies as a means of expressing discontent with the 'new' cinematic and world order.

Neubauer's education at art school coincided with the height of political and social upheaval of the late 1960s, and she has conceded that her work was inevitably informed by that era, but the films never seem like polemical tracts or sterile exercises in radical filmmaking. In contrast to the worthy agit-prop of some feminist animators, Neubauer's films refuse to preach and seem to prefer to problematise through abstraction and personalise through the use of autobiography that declines to claim for itself any universal application, while still inviting the viewer's identification.

In an interview with this author,[1] Neubauer said that her work grew in part from the perception of telling accidents, from using what was at hand. Sometimes this use of the 'found' yielded images which are simply striking, apparently just aesthetically pleasing or disturbing. At other times, however, an event, for example noticing that after a car crash the police tend to arrive before the ambulance, or the reaction of a crowd to a disturbed woman raging in the street, would seem to resonate with larger implications about social conditions. Her work often seems to try to address such conditions on a microcosmic scale, paying particular attention to the politics of gender, which becomes the point of origin in her films from which conflict emanates on a more macrocosmic scale. *Mid Air* (1986) is an excellent example of this movement, where a wife's use of witchcraft to subvert her husband's authority leads eventually to its use against the police.

It is while prising open the gates of the Garden of Eden, investigating the beginnings of sexual difference, that Neubauer's films are at their most shocking, pointed and effective. She noted in an interview with Claire Barwell that her favorite part of *The Decision* (1981) is

> the little piece every projectionist cuts off or projects against the curtain, the piece everybody turns up too late to see. It's the title that says 'That is where everything begins' followed by a close shot of the backside of a newborn female baby. [Later covered in excrement.] When I got the rushes back and projected them in the viewing theatre I could hear the reactions of the male projectionists. They were disgusted and angry – so I knew it was good! These men must see hard-core porn films by the dozen yet they could not take the mess of a newborn baby – something a mother has to deal with twenty times a day!' (2003: 173)

Indeed, this shot is a condensation of where 'everything begins' in a multiplicity of ways.

On the most superficial level it reminds us that we all begin as babies, incontinent and helpless. But more subtly, the image of the newborn's vagina metonymically reminds one of the vagina from which the baby itself emerged – this is truly where all of us, 'everything' begins in the cycle of matrilineal descent. Ever since Laura Mulvey's influential essay on 'Visual Pleasure and Narrative Cinema' (1975), film theory has been obsessed with the centrality of the female genitalia as the structuring absence around which the scopic regimes of cinema are constructed, either through voyeurism or the disavowing mechanism of fetishism. Neubauer's close-up of this organ literally strips the woman, and exposes the empress's nakedness, and thus lays bare the 'lack' over which cinematic visual pleasure erects its defences. The projectionists and audience are shocked because by its clinical frankness, the elemental simplicity of the baby girl's body undermines those very defences of which 'hard-core' pornography is another symptomatic manifestation.

The film's later use of Zoetropes, old silent film footage of couples kissing, and peep show reels emphasises the masculine power of 'the look' in cinema's heritage. Neubauer's films attempt to deconstruct these systems, but (thankfully) without denying the possibility of pleasure or humour; instead the films return to origins in order to rediscover the sources of pleasure and 'unpleasure', by an examination of the origins of sexual difference, of conflict and, most innovatively, of cinema itself through this very melding of live action and animation which harkens back to early films, like those of Georges Méliès and Emile Cohl, which similarly enmeshed the drawn and the 'real', fantasy and the fantastic with the prosaic, myth with cultural specificity.

The Decision typifies this mixture. After the opening shot of the baby's bottom, the film proceeds to tell the story of a beautiful princess, who has to decide which prince she would like to marry. A man's voice-over describes the tale in a dead-pan parody of fairy-tale discourse, while animation and live-action sequences intercut, now illustrating the story with drawn footage, then suddenly cutting to live-action shots, to provide ironic counterpoint, for example as the voice-over intones 'One prince had the most beautiful words and with them he could spin dreams,' the film cuts to a washing machine spinning clothes.

A steady rhythm is gradually built on these sort of juxtapositions: an animated couple make love in blackened frame, their outlines quivering and blending into each other in vibrant colors, while a peep show reel scrolls on in a boxed corner of the screen; the drudgery of housework and childrearing is contrasted with the images, drawn and from a 'sampled' live-action film, of a couple dancing joyously. The King, as an animated character, enjoins the princess that she is free to choose, but choose she must. An empty screen appears with the words 'Fuck that Freedom' written in type. The montages seem to suggest that there is really no choice, all decisions lead to the same final drudgery. In desperation, the princess seeks advice from the castle witch, who suggests two courses of action. First, disfiguring her beauty to see which suitor will still want her afterwards; but the princess rejects this nihilistic option. Then the witch offers her a zoetrope made from a tin can, saying 'this box will show you the ending of many stories', but all the film shows is a simple drawing of a skeleton repeatedly losing its head, as the Zoetrope revolves.

As the princess becomes hypnotised by this magic box, the film could be read to imply that all stories, especially cinematic ones, are seductive illusions, death is the only closure, and to make decisions of any importance one must try to escape the ideological control, or, as the voice-over concludes 'let us hope that by the time she awakes she will no longer be a princess, but someone capable of making a decision'.

Such would be one interpretation, by no means the only possible one, as this film, like Neubauer's *Animation for Live Action* (1978) not only resists but openly parodies the imposition of a univocal reading, represented by the male voice-over whose seemingly assured narrativising is undermined by the polyphonic proliferation of images. In *Animation for Live Action*, the cartoon character that is both a representation and a product of its creator 'says' in a scroll of text that passes over the screen, 'Artistically, the animation film is the medium which by its nature can accommodate most easily a simultaneity of viewpoints, and demonstrate clearly the indivisibility of events.'

Her film *The Mummy's Curse* (1987), *Mid Air* to a lesser extent, and *The Decision* especially, all attempt to put this observation into practice. *Animation for Live Action* has at least three 'narrators' or viewpoints, a male voice-over who claims the film as his own, a 'dramatised reconstruction of the life of my ex-wife', Neubauer herself, who we observe filming in the reflection of a shop window, and the animated figure she creates, who in turns draws Neubauer herself in a parody of the Fleischer Brothers' *Out of the Inkwell* (1919–29) series, carries a camera, and cuts film stock into pieces.

Neubauer has said that editing is probably her favourite part of filmmaking, and it is through her subtle use of it that most of the impact of these films is made, and by which 'the indivisibility of events' is suggested. By repeating cycles, returning to images already seen, and disrupting what little narrative remains in this manner, these films convey the impression not just of fairytales or stories told, but of dreams remembered. For this, the 'uncanny' quality of animation is well-suited, conveying as it does the primal pleasure of seeing the inanimate move and speak, of the impossible being made manifest.

This was in part the attraction of the earliest cinema, and one that animation consistently replenishes.

Neubauer's use of the medium stays close to these roots, and the rejection of polished technical perfection lends her work a spontaneity that is often lacking in her peers, and adds a visceral impact to the strong images she creates. By rejecting the glib perfectionism of mainstream animation and its fetishism of fluid movement and cleaned-up graphics, these films force the viewer to confront their own expectations about the animation, and indeed film. Furthermore, Neubauer's work insistently reminds the viewer of its own constructedness as art, and thus of the construction of the themes with which it deals, such as sexuality and power relations.

Note

1   Interview with the author, December 1991 in London.

References

Barwell, C. (2003) 'Interview with Vera Neubauer', in N. Danino and M. Maziere (eds) *The Undercut Reader: Critical Writings on Artists' Film and Video*. London: Wallflower Press, 170–3.

Burger, P. (1984) *Theory of the Avant-Garde*, trans. M. Shaw. Manchester: Manchester University Press.

Mulvey, L.. (1975) 'Visual Pleasure and Narrative Cinema', *Screen*, 16, 3, 6–18.

Vera Neubauer's *Wheel of Life* – Interview

Leslie Felperin's 1992 article is reprinted here because it is a useful and insightful introduction to Vera Neubauer's earlier work. In light of Neubauer's subsequent films it also points up both continuity and change, as discussed in the interview below. Neubauer diversified into making live-action for a number of years, experimenting with a range of genres, such as a musical about rebellious mixed-race teenagers, *Don't Be Afraid* (1990), and *Passing On* (1988), a contemplative documentary essay on varying attitudes towards ageing, dying and the hereafter in different cultures. She then developed a fascinating form of knitted animation, first seen in *La Luna* (1999), an ambitious drama that combines live-action with animation, and in *Hooked* (2003), a form of animated documentary, pursuing an interest in knitting on a journey through several Latin American countries. She animates knitted characters in traditional stop-frame manner, but also unravels them for dramatic narrative purposes, as in the playful *Woolly Wolf* (2001) which revisits the story of Little Red Riding Hood with characteristic acerbic humour. Much of the later work takes on a more narrative direction.

Neubauer attributes her shift to making a film that draws on more mythological sources, such as *Wheel of Life* (1999), rather than fairy-tales, in part to her struggle to escape labels such as 'feminist agit-prop' and 'militant feminist'. 'I found the feminist label very limiting, I didn't want to preach. When I started making films, I thought I was making films about my everyday world, as it was happening around me, and questioning the roles imposed on men who are just as trapped as women are.'[1]

Wheel of Life recounts and refashions the stories of Adam and Eve and Cain and Abel. Most of the film, which combines live-action and animation, was created on the beach, through making and re-making drawings in the

 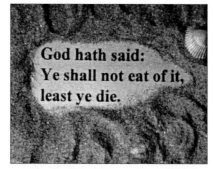

Images from
Wheel of Life
(1999)
© Vera Neubauer

sand, and using shells, stones and detritus washed up by the waves, such as the frayed length of rope that she animates as the tempting serpent who offers Eve the forbidden fruit. Intermittently, a stretch of sand is blown away to reveal printed phrases from the Book of Genesis.

Filmmaker Steve Dwoskin comments that Neubauer's films explore

> the confrontation of assumed roles thrust upon women (and men) by the very core of our social indoctrination. Here one has to go back to the very beginnings of mythology, legend and historical tradition... *Wheel of Life* travels directly to the Book of Genesis as source material... These fundamental gender divisions are not merely stated, but are extensively explored. The exploration is rendered through the cycle of life, the bearing of children... Though gender roles are forever in the forefront [they] nevertheless always go beyond the simplistic symbols. Her point seems to be that there is a harsh conflict between the sexes and an equally harsh history behind this conflict. There is the constant reminder that the roles are a composite of different physical bodies embedded and compounded in a complex intersection of social values and sexual expectations. (2002)

Unlike many of her earlier films, which collaged live-action, puppets, cut-outs and drawn animation sequences, *Wheel of Life* has a much more organic feel, due to the nature of the materials used. Scenes on the beach are intercut with others of a mud-smeared potter at work, and flour-spattered hands making dough, these human agents clearly standing in for God the Creator.

Neubauer comments that she is not religious, and confesses to 'feeling almost blasphemous, when I started discussing it with other people, to say I could see God as someone really vicious, who put the tree of knowledge there only to tempt two people he created, for his own entertainment because everything being so perfect would get boring. The Potter is the face of God, closing his eyes every time something bad or evil happens, when he conveniently goes back to sleep. But it was amusing to me to portray him [in the drawn-in-sand scenes] as a bit of a Peeping Tom.'

Wheel of Life alternates rapid cutting of the actions drawn in the sand, with slower, more contemplative sequences of sky and clouds, the movement of the sea and waves, pointing up the contrast between human activity and indifferent nature/God.

The apparent simplicity, indeed crudeness of the film, in terms of technique and imagery, vividly emphasises the raw, elemental and violent aspects of the Biblical creation myths. The use of sand and shells lends grit to the sexual imagery, the emphasis on genital difference is a constant reminder of issues of gender. As the waves efface the drawn outlines of the characters, only shells representing eyes and mouth are left, as though turning skeletal before our eyes, underscoring the passage of time. The final images of the

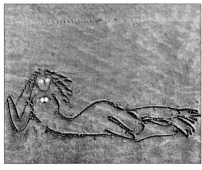

film are of handprints in the sand, an echo of both the Potter as God, and the artist/filmmaker's authorial imprint.

Neubauer: 'Most of the film was shot with a camera on a tripod on different beaches at different times, over the course of a year. Ideas are triggered when you're there, with the tide going in and out; it makes you think about generations of people doing the same things. That took me to something Biblical – the Book of Genesis and the dimension of time – and the fact that stories repeat: love, hate, revenge, jealousy, murder. All the ingredients are there, generation after generation, washed down by time – the story stays the same but the way you tell it, change it, is different. On the other hand, some would say all my films are the same, regardless of the different techniques and different narratives, they all deal with relationships, love, birth, death.

'I'd find my canvas on the beach itself, sand as formed by the waves. It wasn't shot in chronological order, but intuitively, and depending on the particular beach, that would trigger which bit to shoot. I'd get the rhythm of the place, and the tides, which often varied from the published calendars. I developed a sense of it, and would do the drawings in the sand, knowing when the wave would wash over it and wash it away. I had to take the sun into account, but sometimes I left in the differences in the lighting, and made it work for me, for example in the birth scene where you can hardly see her. When I got the first answer print back, they'd graded it so it looked like it

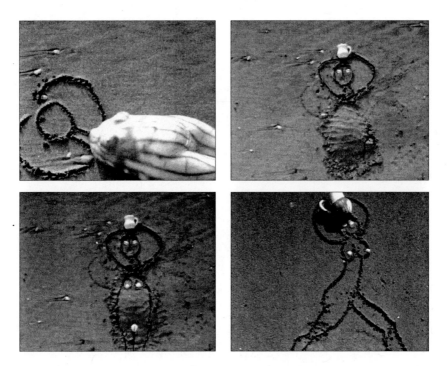

was all happening as if in Sinai desert, hot, but I said no, I wanted that dark cold beach.

'It was kind of thrilling, the tension felt on the beach, really sensual, because I was dealing with the elements, and because the story was almost found there. Sometimes I felt like a medium – with the clouds and the thunder. Sometimes the waves took the tripod away.

'As all the beach material was all done in the camera, I'd come home hoping it was all there, as otherwise I'd have nothing to show for the day's work, and hoping that others would read it, feel it, as I did. I always overshoot, I do both close-ups and long-shots then choose when editing. I don't follow a storyboard, but work off what's there. I know what shots I need to do, and draw it in a circle/cycle rather than pre-planning it. I have some stamp-size images, some words, although going through notebooks retrospectively it is always surprising at how much of the film is in there.

'My approach with that film, and most of the time, is like that of a painter, letting it develop on the canvas; there's no going back. But then, in another sense, I could come back to a beach where the drawing would still be there from a few days, a week, before. Time and the wind had shifted the sand, altered the drawing, so I'd shoot it, then compare the different footage at editing stage. Time would be written into the fabric, and I'd see how the elements worked on my artwork.

'I liked working with the archaeology of the beach, with what's washed up. The skeletons and sheep skulls were a fulfillment of the time element, life and death, and also have echoes of the Biblical sacrificial lamb. There was also metamorphosis through natural means, the skeletal remains you find on the beach, coming back days later; that's why the sheep's head is in at the end credits. And then it also seemed important, and brought the film into contemporary reality, to use the dead birds from a recent oil spill.

'I have some regrets: if it had been 35mm I could have gone in a lot closer, and got more of the grain of the sand. The Biblical quotations were inserted at the end out of cowardice – as a guide for the audience. I was invited to Turkey, where the film showed in a huge cinema. I was amazed by the audience's fascination, because they didn't know the story. Someone in the audience said they didn't need the quotations, and I do find them disruptive, but then, I did want the Book, to find the Book in the sand. I feel there is also an element of self-censorship to the film: it was commissioned by S4C, the Welsh television channel, and I didn't want to be too provocative – it could not be too offensive – and now I wish I'd spent more time with Adam and Eve, i.e. on the their relationship.

'But I was totally happy with the soundtrack. I was hearing the sound I wanted as I was making it, African drums shaking the earth, which was unusual for me. But I couldn't find an African drummer who could do what I wanted. I asked a Japanese musician, Joji Hirot, and he did it beautifully, with very little direction from me. I was totally blown away by the sculptural way he organised his instruments.'

Note

1 Interview with the author, July 2008, in London.

Reference

Dwoskin, S. (2002) 'Vera's Telling Films' in *Animac Magazine*, www.animac.info/ANIMAC_2002/ENG/animac_magazine03.asp

Truth Under Oppression:
The Films of Ruth Lingford
by Simon Pummell

The zoom out from the constituent pixels that opens *What She Wants* (1994) can be seen as a clear statement of intent. The flat slipping and clustering of pixels is more dominant than any illusory movement in depth created by the zoom: the zoom takes us not through a fictional space, but across a picture. Ruth Lingford made her early films in a software package for the Amiga computer, Deluxe Paint, and it is through analogy with painting as a medium that her work is perhaps most usefully viewed.

As we move into the film, and watch a woman walk through the city, it is the architectural surfaces of the city that are alive with images depicting her sexual fantasies; in the same way, the surface of the screen is alive as the pixels slide, slip and cluster to reveal the changing shapes.

In classical figurative animation, the illusion of 3D is a prime aim and the draughtsmanship is disciplined to allow this rendition of form in three dimensions. Historically this was achieved through developing a sculptural sensibility combined with traditional life-drawing skills, and with the advent of the computer as the dominant tool in animation image-making, this tradition has found a natural development through 3D CGI animation; drawing is subjugated to the creation of 3D elements that can then be organised and moved in a 3D space. This is a process closer to the traditional 'blocking' of action in live-action drama, the stop-motion techniques of puppet animation, or the arrangement of painter's models into a suitable tableaux, rather than the mark-making on a flat surface that used to be the staple occupation of either painter or 2D animator.

It's perhaps interesting to view Lingford's first broadcast film as an essay in another kind of computer animation: a form of digital animation that does not render fully realised three-dimensional shapes, and hold them consistent; rather it renders forms through the arrangement of pixels on the flat surface, a form that holds onto the tactile emphasis of marks on a surface. And indeed, once looked at like that, it is not hard to see the analogy between the sliding of pixels across a surface and the more traditional sliding of pigment across a surface, especially the loose expressive brushwork of several developments within painting that range across the late nineteenth century to the mid-twentieth century.

Perhaps the most significant aspect of this choice for Lingford is that it associates all the forms you see with a *hand*, and so with the consciousness that controls that hand. Though made on a computer, this film is in very significant ways a *hand-made* film.

It is this refusal to sever the link between hand and consciousness, this acceptance that the gesture may contain knowledge that cannot be pre-planned, that links her techniques to a line of exploration that runs from expressionist draughtsmanship and surrealist automatic drawing through abstract expressionism and later neo-expressionism in painting: traditions that prize the unconscious content of gestural drawing as highly as the pre-considered representational content.

It is consistent with this that when we first see the city through which the protagonist walks it is as flat and distorted in its perspective as the sets of Robert Weiner's German Expressionist film *The Cabinet of Dr. Caligari/ Das Kabinett des Doktor Caligari* (1920). And as she walks further and enters the London Underground station the elements of the city have ceased to retain any element of recognisable architecture and the vaginal tunnel we enter makes it clear we are now entering a body.

Although the perspective of the rendition of the tube train is more optically accurate than anything we have seen previously, the instability of form reaches new heights in the film's depiction of the metamorphosis of the woman; whether it is the transformation of lover into wolf/dog, or the birthing of a wormlike baby, or the final rush of the world into the vagina (a fish is perhaps within expected metaphoric bounds – but a three-piece-suite of furniture?), the film enters a world where form breaks down and becomes chaotic.

And yet the film is not chaotic – the 'hand-writing' of the images remains the same. And so we believe the consciousness motivating the images remains the same – it reads above all as a confessional film. In this film – made as part of the ANIMATE! Channel Four and Arts Council of England commissioning programme, immediately after her studies at the Royal College of

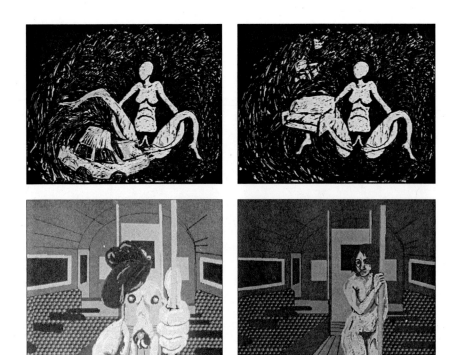

Images from *What She Wants* (1994) © Ruth Lingford

Art – the hybrid technique of painting with pixels allowed Lingford to create a form that directly enacts a breaking down and slippage of the defining
edges between form and gesture: thus writing the artist's body within forms
created at many levels, unconscious and conscious. And this revelation of
desire is made more naked by the choice of the filmmaker to clearly draw the
protagonist as a self-portrait. As a work made in an expressionist tradition
it is an unusually pure and undiluted form: indeed a revelation of *What She
Wants* – or perhaps more accurately '*how she wants*' – or the chaotic form of
sexual desire itself.

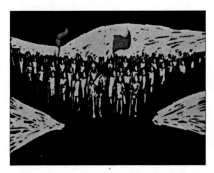

Images from *Pleasures of War* (1998) © Ruth Lingford

The first shot of *Pleasures of War* (1998) flags a very different set of graphic strategies. Simple hills are made from marks that seem to conjure printmaking techniques (first associations might be the linocuts of Frans Masereel, and the woodcuts of Kathe Kollowitz). However set into this – collaged in a non-naturalistic way that refers more to a fine art tradition of collage such as Robert Rauschenberg's use of newspaper photographs than contemporary film compositing's creation of illusory space – is newsreel footage of war and the victims of war.

Throughout the film, these newsreel images appear in the lacunae and negative spaces left by the composition of the drawn animation sequences. In

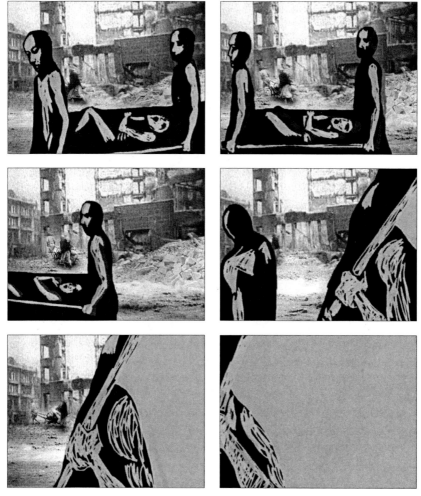

Images from *Pleasures of War*

this way the two types of image are set in opposition rather than in compositions that cohere. The images are literally formally incoherent, and in this way give the film a chaotic edge that usefully breaks up the narrative, and suggests a more provisional, less confident form of allegory than might have been the case with the animation alone.

The drawn animation's images are archaic both in the simple mythic narrative they convey, and in their graphic approach. The narrative of a besieged castle and the revenge of a Queen on the destroyer of her realm is essentially a re-telling of Judith and Holofernes.

However, a key image in the story of Judith and Holofernes – the decapitated head of a man held triumphantly by a woman – has always been hard to differentiate from Salome and John the Baptist. Erwin Panofsky in *Studies in Iconology: Humanistic Themes in the Art of the Renaissance* (1939) devotes a substantial section to the complexities of unpicking the differences in Renaissance paintings between depictions of the two characters: in that period a variety of deployments of chargers, swords, baskets and platters were used by artists to signify which character they were depicting. In *Pleasures of War* the iconography of these two very different figures seems deftly interwoven. Salome's killing for pleasure is woven into Judith's killing of Holofernes to create a two-faced narrative: the woman is not simply represented as a force of good; she is both Judith (a traditional figure of virtue) and Salome (an archetype of woman as corruption and narcissistic evil).

In the universe depicted by Lingford there is no overarching good to justify violence: there is only the sexualised current of feeling that expresses itself through penetration, domination, submission and loss of identity. Sometimes this instinctual current expresses itself in sex, sometimes in violence.

Formally the animation embraces this depiction of desire as two-faced – looking to violence as well as sex – by its undifferentiated depiction of both sex and violence as a constant flux of bodily interactions, inter-penetrations and transformations.

In this way the drawn animation is aggressively amoral: rather than set very particular depictions of individuals into archetypal situations, and so trigger pity and fear – the strategy of Kathe Kollowitz – Lingford's figures are largely impersonal, as anonymous as the powerful instincts that animate them. We feel little for Holofernes, or indeed for any mythic figure depicted in the film – their bloody ends are consonant with their blindly instinctual level of characterisation – they are instincts embodied and so we finally relish their violent pleasures. It is the faces in the newsreel footage with brings a sharp reminder that for many victims of violence there is no sexual triumph, only anonymous suffering and death without any memorial. In this way the clips of archive footage act as the faces of the figures: supplying the individuality that triggers the clearer dramatic emotions and identification that leads to compassion.

In this way the film embodies perhaps both the great potential of her chosen medium of expressionist line animation and its radical limit. While skilfully exploiting the natural affinity of her chosen medium for the shifting grotesque of metamorphosis, and its ability to render highly plastic bodies in flux, Lingford also seeks to move the meaning of her film towards a wider, more humanistic political perception of human conflict: this is the point at which she chooses to give up her primary technique of digital line-drawn animation and engage with indexical images, photographic representations of precise historical events.

Does this shift in technique perhaps mark a significant boundary not just for Lingford's chosen technique, but also perhaps for the reach of line animation as a medium? The last piece this chapter discusses could be seen as both a confirmation of that tentative thesis and of its refutation. This work is a music video, *U.N.K.L.E.: Eye for an Eye* (2002).

Lingford made this work in collaboration with the animation collective Shynola. It depicts a giant mother figure, the size of a blimp, towed through the sky by a phalanx of planes, and its arrival among a population of tiny suckling figures. As the story develops we see the dire consequences of this population of tiny figures succumbing to its desire to swarm over the recumbent maternal flesh/balloon and suckle on grotesque dummy-like nipples studding the whole figure.

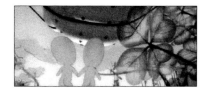

This music video goes beyond the oppositions established in *Pleasures of War* to make a work that works both as a sublimely creepy evocation of the biological drives and desires that have pre-occupied Lingford in all her films, and the inclusion of formal and narrative elements that open the film out to a wider, more political cultural space. Yet these elements are not obliged to act as a counter-point, or corrective, to her core aesthetic.

The music video does not attempt to set material *in opposition* to the anonymity of the animation's

Images from *U.N.K.L.E.: Eye for an Eye* (2002) © Universal Music Group

depiction of its simple mythic narrative. Blank-faced figures, the menacing arrival of the unmarked black passenger jet that tows the blimp (echoes of CIA unmanned drones), the echoing of the cutting patterns, camera angles and iconography of inter-species mating from Hollywood science fiction movies, are all used to achieve a sense of contemporary social relevance not in balance with, but *as an extension of* the mythic, abstract and grotesque elements that Lingford has always employed in evoking sexuality.

The piece reaches beyond the expressive powers of the animation in itself as purely formal expressive draughtsmanship; but does so not by referencing material in opposition to that form, but rather inflecting that form itself with an awareness of the grotesquery of popular culture, and using Shynola's 3D CGI expertise to expand the complexity of the space depicted.

In *U.N.K.L.E.: Eye for an Eye* the co-operation between Shynola and Lingford succeeds in embodying the truth that the literary critic Rosemary Jackson has argued is the defining element of the grotesque, of the fantastic, as an aesthetic strategy:

> It could be suggested that the movement of fantastic narrative is one of metonymical rather than metaphorical process: one object does not stand for another but literally becomes that other, slides into it, metamorphosing from one shape to another in a permanent flux and instability. As Lacan points out, 'What do we have in metonymy other than the power to bypass the obstacles of social censure? This form ... lends itself to truth under oppression.' (1981: 41–2)

Throughout her career Ruth Lingford has made a series of self-described 'feel-bad films' that in actual fact celebrate key aspects of our experience that are often suppressed. Increasingly it has become clear that 'what she wants' is what all of us want, but rarely speak out for; and it is for these suppressed aspects of our sexuality, and so our humanity, that Lingford continues to speak out for in films that are employing a greater and greater range of filmic language to express this 'truth under oppression'.

References

Jackson, R. (1981) *Fantasy: The Literature of Subversion*, new ed. London: Routledge.
Panofsky, E.. (1939) *Studies in Iconology: Humanistic Themes in the Art of the Renaissance*. Oxford: Oxford University Press.

Ruth Lingford: *Pleasures of War* – Interview

Pleasures of War (1998) is a radical retelling of the Biblical story of Judith, a beautiful Hebrew widow, and Holofernes, commander of an invading Assyrian army laying siege to her home town. Judith gains entry to the enemy camp's fortress, ostensibly to offer a personal surrender, but in fact to seduce then kill Holofernes in order to save her country. Radical because of its extremely explicit sexual imagery, but perhaps more so because that imagery is used to raise disturbing issues about the connections between sex, violence and war. The wider context of war's brutalising effects is suggested in the film's integration of archival documentary footage from twentieth-century wars into some of the animation.

The film came about as a result of a television commissioning initiative to encourage collaborations between animation filmmakers and established fiction writers.[1] The project enabled Ruth Lingford to make one of her most provocative films to date, and develop a longstanding interest in exploring the transgressive in animation, the subject of her Master's thesis as a mature student at the Royal College of Art in London, from which the following excerpts are taken.

> Most visual artists work within some sort of physical limitations imposed by their material. To a great extent, the animator can create a space in which no rules apply. Anything that can happen in the animator's head can happen on the screen. Working in a medium in which anything is possible holds many terrors. There is a constant compulsion to set oneself boundaries and barriers in order to have a defined space and structure in which to work. These boundaries are dictated in part by notions of good taste and the expected reactions of others. For me, at times, it has seemed important to consciously try and cross these

boundaries: they are ill-defined, but have to do with a prevailing notion of what is suitable subject matter for animation, and what are the acceptable modes of portraying, say, sexuality or human physicality.

Film historian Bruno Edera may be right in saying that identification is difficult to evoke in animation,[2] but a visceral and perhaps emotional reaction can be achieved through use of movement, unexpected juxtapositions of ideas and a stretching and confounding of assumptions, as in the shifting of perspectives or meanings. The repetitive nature of animation drawings can produce a state in which the internal censor may be lulled into inattention ... I like to leave some space in my working method for the rogue voice of the unconscious. Also, like many animators, I derive some inspiration from my dreams. Animation is the medium of dream-logic, of shifts in time, place and meaning. Many of my ideas come from the moments between sleep and wakefulness.

In some films I have tried to create images that are difficult to look at, and in this I find feedback from others very useful, as the familiarity with the images that is inevitable during the animation process blunts their emotional impact. I suppose that in this sense my work has a therapeutic aspect, as it involves confronting things that I have found extremely anxiety-provoking, but it is also very important to me that my work moves others.

It has been my experience that it is when I am working on material that is sincerely, intensely personal, rather than on issues that I feel I ought to be concerned with, that my work is most likely to find resonance in the experience of others. The key, I feel, is to work with one's most obsessive preoccupations.

It is sometimes hard to own and take responsibility for the more disturbing images in the films. Paradoxically, when trying to tread new ground, it is a great comfort to place myself within a tradition of transgression in the arts, and to remember what Georges Bataille said: 'The pinnacle of being stands revealed in its entirety only through the movements of transgression' (1990: 41).

Considering potential writers with whom to collaborate, Lingford remembered a novelist and short-story writer Sara Maitland, 'whose story about a woman who loves her baby so much that she eats it I had read a couple of years earlier: the concept and logic of it stayed in my mind.'[3] The fact that Maitland was also a Christian theologian seems apposite, given Lingford's interest in Biblical narratives.

Lingford: 'I've always loved Bible stories – particularly those in the Old Testament, because they are so dark and primal. They're not simple stories; Abraham and Isaac, for example, is a huge and complex narrative. It had also struck me that these stories were leaching out of our culture; people in the UK do not know the Bible stories anymore – similarly with fairy-tales. So there is no longer that bank of shared stories.

'Sara started talking about Judith and Holofernes, from the Apocrypha, in the Bible. What attracted me about this story was the violent female figure who is a hero – there are plenty of other violent females in Bible but they're usually "baddies". I knew the story through Artemesia Gentileschi's fantastic painting of Judith, with a strong forearm, sawing Holoferne's head off as though it was the Sunday roast. There was something very business-like about it, very female like, a task that has to be done – which I'd also seen in Almodóvar's film *Volver* [2006], where the women get together to dispose of the body; it's a case of "just steel your jaw and get on with it". So we discussed the Judith story, and the conjunction of sex and war, which seemed to be a fertile topic. We would get together, unpack ideas, and give ourselves permission to think further and more widely about it. Often Sara was thinking in pictures, so it wasn't just her providing words for a script.

'I looked at a lot of art, as the story was a common subject in Renaissance paintings. Although the Bible story is a little coy – it says she got him drunk, and might even point out that she did not have to have sex with him – everyone who painted the scene seemed in no doubt that it is very definitely post-coital violence that is being done. Holofernes is always naked, Judith is always dishevelled in her dress.

'It's often difficult to distinguish paintings of Judith from paintings of Salome; usually the only marker is that Salome always has a plate, Judith a basket. They're both depicted in a similar way, which is very sexual. Then there's all the art with that sense of *fin-de-siècle* and syphilis-ravished Paris, the *femme fatale*, Beardsley's sick and tainted rose.[4] In Symbolist art generally, fatal sexuality is personified as a woman; and there's a sense of cruelty and sexual potency as a threat in itself in its female incarnation. (I understand women were blamed as the cause for syphilis.) The Renaissance art is more interesting, although in the film there are also some visual references to Beardsley and to Munch. Judith straddling Holofernes, standing on one of his hands and his thigh, where she's about to cut his head off, came from a Donatello statue

Images from *Pleasures of War* (1998)
© Ruth Lingford

– although it is a very unconvincing pose if taken literally. In the film this becomes a rather bizarre sexual position, but that's where it comes from.

The sequence where she lowers her veil was inspired by a fantastic scene in the Gilles Pontecorvo film *The Battle of Algiers* [2006] – in which, as the women prepare to go and bomb the French, they remove their veils and put make up on to go to war. It was such a strong image, almost the revealing of themselves putting on war-paint.

'Throughout the development period the story went through many incarnations. We spent a lot of time discussing the sexual encounter between Judith and Holofernes, which is the important part of the film. The scene of anal penetration was something we introduced; we had long talks about this. We felt we needed one more thing, to show that Holofernes was embracing his own destruction. The power relationship had shifted to that extent – Sara has a lot to say about men's enjoyment of anal sex, and what a very potent taboo/desire it is for men. It stands for a reversal of usual submissive/dominant model of sex, so it's both a humiliation of Holofernes and something he both wants and accepts, and leads from there to his accepting of his own death; the eros and thanatos connection.

'Looking back, I sometimes wish I had just made the sexual encounter between Judith and Holofernes the film, or started it with Judith's journey across to the tent, with maybe a title card – just 'cut to the chase' as it were. I struggled so much just telling the story and ... it is still rather confusing! Part of my motivation is about storytelling – so I should have had the confidence or the broader vision to leave out bits of story, but I was worried I had to point it all out. I needed the audience to know that Judith was a woman who identified with the city that is besieged, in a desperate situation, so she goes to the city fathers to suggest this last tactic.

'What's important when you're animating, is to be animating something you feel obsessively about: you need that obsessive energy to get the damn thing done. And this introspection into the darker sides of my own sexuality I find endlessly fascinating and like to discuss with others so in a way that was the juice of the film.'

No reference footage was used for the actual animation, most of which Lingford did, although she stresses the collaborative aspects of the film here too, working with animator Ron McCrae on some scenes.

Lingford: 'To me that was very important, because if you're making a film about sex it seems important to get the other side's view in there somehow. He has a luscious, very embodied animation style; there's a real sense of inhabiting the body in his animation. We animated the sex scenes together almost – often he'd animate Judith (such as the scene where Judith is preparing herself to go and see Holofernes) and I'd animate Holofernes. Although I had already decided most of the action, the scene when Judith rams her breast into Holoferne's mouth came out of a discussion with Ron.

'For the archival material, I spent a lot of time at the Imperial War Museum, working with a picture researcher, to find images of women soldiers and child soldiers. I wanted a spread of war images and used a lot of different wars and places. Integrating the archival material was more a process of trial and error (i.e it was not planned or included at the animatic stage). There was a choice of things for every scene, we'd try them out and see what worked.

'The problem with the Holocaust imagery may be that it is still so charged it's difficult to use in a balanced way, it almost blinds people to the other footage, it is all they seem to see in the film even though in fact it occupies only a very small proportion of screen time. Indeed it is this aspect of the film that has provoked unease amongst some viewers, for a number of reasons, which both overlap and diverge, making it more complicated to disentangle. One reason may be to do with content and context.'

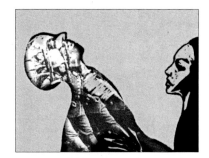

Lingford is quite clear that 'the use of sexual imagery throughout the *mise-en-scène* was quite intentional – for example, the vagina-like shape of the door, the battering ram against the fortress tower, to suggest the aggressive impulse has something sexual embedded in it.' The use of visual metaphor is not uncommon in animation: and the viewer may well have been sufficiently cued by the title of the film to take this on board. Yet the scenes between Judith and Holofernes are not of a metaphorical order, they are detailed, as opposed to generalised. Both the long-drawn out sexual encounter and murder are very explicit. For the viewer who finds the sexual imagery and actions shocking, the integration of documentary footage into the animation, however fleeting, may well cause further anxiety because it blurs the conventional demarcation between 'reality' and the 'imaginary' world of animation. Unease with the former is likely to be exacerbated by its integration and juxtaposition with the latter, because the most familiar, therefore identifiable, images in the documentary material are those of the Holocaust, which raises other issues.

The words spoken at the beginning of the film, 'you are sowing in blood and I will reap the whirlwind', suggest the bloodlust that begets an endless

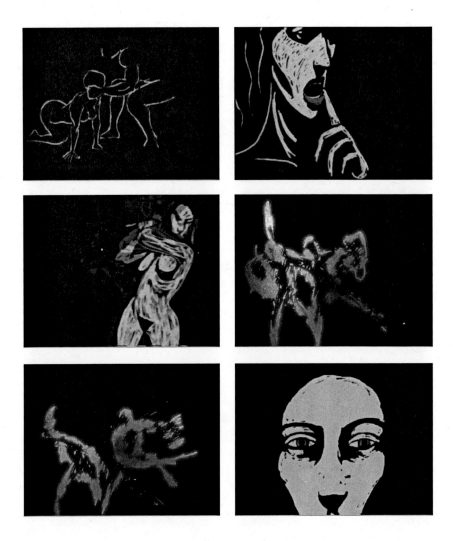

cycle of revenge killing to be a primary fuel for war. This impression is reinforced by the violence and furious energy of both much of the action depicted
(the soldiers killing, raping and pillaging), and the animation itself. Yet in
one sense such an interpretation seems to conflict with what we know of the
coldly calculated, inhumanly efficient killing machine the Nazis developed
for the Holocaust. There is also the fact that wars may happen for many and
complicated different reasons, often rooted in specific socio-economic conditions, which makes the film's conflation of so many different conflicts from
around the globe somewhat problematic.

Lingford responds: 'When the film was being made, Israel and Syria
were fighting and Judith and Holofernes was a Jews versus (As)Syrians story.

Whatever we did, it would be read as something about the Middle East, so we thought we might as well take that on board. My feeling was that what was happening in Israel was a turn of the wheel – from the Holocaust, the brutalisation of the Jews, but they somehow internalised some of it and were playing it out, they are now the brutalisers. *Of course* it is not as simple as that, but I feel there's a dynamic to that situation ... it's not just revenge, because it is pointed at someone one else entirely. But it is the fact that the experience of a victim being treated so very badly infects the victim and takes part of their humanity away.

'More generally, most war films feature the pleasure of striking back; for that matter in most films, there's the joy of killing off the baddie, the pleasures of righteous anger. Yet righteous violence is at its heart tainted with a future taking on of the cycle, the seeds of the infection. So to defend my use of Holocaust imagery I wanted to identify Judith and her people with this abject victimhood which by fighting back you then turn it around.'

Another complication in working out one's response may be due to the sheer bravura of the filmmaking, which suggests the film's real focus and energy lie in what happens between Judith and Holofernes, deriving from Lingford's interest in the complicated dynamics of human sexuality. Almost every scene moves forward into the next via transformations from one element of décor or character pose in a rapid, relentless narrative, sweeping the viewer along with its furious energy. The stark black and white 'woodcut' style, allied to brilliant use of primary colours – yellow, red and orange – also contribute to a sense of the inevitable, the primal. All of this makes it difficult to be anything other than awed by the virtuosity of the *mise-en-scène*, horrified at its visceral impact, yet left with a nagging concern about the multitude of possible political implications and a sense of being taken hostage by the forcefulness of the film. Lingford herself feels the powerfully evocative soundtrack 'might be too intense, leaving the viewer feeling they have no time to think, or to process what they are seeing'.

She adds: 'Another motivation for the film was that of exploring women's violence, as opposed to the idea that if only the world was run by women it would be a soft and gentle place and we'd all be very happy. And that men own all the violence in the world. If you think women are non-violent, just ask any child. Being a mother, it's frightening to discover things you didn't know you could feel or express, feelings of rage and violence. It felt important to say women can be violent.' This is clearly expressed in the depiction of Judith's pleasure as well as aggression in the scenes with Holofernes. 'Earlier in the film, we see women raped by a group of soldiers, and clearly this is about aggression, power, domination. Then later we see Judith's pleasure in domination and power, in the act of seducing, in making him pleasure her.'

Technical notes

The technique and graphic style of *Pleasures of War* were developed from Lingford's earlier films, such as *Death and the Mother*, (1997) which was made on an Amiga computer, using a very basic programme called Deluxe Paint, which allowed onion-skinning and instant playback, but limited the number of colours – 'a limitation that suited me (life is more difficult now with so much choice). The pixels look much larger than on my later Mac work, mainly because I wasn't anti-aliasing the lines (visual softening using intermediate colours). I drew straight into the computer using a very basic digitising tablet with no pressure-sensitivity. This required quite a hard gouging action, which felt a bit like lino-cutting. I would draw with white on a black background, then draw with black into the white to vary the very uniform line. I used a mixture of Keyframing and in-betweening and some straight-ahead animation, sometimes leaving traces behind (like where the mother goes out of her house).

Pleasures of War was made the same way, but the drawn animation was transferred on to a Mac, and the image softened, and the archive footage added in After-Effects. The same application was also used for some other effects, for example the flames in the bodies. The clever technical stuff, like layering in the archival material, was done by Caroline Parsons.

Notes

1   This was Channel Four television in the UK. Channel Four's commissioning editor and freelance animation producer, Dick Arnall, had felt for some time that many animated shorts suffered from weak scripts, hence this initiative.
2   Edera, B. (1980) 'Eros Image par Image', *La Revue du Cinéma et Ecran*, 354.
3   This and subsequent comments are from an interview with the author in Boston, May 2008.
4   Images referencing Beardsley also appear in Lingford's earlier film *Baggage* (1992).

Reference

Bataille, G. (1990) *Eroticism*. London: Marion Boyars.

Interrogating Masculinity

Revealing Men: The Y Factor
by Ruth Lingford

In the hundred years since its birth, live-action film has done a pretty thorough job of showing us what sex, in all its variety, looks like. Maybe it can be the task of animation to tackle the far more interesting question of what it feels like.

In live-action film, sex can be pornographic or erotic, confrontational or titillating. A key element is the ability of film to allow identification with the protagonists. Sexually-charged visual images operate directly on our nervous systems, arousing or repelling the viewer. Animation may not be as good at arousing us or at allowing identification. But it can help us to examine the tangled elements of our experience of sex. Layers of contradictions and ambivalence can be expressed through metaphor, metamorphosis and layering of images. We can be drawn into unexpected somatic identification using movement, and that identification can shift fluidly between protagonists. Sex often obsesses us as human beings, and that obsession can fuel the repetitive work of animation. We can interrogate our own experience and imaginatively inhabit the experiences of others, and we can cross gender boundaries in the process.

There was a time when there seemed to be a clear divide between men's and women's animated films. Mens' films, it seemed, were preoccupied with action, conflict, gags, punch-lines and technical pyrotechnics. Womens' films were where emotion and soul-baring happened, where the body was given space to speak. Maybe women were pioneers in animating the unconscious, but in the films in the *Desire and Sexuality: Animating the Unconscious* DVD collection (2007) we see that men are using this medium to examine their darker places, and to explore and empathise with the female experience.

In *The Secret Joy of Falling Angels* (1991), Simon Pummell examines the complexity of a sexual encounter between a woman and a bird-like creature of indeterminate gender.

Secret Joy... is a film made at a time when our perception of sex was inflected and infected by the fear of AIDS. Sex had become a barbed thing, and a generation was newly aware of the links between eroticism and death. We can maybe trace the shadow of AIDS in the art of this time as, with the benefit of longer hindsight, we recognise the shadow of syphilis in the art of the *fin-de-siècle*, in the unwholesome beauty of symbolism and art nouveau.

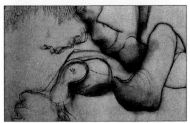

The point of departure for *Secret Joy...* was Renaissance paintings of the Annunciation. Pummell was interested in the nuanced layering of gesture – resistance, fear, awe and acceptance. The figure of Mary holds her hands up, or crosses them across her breast. She gestures to say 'Me?' and 'Not me!' and to question and repudiate. But her head and face incline towards the angel, in a gesture of submission. Pummell recognised these contradictory gestures as expressive of the complexity of human eroticism. The film imagines an erotic encounter between a woman and a bird/human creature that looks less like an angel than a monstrous chimera. The woman is fleshy and sensual, morphing between a sensual realism and a grotesque glamour.

The film is constructed with several contrasting techniques; graphite drawing, coloured pastels, stop-motion with articulated bird skeletons, and acrylic paintings. The paint suggests feathers, interior body spaces, abstract images mirrored to create a vaginal Rorschach pulsing. Still paintings are moved under the camera. Pummell cleverly integrates the disparate elements by echoing movement across techniques, and by making the drawing appear initially as a shadow occupying the same universe as the birdcage. Backlighting is used throughout, unifying the look of the piece. Sound enhances an unsettling and sensual world of textures.

Although this is a film by a man, we feel a convincing female subjectivity at its core. This is in part created by the intimacy and emotion of Annabel Pangborn's voice. The constant shifting of the

Images from *The Secret Joy of Falling Angels* (1991) © Channel Four Television

woman's body between desirable and grotesque feels like an expression of a mobile internal state rather than the product of misogyny. This is both a cool and a passionate film.

Early in the film we are invited – first via the letter O, then via a mirror – into the woman's vagina, as experienced subjectively, into an inchoate pulsing world. The music suggests melancholy, even the presence of death. The sexual act in the film often seems to be happening between two versions of the same woman. The vagina is maybe the most important and most insistent protagonist in the film.

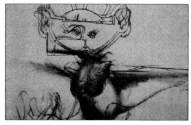

The only time we see male genitalia is in the distortions of the woman's body, and implied in the aching voids of mouth and vagina. It is only the clear act of impregnation that tells us that this is definitely a coupling of two creatures, male and female. The angel often has breasts. Maybe the idea of the angel suggests a freeing of the sexual spirit from the confines of the gendered body. It is the skeleton bird that most clearly represents the penis; it's blind, frantic thrashing with its creaking sound effects contrasting with the deeper pulsing rhythms of the female images. The bird, according to Pummell, comes from the dove often seen in Annunciation paintings as the embodiment of the holy spirit. But birds to Pummell are also objects of a certain revulsion, seeming to him to be mindless bio-mechanisms.

The insistence and urgency of sexual desire are built up by the abstract rhythms of the animated painting, the beating of the wings, the growing intensity of the pace and cutting. Bird skeletons couple in a frantic spasm, an abjectly physical counterpoint to the psychic transcendence of orgasm.

But it is the drawings that allow us to experience the particularity of the erotic experience. The drawings recall several things at once: anatomical drawings; Disney line-tests; and the exquisite unwholesomeness of Hans Bellmer's drawings. But animation can go further than still drawing when it comes to Bellmer's quest to disrupt the syntax of the body. Breasts morph into testicles, into the wattles

Images from
The Secret Joy of Falling Angels

89

on a grotesque face, man into woman, realism to grotesque caricature, the boundary line of the body is stretched into abstraction and geometry. The drawings suggest the loosening of boundaries that make eroticism dangerous. They are repeated backwards and forwards, creating a repetitive, swinging action which is in contrast to the frenetic rhythms of the skeletons and the pulsing paint. Ripple-glass effects give us a different sort of pulsing, with an underwater feeling. These rhythms recall breathing, heartbeat, the involuntary spasms and contractions of digestion and sex.

The drawings mix gestural line, indicating the dynamics of movement, shadow, creating weight and a sense of flesh on the bone and a controlled but mutable boundary line that defines and describes. We also see the traces of movement in the layers of backlit drawings. Although loose and mutable, the drawing is sufficiently anatomically convincing to allow us to experience the sensuality and the burden of flesh, with its weight and pendulousness. The painted acrylic sequences gives the impression of feathers, of fingerprints, of the inner space of the body. They are tactile in a double-edged way, attracting and repelling with a sort of unwholesome stickiness. At times they imply a moist meatiness.

The portrayal of orgasm in this film is something that feels authentic. The drawing allows the loosening of boundaries, the shifting of identification. As in the best sex, we are unsure where one body ends and the other begins. Body parts morph and change gender. Emotionally we take a journey through fear and resistance, through a frantic montage of skeleton shots, into a strangely calm centre, where time slows and there is an intense sweetness. It is no longer clear who the wings belong to. This is sex act as narrative, where the dénouement is the beginning of a new life. The bird-foetus is glimpsed in the woman's belly, while the resolution of the voice tells us that everything is going to be all right.

Pummell's evocation of meaty subjectivity, the mortality of the body, its weight and the way it binds us to the earth and offers moments of transcendence is something which we may associate more with womens' filmmaking, with animators such as Vera Neubauer, Joanna Quinn and Michèle Cournoyer. And Pummell is one of few men whose work approaches the self-exposure of women animators like Alison De Vere, Alys Hawkins and Emily Hubley.

Image from *Ring of Fire* (2000)
© Andreas Hydake

One other is Andreas Hykade, who subjects male sexuality to a merciless gaze. In his world, masculinity is a problematic burden and its integration into a fully emotionally functioning selfhood is a moral challenge. Hykade has been accused of misogyny, but in fact he tends to idealise women – the dandelion girl of *We Lived in Grass* (1995) and the water-haired

love-object of *Ring of Fire* (2000) are personifica-
tions of the female principle as life-giving and of
central importance. The mother in *We Lived in Grass*
can be seen as an abject baby-machine but in fact
she is a strong and complex character, though we are
given a strong sense of the depredations of being a
wife and mother on her body.

And the gipsy prostitute in *Ring of Fire* is a maj-
estic figure, allowing access to her mysteries only
on her own terms. The more abject images of sex
in the film seem clearly to be mere projections of
male desire. Through the cowboys' eyes, we see the
world of sexual relations as an excessive carnival of
disembodied body parts offered for commerce. This
commerce depends on a performance of masculinity, from which the inept cowboy runs, humiliated,
only to stray into the heroine's territory, where he is
bathed in the generous waters of the female principle. The beautiful heroine is suborned and raped by
the competently evil cowboy, while the inept cowboy
enters the gipsy's tent, where he is awe-struck at the
revelation of her endless sexual mysteries.

Images from *Ring of Fire*

Hykade's drawing is permitted by its intense
stylisation to show sex graphically and in a perverse and dizzying variety.
But the most intense expression of eroticism in his film comes in the form of
a metaphor, that of the pouring of water. The end of the film, where the softer
cowboy washes the damaged heroine, is at once erotic and moving. Here we
see the equal erotic exchange between a man and a woman as healing and
life-giving.

Igor Kovalyov's films deal with eroticism as part of the complex web of
relationships. In *Milch* (2005) the love object is a personification of healthy
carnality, desired both by the father and the son. But the film is equally concerned with looking at power relations within the family, and the learning
of masculinity by the son. We see sex through the boy's eyes as a rich and
disruptive force. His pent-up energy in the oppressive silence and tension of
his home is expressed in the repetitive banging of his wooden car against the
wall, his kicking a ball which we hear breaking a window, and by his sexual
obsession with the girl. The rich visual textures of the film, along with its
evocative sound, allow us to experience the film with all our senses. In the
alley where the father and the girl have a highly charged encounter we can
smell the caged circus lion. Kovalyov's work is full of musical rhythms and

tiny gestures which illuminate human relationships.

In *How Wings are Attached to the Backs of Angels* (1996), the woman's sensuality is contrasted with the controlling reductionism of the man's desires. This is beautifully expressed through the graphic style – the male world is depicted in a mannered Victorian style, obsessively mechanistic. In this world, observation and science are all about control. Nature is there to be tortured and manipulated with tiny surrogate hands, putting touch and feeling at a distance. The female, depicted in live-action, is grainy, real, capable of pleasure and emotion. The fear she inspires in the man is that of his own mortality. She defies his control and makes him experience himself as flesh, vulnerable to being decapitated/castrated by his own machines.

Images from *Sucré* (2005) © **Folimage**

All these films examine the relationships between men and women, their conflicts and similarities, with eyes that seem not to have a partisan gender stance. But it is in Gaelle Brisou's *Sucré* (2005) that the divisions between the 'men's film' and the 'women's film' seem most thoroughly broken down. The film seems to exude the female principle in every frame. The sensual curves of the landscapes and of the female protagonist express not just an eroticisation of the larger female form, but an understanding of what it is like to inhabit a body with curves and weight, prey to desire and excess. The eroticisation of food, and the voluptuous self-abandonment to over-eating seem somehow definitively female, and it is a real revelation to find that this film is made by a man, and that things we may have thought of as gendered are maybe more universal than we thought. The sex scene between two obese creatures could have been played for laughs, or as bizarre. Instead we see a joyful eroticism that transcends stereotype and celebrates human diversity.

Extracts from Simon Pummell's Notebooks

<u>Art and Psychoanalysis</u>
<u>Peter Fuller.</u>

Animation in itself is an artform, and that's the point I always think needs clarification. The animation exists without any background, or any colour, or any sound, or anything else. You don't even have to have a camera. I don't know if you've ever taken any of the great Disney animation, or even some barfly animation, and held any of those big thick scenes in your hand and flipped them. God! Its so beautiful, you can't believe it. That pink elephant sequence in Dumbo 1941 is a perfect example of what I'm talking about; there are no backgrounds, no nothing. Animation does everything.
<u>Chuck Jones.</u>

Gesture is that expressive power of the body by which we simultaneously break through the boundaries of our skin and learn the limits that exist outside us. When we, Rilke says what we hold back will express as much as what we give.

The paradox of the body is that it is meat, and it is something that leaps, gestures, speaks, touches.

"Hang the meat on the hook" Charles Simic says, "So that I

may see what I am." At other times, our bodies are as loose and liquid as water, and are completely swallowed into our actions, into walking, running, making love, speaking.

<u>Poetry and the Body</u>.
John Vernon.

PROCESS

ANIMATION IS THE ONLY GRAPHIC ~~FORM~~ THAT ALLOWS
A PURELY DYNAMIC PRESENTATION OF A FORM.
THE FORM SHOULD NOT BE PRESUPPOSED BUT ~~XXXXX~~
REALISED THROUGH A DYNAMIC PROCESS.
IT IA A FORM WHICH EMBODIES THE POSSIBILITIES OF
THE DYNAMIC RATHER THAN ATTEMPTS TO REPRESENT IT
BY A DISSOLUTION OF FORM. IT IS IN THE POSSIBILITY
OF SIMULTANEOUS PRECISION AND FLUX THAT THE
PROBLEMS AND POTENTIAL OF THE FORM LIES.

THE SKILLS AND PREOCCUPATIONS OF TRADITIONAL
DRAUGHTMANSHIP MUST BE TRANSFORMED FOR ANIMATION,
ALTHOUGH ENGAGEMENT WITH THEM GIVES SOME CONTEXT
TO ITS CONCERNS.

THE GROTESQUE REQUIRES A PRECISION OF OBSERVATION
OF THE INTERACTION OF LIFE AND DEATH, AND ITS
TRANSFORMATION INTO FORM/FORMLESSNESS. THE
VIRTUOSITY OF THIS ALLOWS THE FESTIVE WHICH
CELEBRATES SUCH AMBIGUITY.

The possibility & the use &
rigid /plastic tension the basis
of animation Convention.
The use of skeletal structure
as a discipline to rework
Disney's plasticity.
Strict perspective and attention
to anatomical accuracy.
Double Tension:
Skeletons essentially beyond death
Muscles particularly clearly reflect
aging
Opposition is the essence &
anatomical basis & movement;
rigidity and flexibility allow
systems & leverage.

A logic based on reconciling
opposition

Muscles: use 'disadvantage' & airbrush to
give plasticity - use transparency
& airbrush layer to reveal structure
beneath.

re
er
u
/

Animation allows a predominantly formal narrative - a 'logic of energies transferred and opposed a physical and biological' progress which is anonymous.

Conventions

Uses of pause in flux - detail action within stillness.

Total distortion of body beyond normal structure at expressive peaks. look for expressive archetypes.

Use of ghost image trains converging at peak moment.

On Simon Pummell's
The Secret Joy of Falling Angels

'The Aim: To move Disney's rhetoric of gesture from the realm of the conscious to the unconscious.

... So cartoons can provide a subject, or rather an approach which allows a subtle appreciation of fixed meaning, vex and disrupt that and also convert that disruption into aesthetic pleasure.

At the most fundamental, the possibility of the uses of tension between the opposition of rigidity and plasticity as the basis of animation convention needs to be explored. The use of a skeletal structure to rework Disney's plasticity. Disney's figures were uniformly plastic and their whole bodies move with the convention of squash and stretch. To stretch such plasticity across a more rigid skeletal framework (eg. breasts and belly move against a more rigid structure defined by the neck and shoulders) sets ups a tension fraught with possible meaning. Opposition is the anatomical basis of any movement, flexible muscles contracting and expanding act on the skeletal system of leverage; movement is a never-ending dialogue between the two. An energy runs through the body as a series of weight shifts and muscular contractions, it is transmitted by the interlocking structures of the anatomy and so illuminates that anatomy. There is an added layer of meaning in the relative agelessness of the skeleton coated with flesh and muscles which particularly reflect aging. Movement also produces unlikely distortions of the body, allows expressionist distortion disciplined by the context of function, of movement. In such organisation of movement and gesture lies the possibility of an animation that speaks a bodily language, a language that allows to some extent a productive suspension of the structures of rigid meaning. A purely material language. Animation that embodies the qualities Roland Barthes seeks in the forgotten rhetorical figure 'actio':

*It's aim is not the clarity of messages, the theatre of emotions; what it searches
for (in a perspective of bliss) are the positional incidents, the language lined with
flesh, a text where we can hear the grain of the throat, the patina of consonants,
the voluptuousness of vowels, a whole carnal stereophony: the articulation of the
body, of the tongue, not that of meaning, of language. A certain art of singing
can give an idea of this vocal writing; but since melody is dead, we may find it
more easily today at the cinema. In fact it suffices that the cinema captures the
sound of speech close-up (this is, in fact, the generalised definition of the 'grain'
of writing), and makes us hear in their materiality, their sensuality, the breath, the
gutterals, the fleshiness of the lips, a whole presence of the human muzzle ... and
in throwing so to speak the anonymous body of the actor into my ear; it granu-
lates, it crackles. It caresses, it grates, it cuts, it comes: that is bliss. (1975: 66–7)'*

The extract above is from an essay, 'A Popular Art', written by Simon Pummell
as an MA film student at the Royal College of Art in London, accompanied
by excerpts from a notebook of ideas and reading he kept during that same
period.[1] It is a measure of both his consistency and his relentlessly enquir-
ing artistic project, a rather unusual combination of very visceral attack and
intellectual ratiocination, that these extracts reflect concerns still resonant in
a film which he was to make almost a decade later.

The Secret Joy of Falling Angels (1991) is, to date, his only purely animated film, although all of his subsequent work, including the feature-length
film *Bodysong* (2003), a roller coaster tour of the human body and life cycle,
made entirely of archival film footage, have similarly used a range of old and
new technologies to develop a new form of hybrid filmmaking, and continued
his interest in the body. He is currently working on a 'revision' of *Secret Joy...*,
this time combining live-action and digital technologies.

The technical aspects of his filmmaking process in *Secret Joy...* have been
documented elsewhere,[2] so this interview concentrates largely on an account
of the genesis of the film, the ideas and thematic concerns that inform it, and
more generally his thoughts around how representations of the body inform
our experience of being human.[3]

Genesis

Pummell: 'The film was initially part of a much larger project about the
Passion story as a whole, and the Annunciation was only ever the first part
of that. And when that got split off into a smaller, more do-able film, I kind
of lived with that for two years until it got financed, so I think it evolved a
lot in that time.'

After taking a first degree in literature, where he developed a fascination with Elizabethan and Jacobean writing, in particular the work of Thomas Nashe, he was unsure about what to do next.

'Nashe's prose is very violent, very grotesque ... I use "grotesque" in a very literal, technical sense, as literary academics use it, which is to represent a type of writing that prioritises the life cycle, the shared physicality of people over their individual personalities. The physical processes we share are actually more significant than our personalities and idiosyncrasies.

'I knew I wanted to make something but was struggling as to what that something would be. If you had asked what my conscious project was, I kind of thought that I was going to try and find some prose equivalent of that; which I simply couldn't do. I had no sense of making a visual equivalent of that writing, I just liked the sense of physicality about it, and poetic quality of the texture. And then I started drawing, and that sort of met me half way, so I suddenly had a tool I could use. The next step was to feed that into animation.

'The first thing I drew, was in fact a birth scene. A woman giving birth to a shapeless... what looks like part of a self really, rather than a baby – and it's bouncing, trying to get back into her. So the body is all very kind of liquid. That clearly expressed something that I needed to get onto paper in some fashion but I was not clear what it meant. You could understand going to film school as me trying to see what that first sequence was about. And the first piece of animation I ever did is actually in my graduation film four years later. So I clearly wanted to keep it in there; it's not like I threw it away and developed these other conscious things. And it was a puzzle, what to do with these incredibly volatile, fluxive shapes I had made, bouncing around, metamorphoses.

'The desire to make it move was connected to an interest in narrative development, mainly of an oblique sort, but I do like things to develop. I guess quite often, without meaning to, I have treated my visual work as something to interrogate. If you contextualise it in some kind of narrative you are forced to engage with its meaning yourself. I don't think I have ever just made visual objects and left the meaning completely up to other people. That's every important to me. I work through it, which in the end is a very classic therapeutic thing. It's treating the drawing as a symptom, and narrativising it and then it becomes something else.

'So the various attempts I made to make some kind of narrative film that had drawn animation in it, was an attempt for me, completely parallel to the academic essays I wrote, to ask the same question of this very fluxive particular anatomical form that I found spoke to me. And the question is "why did it speak to me?" And if you can put it a narrative context that makes sense to people, you have partly answered that.

'*Secret Joy...* basically inverts the Annunciation. It is very important that the angel does not have arms. The angel is not a superior being to the human, the angel is an alternative being. You could even see it as a less dextrous being, so it's kind of stunted, as it lacks something defining: since hands are a key human thing. The angel is like an autistic figure in a way. He definitely has some special powers but he pays some prices for that. And the fact that he literally has sex with the woman and then at the end the cycle is closed and you see the baby bird inside the woman: an incredibly literal version of the Annunciation.

'Something I am interested in is what happens when you take things incredibly literally. (I recently read this sentence in an analysis of Kafka's *Metamorphosis* by Stanley Corngold: "The intent to literalize a metaphor produces a being wholly divorced from empirical reality." It seemed relevant to this discussion). I think that's what happens with the Annunciation; it gets very quickly talked about and symbolised. But what is it? What's happening? God impregnated a woman. You can sort of quickly say it has theological implications but actually on some level that means you do not have to engage with the brute story of the myth. One of the things I really liked about the form I discovered in animation is that it is really mute, and in that way you can say it is quite resistant to my desire to explain - that it's actually quite related to the fact that a lot of the stuff that goes on between people in life is actually not that explainable but it's mute. I remember I wrote this sentence: "Muteness and inexpressiveness of the pre-verbal, like blind role of instinct" at the beginning of the funding application and presentation of the film. By this I mean that we actually exist in a world of drives and compulsions rather than metaphors and meanings, which I do fundamentally believe.

The angel and the woman

'The angel is a more broken, patched-together figure than the woman. He seems to be more aggressive but is much more provisional as well. He is very prone to collapse back into his element. There is a point where he becomes a bird-skeleton again and then he is fleshed again, there's a wing and then there's two wings. He's actually more vulnerable than she is, I think, although she is more aggressive as well, and that produces the feeling of ambivalence. I think a lot of the time that came out first, before I thought about it. But there was one moment just before the union of the two figures, when he hovers above her and he changes size, at one point he is very small. That was a conscious decision, to make him seem dependent on her. He becomes like a flying cupid for a moment and then he goes back to being bigger again. The scale between the figures shifts quite a lot, in terms of who is what size: a see-sawing of who is the big, powerful figure and who is the small, vulnerable figure. I guess the most vulnerable moment of the woman figure, I always think of it as the "Alice in Wonderland" sequence, where she starts changing into grotesque shapes, and she is coloured with watercolor and her head is massive. For me it's childlike, but it's clear she is an adult woman. There are a number of things going on, but that's the moment where her identity goes into the kind of volatile slippage that his identity is in pretty continuously.

'I was aware that it was one of the effects that she became simultaneously older and younger than herself, at this point. She physically breaks down into her components less than the angel does. The angel tends to break down into components: his bones show through, he becomes only a bone bird, he is always part animal, part human, but one of the things that happens with the woman figure is that somehow her stable identity goes into slippage in a different way and that could be read as her simultaneously becoming all sorts of different ages. It is also not unrelated to the fact that the way that sequence is coloured gives it a nursery book quality, but it's not nursery book images, so there's something unstable there again. So it might also be that your own perspective on her as a viewer keeps shifting around at that point when the angel literally just falls into component parts, but when the woman's identity shifts, your point-of-view changes, the point-of-view it puts you in changes but your age as a viewer changes in some way. I think the way she is depicted when the film starts is a much more agreed convention of a certain kind of life-drawing rendition of the female form and thus positions you as a culturally knowing viewer.

'In the original storyboard things actually transform from one thing to another – i.e. there are two stable states and a transition – whereas later I realised I was much more interested in forms that distorted and shifted and never resolved into some kind of single stable state. When it came to the crunch I felt that was not what I was describing at the beginning, it wasn't mute and preverbal, it was actually a perfectly traditional metaphor (A = B). Two stable entities linked, so that went.

'Adding movement to the mixture ... if what you are interested in is the unfinishedness, the shifting of any identity, then what I like about drawn animation is that most of my drawings are very incomplete so there are things appearing and disappearing at any moment. (I have been thinking about this for a new live-action reinvention of the same work.) Which gives a sense of the figures being about your sensorium, not about a visual image of the body.

In other words even if you really monitor your inner sensorium you're not aware at every moment of your own body. You know if you pick that bottle up and close your eyes, and feeling what parts of your body you can feel, you could feel your cheek and elbow, and your hand holding the bottle, maybe your bum where you are sitting on a hard seat. But you cannot feel your ankles, whether they are there are not, they kind of disappear. Therefore the animation becomes much subtler than a single drawing because that gets written into it, because everything is actually on a very micro level in flux, which you can't get with a storyboard, which looks much more graphic-y.

The life cycle

'The important breakthrough for me in writing other more narrative films, quite long after this film, was a realisation that I actually am interested in making cyclical films. We were talking about the grotesque, Thomas Nashe and those Elizabethan writers ... they were very influenced by Rabelais, and something that had a massive impression on me when I was studying Mikhail Bhaktin's book *Rabelais and His World* [1984] was that it is about the tension between a moment a culture shifts from believing primarily in a cyclical view of the world into one where it starts to attach importance to individuals, and that produces an incredible tension.

'In the end, the crudest, simplest but most effective definition of tragedy and comedy is that tragedy is the individual story that has to end in death, but comedy is about the larger waves of humanity which actually is purely cyclical. So I think whether *Secret Joy...* is comic or tragic, in those terms, it's more like a sounding board for what you feel, yourself, about the world. For me, in the end, it's kind of important that there's a little angel, for better or worse, in her belly. I think that implies that the whole dance carries on. For me, it's definitely a yearning film, but it's not particularly a sad film. The things I tend to like best in culture are both those things simultaneously. So therefore I wouldn't say its either way for me, it's not about loss, but it's about the loss within fullness.'

To comments about the film being about sex and death, and Pangborn's feeling of a sense of loss at the end of the film, Pummell responds: 'I think that that's true. One of the reasons that sex is an interesting cultural topic of our time is because it is one of the times/places people experience that feeling. Where people lose themselves in something else. With Bataille's sex/death thing, there's a bit too much death in it for my taste. I feel that he was writing as someone who was a librarian in 1950s France, that he perceives utter loss of control as absolutely deathly. It has to be an annihilation. Whereas it can be seen as an enlargement.

'That's become more popular post-60s; it's become a more culturally viable way of looking at it. The loss of control is not necessarily a negation. I definitely think it is about totally losing yourself and the fact that you move in and out of that.

I guess I would call that, also in sex I think they call it, power relations, because people have to negotiate that quite trickily, because that's definitely a vulnerable thing, and once vulnerability is involved, it's about what you withhold and what you give. So yes, but I would term it rather differently.

'It's a rather difficult thing to express ... possibly because Western vocabulary is not very good with these areas. *The Secret Joy of Falling Angels* is kind of anti-Western religion; the dichotomy of Western religion is in the title. Because the Western religious myth is that falling is damnation and joy is to rise. I spent a term at university being very stoned and reading 'Paradise Lost', and what you can never get around in that is that Milton loves Satan, everyone in heaven is bored out of their brains, they don't know what to do, all they do is dance round in circles. Whereas Satan finds himself, in a way. But I think that other traditions have a slightly more subtle way of looking at those things ... in Buddhist traditions people talk about fullness in emptiness: basically that the binary division is not there and that's a little bit what I think people touch on in sex, the togetherness and loneliness, the negation of your identity and the fulfillment of your identity cease to be binary opposites.

'I think in the little I have read outside Western traditions, something like Buddhism gets closer to that. That is where my interest in deconstruction, Jacques Derrida, comes from, that any concept has inside it a negation, an irritation, a tiny grain of its opposite meaning within it. It's intrinsic to it, to be able to have its own meaning. There is a point where you come really close to the division and you examine the division between opposites, that such divisions must break down, and that each must incorporate the other. And I don't think that we feel that very often emotionally in our lives but there are definitely a few moments when we do feel it. It's not even a sense, it's a feeling, just a feeling, but in that feeling you find those divisions don't hold.

'I think out of anything else in particular that I have done, the moment that comes into my head when I was trying to get that feeling again, was when you see fifty babies being born at the beginning of *Bodysong* and they build and build and build, wave after wave. Because that's a key moment, where you are your most intensely individual yet at the same time most intensely connected to the broader cycle.

'Particularly in the culture we live in, we are highly developed individuals and we have CVs for our individuality, but we spend a lot of time emotionally trying to obtain the points of experience which we share with everyone else; be that having sex, giving birth or more simple things.

'Is the male figure less resolved than the female character?[4] I guess that relates to the fact that the male figure is more patched together and keeps falling into his constituent parts. Whether that's a particular accident of me making that film or whether it's some observation about maybe the male and female psyches, I'm not sure. Or at least it may not even be male and female psyches, it may be male and female mythic figures as well.

'Mythical female figures often tend to represent completeness in some ways, whereas often mythological male figures kind of fall apart or are torn apart as well. If you see Prometheus as a male figure, it's the fact that he is damaged that is part of his myth. He is destroyed to achieve something astounding because he steals fire, rather than he has within him intrinsically the power to do something astounding, like reproduce. I think the difference is there are certain male archetypes which are more about ... you have to dash your self against the world, and the world will eventually destroy you but you will alter it, rather than have within you a generative power to make a new world. So there is a different kind of mythos.'

Digital drawing

Pummell has recently completed a new feature-length film, a drama-documentary, entitled *Shock Head Soul* (2011), about the outsider artist Daniel Paul Schreber who wrote an autobiographical account of his psychosis. For this project explored new forms of digital drawing (hence his interest in looking back at *Secret Joy...*) and sought to achieve visual representations of the body that were not possible when he made that earlier film.

'These are some storyboard images for the idea of taking an actor and pulling and twisting him like the characters in *Secret Joy...* which interests me the most because you can then drop it into any kind of film. One of the problems with animation and live-action is that the indexical quality of photography is in contrast to, in conflict with, the abstract notion of drawing; they are basically expressions of a different order, so when you put them together they will only ever be in conflict. If you use the procedure of drawing on photographic material, you set up something new, sort of strange.

'But there is something actually even deeper than technique. I believe that photography has some fundamental magic, about being a kind of magic mirror, something that part of the century responded to massively, and that erased drawing, because the photograph has this other thing, it has presence. So if you can retain that indexical quality of the notion you are looking at something real because the light bounced off something, bounced off of a real body, but then you can actually use all of the procedures of drawn animation; in terms of compressing, stretching, twisting and erasing and making the image partial. You actually end up with some new, hybrid form that really is something new in terms of what film language is, because you are literally combining what previously were two distinctive indexes.

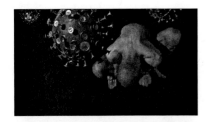

Images from *Shock Head Soul* (2011)
© Simon Pummell

'You have actually no drawn markings, you are picking the hand up and reshaping it, as if you were a drawing but it remains a photograph. You will be aware of gesture because everything will be shaped different, but there is no mark that is distinct from the photographic index, you are not marking on, in any way, you completely let the indexical image eat the drawing.

'For me this digital re-drawing is part of a kind of spiral I'm beginning to see in my work, and which I'm very happy about. The digital techniques within the film element of the *Shock Head Soul* project are ways that animation is embedding itself more and more in the live-action and cross-media projects I'm making. The project intertwines rotoscoping, CGI and the re-drawing of live-action images we talked about earlier to make a very fluid, elastic world that the main character inhabits. And the installation version of that project also uses the obsessional looping that I explored in *Secret Joy...* - though to rather different purpose.'

'The Writing Down Balls (figments of the main character's delusions) flock randomly around him, while he stubbornly, even obsessively repeats the same actions, his body twisting and distorting as he moves.

'And in an even more direct return to the pre-occupations of *Secret Joy...* I have just now started work on a new installation project that is taking the drawing approach of *Secret Joy...* in new directions. The key frames of these installations are large scale acrylic and watercolour drawings. When they have been scanned the inbetweens are created digitally to create smooth, plastic movement, that represents translucent bodies performing obsessional looping actions. The focus is on the body as an intricate mechanism, the detailed shifts within the body through movement. It's planned to project them large scale in galleries as contemplative, looping images: moving large scale drawings. It's kind of a complete spiral around to the pre-occupations of *Secret Joy...*, hopefully in a more fully developed way.'

Notes

1   Other suggestive texts cited in the notebooks, which illuminate both Pummell's work as a film-maker and some of the other filmmakers' featured in this book, include Rawson 1969, Vernon 1979 and Pummell 1997, his own essay on John Berger's critique of Francis Bacon and Walt Disney which more fully explores ideas about representation of the body.
2   See, for example, Pilling 2001: 28–37 and Kitson 2009: 118–22.
3   Interview by the author, July 2008, in Holland.
4   A response to a comment made by the film's composer Annabelle Pangborn, in the interview included in the present book.

References

Barthes, R. (1975) *The Pleasure of the Text*. New York: Hill and Wang.

Kitson, C. (2009) *British Animation: The Channel 4 Factor*. London: Parliament Hill Publishing.

Pilling, J. (2001) *Animation: 2D and Beyond*. Crans-Près-Céligny: Rotovision.

Pummell, S. (1997) 'Bacon and Disney Revisited', in J. Pilling (ed.) *A Reader in Animation Studies*. London: John Libbey, 166–82.

Rawson, P. (1969) *Drawing (Appreciation of the Arts 3)*. Oxford: Oxford University Press.

Vernon, J. (1979) *Poetry and the Body*. Urbana: University of Illinois Press.

On Andreas Hykade's
We Lived in Grass and *Ring of Fire*

"'All woman is whore and all man is soldier" my Papa said. "So go into grass and kill a tiger for the best tits you can find"' says a young boy's voice over the opening images of a grassy hill in Andreas Hykade's film *We Lived in Grass* (1995). As a house appears on the hill, he continues, 'I didn't understand this at the beginning. But at the beginning I wasn't even born.' The

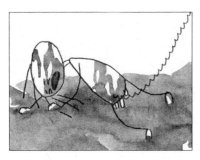

Images from *We Lived in Grass* (1995)
© Andreas Hykade

scene that immediately follows, set to jaunty, cartoony music, features a stick-figure woman bouncing up and down, dealing with a brood of kids' insistent demands on her breasts. Whirling around in a classic speed-blur of cartoon lines, threatening them with the word 'Papa', she then pops out what we assume is the film's narrator, in a wash and splotch of ink. The music stops, replaced by squelchy, watery sounds as a still minimally-drawn, yet remarkably expressive, infant looks up, pained, dazed and somewhat fearful. 'Papa', the mother repeats menacingly, and the jaunty music starts up again, this time with a deep tuba added into the bounce, as the father's massive bulk appears and fills the screen: naked, emphatically large genitals hanging down, looking something like a cross between man and bear.

Coming straight after the harsh, disturbing provocation of the opening words, loaded with adult meaning, such cartoony comic capers are all the more unsettling. The film continues to surprise, switching pace and visual style as it charts the boy's conflicted development,

Images from *We Lived in Grass*

breaking into nightmare under the strain of paternal, peer and institutional pressure, to become a searching critique of the social constructions of masculinity, of the price that is paid, personally and through its effects on others, in attempting to achieve the desire to 'be a man'.

Chris Robinson encapsulates the film's narrative implications well:

> Out hunting for tiger, the boy comes across a young woman ... who offers the boy a lock of her dandelion hair... Her gentle loving nature stirs strange emotions in him. 'Papa didn't tell me about this' he says... As the boy bathes in the warmth of his new discovery, his father dies. With Papa go the whore and the soldier. The nightmares stop. When the boy next sees the dandelion girl, she is standing, almost meditating, her eyes closed. The boy tries to get her attention, but she does not notice him. In frustration he yanks and twists her hair. Unmoved, she straightens her hair and continues her meditation. 'All woman is whore' the boy says. The nightmares return. This time he burns down the dandelion girl. The father is dead, but his words find new life. (2005: 150–1)

Despite the international awards and acclaim that this and Andreas Hykade's subsequent films have received, his work has also perplexed and outraged in equal measure. The films have something of the folktale and Christian traditions of the Holy Fool about them, an ostensibly childlike innocence that speaks uncomfortably adult truths, in the guise of folly (for which here, read 'cartoons'). It is particularly the relationship of imagery to subject matter, especially in the later *Ring of Fire* (2000), that has provoked controversy, accusations of misogyny and even hate-mail. The directness and graphic explicitness of some of the sexual images are in such contrast to the maturity of insight the stories convey that for some viewers the contradiction appears too difficult to overcome.

After earlier films that were strongly influenced by other filmmakers, with *We Lived in Grass* Hykade felt he was beginning to develop his own form of filmmaking. It also signalled the start of a continuing exploration of what he describes, some fifteen years later, as 'almost every subject that interested, and still interests me – the relationship between men and boys, men and women, sickness, death, society, the mother, the father, religion – metaphorical animals, dreams ... every time I pick out a new subject for a film it leads back to this.'[1]

In the edited interview below, the filmmaker discusses the genesis and development of his work, the relationship of the personal to the collective experience, autobiography and fiction, and addresses some of the issues raised above.

The personal and the collective

The title, *We Lived in Grass*, has puzzled many viewers; as often happens, it was an accidentally provoked yet consciously appropriated memory. Hykade explans: 'I had all these scenes for the film, not yet animated, but I had a problem about what's inside, what's outside, that I wouldn't be able to give a clear idea of where they lived. It seemed to be just a white piece of paper. One day I got a very stuffed nose, and difficulty breathing, so the doctor gave me something to open my nose. I'd go funny after taking these pills, I would smell the floor and think, I'm so lucky to be able to smell the floor, and the grass ... and I remembered drawing all that grass in the sketchbook ... and then suddenly I had a defined space. So when looking for a title, it just felt right. Even though it sounds equally odd in German.

'The film has a lot to do with where I grew up, in a small factory town in the Bavarian countryside. Another town nearby had a Holy Mary chapel, where for five hundred years Mary had been performing miracles, saving lives. People there would plaster the chapel with images of their personal experiences; for example, a farmer who'd survived being crushed by a tractor would paint himself, in a very simple way, with the tractor, the Virgin Mary and her child and then he'd write a little sentence, the place and date where it happened. Later, as a student, I would always remember that little church. I was really impressed by the artistry of the simple drawings, touched by what those people felt, painting themselves on the same painting as their God, so it was a combination of the private, personal realm, their own lives, and how that connected with the collective myth.

'It made sense to me as an artistic concept, and I tried to adapt it for myself. In a way, it was rather like the American underground comics that I was gobbling down at the time: Robert Crumb would look at America and look at himself and put these two things in the same space. In the mid-1980s I also saw a lot of British animation films, by the Brothers Quay, Phil

Drawing for *We Lived in Grass*

Mulloy, Vera Neubauer, Jonathan Hodgson, where you could see the same drive, which also encouraged me to think in that direction.'

In a film about machismo and sexist attitudes, a brute of a man dying of testicular cancer might seem a particularly heavy-handed metaphor. Strangely, however, this aspect of the film is based on fact. It also reflects the curious world of Hykade's films in which the literal and metaphorical, the serious and the purely whimsical, often refuse to play to expectations, swap places, as with his switches between comedy and tragedy, violence and tenderness.

'*We Lived in Grass* grew out of a book of around two hundred drawings of what I remembered of the countryside. Looking at them I'd see recurring themes that seemed to be connected. So I started thinking there was probably a film in there. It turned out that the central image was not about myself (unusually, since I was obsessed with my own biography), but rather a neighbour of ours. He died of testicular cancer in 1974, when I was six.' Hykade recalls the man, an alcoholic, womanising bully, and his ever-expanding family, from his fascinated forays as a small child into his house, whose doors were always open, and in more public, communal environments in the village. He also recalls the fear inspired by the phrase 'testicular cancer' and how 'you could feel the pain he was in throughout the house'.

'I remembered him from the pub my Dad used to go to. He'd take me with him, then give me a pencil to keep me quiet, whilst the men would sit, play cards and talk. That man was a massive, awful brute, an old fashioned man,

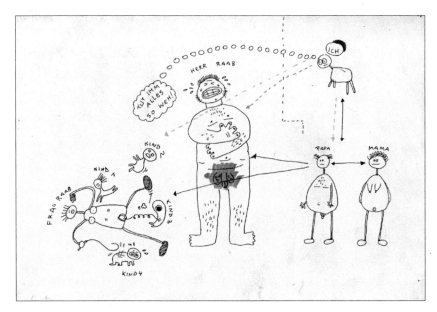

Drawing for *We Lived in Grass*

and he'd always talk the loudest. The way they talked about women, the language they used was so disgusting, I couldn't repeat it into this microphone. I'd sit and listen and feel, this was the world, there was maybe something wrong about it, but this is what they give you, like saying 'this is the landscape'.

'So the idea of the film was to show how these attitudes to women, to sex, were imprinted on his children, the effects of that, and how one of them tries to escape it. In this narrative the man became almost the father to be killed, in a metaphorical way. The image of the man was so strong because it connected a very personal image, something I had seen that had stayed with me for all those years, with a kind of collective image.'

Dreams and nightmares

The conflict between the boy's own nature and the aspirations he is supposed to fulfil, and his subsequent confusion, are vividly conveyed in the nightmare sequences and scenes of his encounters with other, more confident boys, already at ease as they ride on their 'tigers'. Hykade comments: 'The tiger became an important image. The other boys, although they're nasty in themselves, are quite in touch with their animal powers, while the boy ends up not being able to control them, and killing the tiger in his dream.

'The scenes of the demonic toy monster with the music box came from childhood nightmares. I used to watch a TV animated puppet series called the

Images from *We Lived in Grass*

Sandmannchen [translation: the little sandman], shown before bedtime. I was always afraid of the puppet with the two dead eyes. I started dreaming about him on that steamroller in that fire. I was convinced this creature would take control of me and lead me to hell. I had the nightmare so often I had trouble going to sleep. It became nastier each time, I could feel the heat get hotter and hotter. After a year or two I started thinking, 'hang on, this is just a dream, he can't harm me, so the next time I had the dream I'd tell him so, and he'd try to enlist a witch on his side... As the dream kept recurring, it became like a comedy ... it got to the point I would look forward to it, giggling, 'ha ha, here you are again and you can't do nothing to me', and he'd shrink away. The third dream in the film is invented, to get to the ending, but this one is pretty much as it was. The fragmentation, the alternating speeds, in that final nightmare/dream, was planned to be like that. I knew exactly what I was doing in this last scene. Everyone around me would ask "Why?" and try and convince me not to burn down this girl, and I couldn't explain it, it was just the way it has to be.'

The disturbing scene in which a priest-like figure seems to torture the boy with threats of damnation drew on memories of a particularly sadistic religious teacher. 'She would make us stand up to recite the Lord's Prayer. One day she made us all stop, and made one student, who was very quiet, a little bit backward, continue reading alone and he stumbled, hardly able to read any of the words. She went for him, screaming and twisting his ear. He was red in the face, crying from pain, and meanwhile she made us continue the prayer, and in the end she was smiling, saying 'that will teach him to learn the Lord's Prayer.'

Some visual devices in the film are far more opaque, such as the much more faintly-drawn creatures that often surround the father. Hykade sees them as 'auras of the father, such as the phallic tree trunks that represent maleness. At the beginning they're all in harmony and then as he gets sicker these spirits go out of control, as his body fades away they describe his moods and they all die in the end, so they end up hung on the wall. The bit of triangular floating cork is God watching, flying around, being not very effective.' Those phallic tree-trunks reappear in his later film *Ring of Fire.*

Looking back

Like many filmmakers, looking back at their own work, Hykade has alternating and contradictory feelings of satisfaction and self-criticism, but sees this as part of the process of developing as a filmmaker. 'With *We Lived in Grass*, what I was planning to do was to go from comedy to tragedy, back to comedy, but it just didn't work. It starts with the "tit dance", with the kids playing on the father's dick, and you could hear the audience laughing, and then you'd come to the quieter, more serious moments when you find out the father has testicular cancer and then of course nobody laughed. Or the scene with the angels sitting at a table on the hill: I thought, after all this heavy drama, we'll go to the angels and they do nothing and I thought this would be funny, the fact that then nothing is happening is funny. But nobody laughed. Now I think it's quite obvious why: tragedy is stronger, in a way tragedy beats comedy, because you really identify with the character, you're not looking at it from a distance, you're right in there with the story, so you can't get the mood to be light again for the audience to laugh. The boy who did the voice-over before the final recording would ask "Why does he do this?" and I'd explain, and then he'd look at me and say "He's sick" and that's it, I think, why this would never have mainstream success, the audience don't want a main character who is sick. And with the ending, the darkness at the end means the real end of the world, but it is not an end that would satisfy an audience. At that time I didn't have too much experience in creating a narrative, in a way it was all just throwing everything you have into the soup. But when I watch it now, every six months or so, I still like it, and in a way it's amongst my strongest films because it is so uncorrupt, it's very raw.

'After doing this film, I split the two aspects, working in a more defined comic mode on a television pre-school series such as *Tom and Strawberry Jam* and then in more serious mode in the short films. But what I'm looking forward to is trying to bring these two things together again, taking characters from one side to another. That's what I'm trying to do with the Jesus feature film, to have a range of emotions, although with a unified style.'

Autobiography and fiction

'I think the more personal, not autobiographical, a story is, the more capacity it has to speak to an audience. You can't cheat emotionally.

'A film usually gets its inspiration from many sources', he says, and for *Ring of Fire* one was a drawing of himself in a triangular romantic entanglement that then combined with memories of his much earlier teenage self, discovering the feverishly sexual atmosphere of a nightclub that attracted a startlingly heterogeneous crowd from all over Bavaria. 'This was the mid-1980s, a time of great sexual freedom. We'd heard of AIDS, but thought it only happened in New York. People wore the most incredible clothes: there were fantastic gay men with feathers in their hair, and Goths ... It was like sexual inspiration, from all sides, it felt so vital, overwhelming, so beautiful in a way. I wanted to capture that feeling. I felt like a 16-year-old cowboy, all that glorifying and celebrating yourself like you're a new version of Clint Eastwood. The myth of youth, the big horizons.

'Everything starts with and then develops from the characters, the need to tell their story, which often comes from a strong central image. In *We Lived in Grass* it's a little boy seeing his father die. In *Ring of Fire* it's two cowboys walking into a bright shining bazaar. Some characters stay in mind for a long time, so I try to tell their story over several films. You could see *Ring of Fire*'s innocent young cowboy as the father in *We Lived in Grass* in his youth, or as the boy who's grown up.

'In *Ring of Fire*, the sharp, angular cowboy is familiar with the macho rituals, but he only knows how to operate in a defined system, perform the expected rituals (and that's what has corrupted him) whilst the other guy doesn't; that's what gets him into the position of doing what is needed to be done at the end of the film. Insecurity is a vital and constructive thing, only if you're insecure are you really able to deliver something good in art, or in almost any field; you have to be insecure, you have to have a question, not an answer.

'You have to know your whole story, before you start telling it. With

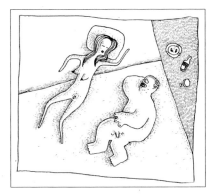

Drawings for *Ring of Fire* (2000) © Andreas Hykade

Image from *Ring of Fire*

Ring of Fire, a big problem was that the strong central image, the two guys going into the sex bazaar, left a big gap. I thought I could leave it up to my unconscious to sort it out, but in fact it led to a big mess. This was my first real artistic crisis, because when I started I didn't know where it would end. Although there was a very detailed script and storyboard, the ending was no good. As a kind of diversionary tactic, I advertised in art magazines and in prisons for people to send in drawings of all their sexual fantasies, which kept me busy for a while. But every day I worked on it I felt weaker, and I was not able to separate the film from myself, I took it personally. It went on for months, until I had to make a decision to either stop or go on, and try to solve the problem and simply do the best I could. So in the end I wrote a completely new third act.

'My whole way of working changed with this. Before, the identification with the film had been absolute, but now I realised the film wasn't me, what might be good for the film wasn't necessarily what was good for me, there was a distance now. I think this is really healthy. Once you stop identifying with the film, you might be able to see the problems with it. Usually an auto-biographical narrative comes to a point where you have to invent something to solve a problem it poses as a piece of art. And the art increasingly takes on its own life. So you start to serve the art and not your own biography. It's a natural process. In the end it's not important for the audience whether something 'really' happened or not – they just have to believe what they see and hear.'

The naked truth

On the graphically explicit sexual imagery, he says, with disarming candour, 'In *We Lived in Grass* the scene of the father having sex with his wife, that's nasty, it's one of the few scenes I did not animate myself. I wouldn't have wanted to do it, a woman animated it. But it's not rape, it's a vital thing, it's more like taking a handkerchief to masturbate. It's the most vulgar moment of the film, but I never thought about not having it. No, that's what it needs. Of course you'd always have sympathy for someone dying, but this guy was a nasty bastard, even in his last moments he is just nasty.'

On the whore-madam in *Ring of Fire* (a prototype previously glimpsed in fractured cuts of her costumed body in *We Lived in Grass*), Hykade comments: 'For me, this represents corrupt love – you could not really be naked with this love. Nakedness has never been a sexual thing, at least in my vocabulary; it's more to do with vulnerability, which I see as a positive thing. The sexual characters are the ones that are decorated, fetishised.

'I was surprised by the nastiness of the hate-mail I got for *Ring of Fire*, the violence of the language in the letters, from both men and women. What it taught me is that people see what they want to see. If you're sensitive to certain images, a naked woman with a big vagina is a sexist image; but you're reacting to an image, you're not reacting to the whole thing. For example, I saw the furry vagina image as nice and cosy, a kind of protection, suggesting nothing will harm this man. They never got the point that the film ends in a different place than where it starts. The water woman and the gypsy madam, the classic Madonna and whore, are a projection of the boys' fantasies. I think it's quite clear, as when the woman loses her hair, that the film moves from pure projection to the human soul, the cost of behaviour. The characters are stereotypes, clichés, at the beginning, but they're not at the end. There is a progression from the fantasy image to realising there is a soul behind the flesh. But it's always a problem knowing how far to abstract a figure, if the audience will get it.

'Such attitudes make it more difficult to talk about things outside of the mainstream. If everything is defined, especially in relation to serious subjects,

Image from *Ring of Fire*

what are you supposed to do? Just not talk about it? Just say "rape is bad"? That's it? Reading Nabokov's *Lolita*, you're in the mind of the rapist. It's a shocking book, but you are vitally involved as a reader. If the book was constantly telling you Humbert is a pervert, a devil, there would be no point to writing – or reading – it, but if you ask how could that ever happen … then just read the book. You have to dig into the subject to show something, you cannot avoid it. But in a way I'm quite glad I got all the letters. On one hand, I try to be aware that you have a responsibility to say the things you want to say, *clearly*, but on the other you don't want to be inhibited by notions of the politically correct.'

Religion

The pervasive presence of religious imagery and symbolism in the two films has been less remarked upon in critical commentary. In *We Lived in Grass*, for example, apart from the direct references to religion, the dandelion girl at one point is in crucifix pose, the flames of hell-fire burn in the nightmare scenes, and the playfully silly angel figures later perform a pre-funeral dance for the dead father (the latter also reference Hykade's memories of local funeral processions in his childhood). The drawing style used for the angels, with their undulating hair, prefigures that of the water-woman in *Ring of Fire*, and the latter clearly performs a redemptive function for the failed cowboy that the boy cannot accept from the dandelion girl in *We Lived in Grass*. The Catholic notion of grace seems indicated here, and the scenes between the water-woman and the 'weak' cowboy have echoes of the parable in Luke: 7 of the prostitute anointing Jesus's feet with her tears and drying them with her hair. Hykade also comments that 'the whole film is saturated with the Old Testament, the notion that evil shall be judged, and the traditional gender roles: a man's a man, a woman's a woman.'

Image from *Ring of Fire*

Image from *Ring of Fire*

Born in Altötting, Bavaria, a centre of Maryolatry, for most of his life, Hykade has been a practicing Catholic, and his early biographical notes always mentioned that as a child he had been touched by the Pope on a visit to Germany. Although his relationship with this religion has had its up and downs, the sincerity of his engagement is unquestionable. 'I'm still a Roman Catholic, and I've reached a point where I think although I still have some doubts, I'll stay part of it, it has influenced me too much. I'd want to stay part of the Catholic Church at least until I've finished my Jesus film [laughs].[2]

There is such a rich store of images and stories that have really inspired me since childhood, and I think this will not stop. It's not easy stuff; you read it and sometimes you think it seems completely mad, but it makes you think. The books of the Bible are like good animated films: their meanings seem to change as you change; you can reflect on them. Most of them are short. Precise. And that's what I appreciate.'

Of course, the Judeo-Christian tradition's influence on gender stereotyping and the cult of the Virgin Mary may be said to be a factor in Hykade's romantic idealisation of the female as emblem of purity and healer of men, and as a pathway to the redemption of sin. And it could be argued that such idealisation is simply the flip-side of misogyny. But that would be to ignore the almost painful honesty of the films' explorations of masculinity. To concentrate solely on the images as evidence of sexist stereotyping is to not recognise what actually happens in the films. In *We Lived in Grass*, the dandelion girl has an autonomy and sense of ease with herself in the world that is in marked contrast to the tortured boy; in *Ring of Fire*, both gypsy madam and water-woman are the stronger characters, the one powerful and judgemental, clearly in control, the other surviving rape without loss of a sense of self or her humanity. The macho male is thoroughly humiliated after his demonstration of gunplay fails to win him sexual favours from the gypsy madam.

Directing and collaboration

'I enjoy animating but I want to direct. So casting the animators is really important. I try to work with other people who can bring their own strengths to the project. For example, on *Ring of Fire*, Anita Otteger, who has a very gentle way of dealing with form, animated the water-woman, and I didn't have to explain very much to Jed Haney, who did the Piano Man, because I knew it would be best if he just did it in the way he thought right. Jurgen Haas, who'd done a lot of erotic animated pop promos did the mass sex scenes. I needed different kinds of animators for the very vulgar rough stuff in the sex bazaar scenes, the ancient old men-trees performing auto-fellatio.

'As I am not a brilliant storywriter, I am always glad to work with people with more experience in this area. Then I try to find the best way to show everything that happens. I show the pictures in the right order to several people, and let them tell me the story they see. This highlights the weak points, and then I can try to tell the story more clearly. When I'm sure of the story, I'm also able to react to new things that other people bring to the work.'

Ring of Fire: style and technique

'The black and white Cinemascope format was of course because it was a western. But although it felt natural, almost necessary, with three characters in shot, it did however cause other problems. I remember reading that Disney said after *Sleeping Beauty* [1959], the only film he did in Cinemascope, that he'd never do it again. I know exactly why: the problem is the wide shots, where a lot of stuff is happening, it's so difficult, almost impossible to fill the picture space. I'd produce forty characters, put them in, but it would still felt empty. Many of the shots using framing and symmetry were partly a way of

Image from *Ring of Fire*

Image from *Ring of Fire*

tryin to find solutions to that problem.

'The artworking technique was quite unusual: pencil drawings were painted onto cel with a heavy brush, so it was lumpy and crude, then a team of people scratched away the paint from the back with scalpels to achieve the wood-cut effect. Using computers became necessary for the scenes of the walk through the bazaar, but the whole process of working with 2D and 3D worlds together was to take the 3D programme and use it as much as possible in a 2D way, as though it had been hand drawn.

'Once I knew that *Ring of Fire* was going to be partly computer anima-tion, I felt it risked a certain coldness, so the musician Steffen Kahles and I decided to use only hand-made music to balance this out. Although I'm not a musician, from the very start I have a concrete feeling about the music for the film. The musician is always involved in pre-production, which makes it difficult for him, but is good for the final outcome. If there are bits in the film, where the music is the guide, we always try to produce a layout music with which we can work. If this is not possible, we define the inner rhythm of the scene and then animate on this beat, so the musician can take it and build the music around it.'

Notes

1   Interview with the editor, April 2008, in Boston.
2   Hykade has, since this interview, officially renounced his Catholicism.

Reference

Robinson, C. (2005) *Unsung Heroes of Animation*. London: John Libbey.

Igor Kovalyov's *Bird in the Window* and *Milch*
by Michael O'Pray

> There is the phrase: 'Be a man' (never: 'Be a woman'), as if it were an exotic role,
> perhaps because the implicit concept of maleness is manic and overwrought.
> (Stokes 1965: 38)

It may be argued that these two films, *Bird in the Window* (1996) and *Milch* (2005), are about the *impact* of desire and sex on families, a different one in each film. They are also about male anxiety with sexuality as a kind of congealed knot at its source, although perhaps not the only such knot. On the other hand, both films depict loneliness and the failure of human communication, or at least its limits. They are equally about survival in its myriad forms: in these films, survival is the acceptance of the loss and defeat central to male desire. This welter of interpretative levels is a testament to the films' complexity and to their oblique, often elliptical narratives and structures, with *Bird in the Window* being the more ambiguous of the two. It is a great part of Kovaylov's brilliant artistic achievement that these various themes nestle within one another.

The quotation from Adrian Stokes above is relevant here for it underlines the demand and its psychical effects on the male found in the two Kovalyov films that I want to discuss in this chapter. Both films have a young boy and a father figure as a central relationship running alongside a sexual one between the father figures and women,[1] and these two sets of relationships are intertwined. Kovalyov's treatment of his male protagonists is always sympathetic and at times expresses a tenderness towards them despite, in the cases of the older men, their often-boorish selfish behaviour, as if their 'manic and overwrought' states of sexual desire were the results of a demand – to 'be a man' – rather than of volition. It is this sense of the male psyche being determined in its sexuality by compulsive uncontrollable forces that permeates all his films and especially *Bird in the Window* and *Milch*. Having said this, the women in the two films are not passive figures. On the contrary, they are tough, independent, resourceful and in themselves, desiring.

Bird in the Window, on the face of it, seems to be as much about thwarted desire (sexual and otherwise) as it is about sexuality *per se*, but what is interesting is how this desire is thwarted and who in the film desires. And perhaps how far are these desires filtered through or attached to or stand in for other kinds of desires? It may be this complexity or subtle nuancing that explains the films' difficulty. But the difficulty is of a kind itself, one that uses ambiguity of meaning for its own ends, for the film's opacity does not mar our understanding of it. This is not so unusual in art. For example, Giorgione's painting *Il Tempesta* (c.1506–08), with its odd couple occupying a landscape threatened by a storm, has puzzled critics and historians since its production in the Renaissance and yet it is thoroughly satisfying in its clarity of feeling, or in its enigmatic tension. While this disjunction between an emotional response and one of reason may bother us (as it did Freud), it remains a perfectly viable way of going about art for some artists and viewers. Interestingly, Kovalyov himself has remarked that 'any art ... must touch you, but you don't have to understand it' (quoted in Pilling 2001: 74). Kovalyov's admiration, for Robert Bresson, Carl Dreyer and Andrei Tarkovsky for example, speaks volumes on this issue, for all three filmmakers are renowned for a certain ambiguity, a certain reluctance to round off, to conclude, to explain things away, we might say.

First, I want to look more closely at *Bird in the Window*. In the film, a swarthy thickset white-suited early middle-aged man arrives asleep by taxi at a large walled-garden house perhaps in a Mediterranean country, or one with a similar climate and culture (perhaps Mexico?). He is a bullish, gangster-like figure who establishes his familiarity and oafish manners immediately by throwing a clod of earth at the old gardener and signalling him not to let on that he has arrived. The man knows this place fairly well and wants to surprise the occupants. He is met at the door by a woman who embraces him and leads him through the house where in one room two Chinamen play chequers celebrating a winning move by pecking kisses and giggles. A little boy appears now and then, only to be quickly gathered up by the woman and carried away before he can approach the man who seems surprised to see him yet disappointed at his urgent removal. This key relationship between the man and the boy remains obscure throughout. Is he the father? And if he is, does he know it or not? We never find out.

The couple (husband and wife? lovers?) who have been separated for

Images from *Bird in the Window* (1996)
© Klasky Csupo Inc.

whatever reason, come together again with mixed results, for while there is sexual desire, there is also aggression, anxiety and deception. She resists his sexual advances. He passes the time, eating, reading and strutting about the house in a restless manner, unable to settle. At one point, the woman screams at a cockroach in her kitchen sink; he kills it and throws it out of the window into the garden, pleased to have fulfilled some masculine role in this alienating house.

The house is rife with sexual desire. The Chinamen's kisses – are they an innocent ritual or expression of intimacy? The scenes in which a young boy (the son?) pulls up his nightgown to show his penis at the end of prayers only to have his face slapped by his mother; the man's clumsy attempts to seduce the woman; and eventually her long reaching arm stretching out to draw the man into her bed, her lascivious drinking from the wine bottle. But we never see the sexual act, which is of little interest to him in this story. And finally, the boy's desire to approach the man ending in his death as he races onto the balcony and promptly falls over the rail into the garden. I will return to this odd incident later.

Chris Robinson has described the film as 'extremely personal' (2005: 44) and about a man 'who is a stranger in his own home and ... sees that he no longer belongs there'. He suggests that the film is emotionally associated with Kovalyov's separation from his wife, and whether this is true or not, and even if it is, then it still may not help much in our understanding the film. Like his later film *Milch*, *Bird in the Window* merges a kind of naturalism and narrative logic with one of the imagination, like invasive fantasies in waking life or a dream. Robinson speaks of an overlap in the film between 'reality and dream'. It is perhaps more useful and more appropriate to speak of fantasy or fantasies erupting in the film or even seeing the entire film as a fantasy, and one reason for doing this is the film's visual, narrative and emotional logic. It is ambiguous and elliptical as if a particular idea or thought is pressed into service by the story. As in a dream where the manifest content often provides clues in its 'insignificant' detail as to the fundamental thought and feeling (its latent content) that determines it. For example, the boy's death is dealt with in a fairly casual fashion as much as to suggest it is not real even within the film's own terms. Kovalyov describes how his films begin with 'just one small detail' (quoted in Robinson 2005: 44); trivial incidents and 'moments' seem to have as equal an authority and importance as larger ones.

Both films have a compulsive feel, of characters under the sway of feelings over which they have no control. But perhaps just as interesting is that these compulsions are not transparent to others. Kovalyov's world is one of opacity, of misunderstanding and of sadness, of loss at a quite fundamental level but a loss that is compensated by a ceaseless activity, often sexual in nature, and it is important that it is men, in fact the fathers and their 'sons' in both films, who represent this in their own particular way. In the case of fathers it is a fully-fledged but futile one, in the boys a nascent, imminent one, with a fatal exuberance in *Bird in the Window* as the boy dashes for the balcony, and a furtive, brooding compulsiveness in the forever watching and distracted boy in *Milch*.

A stylistic feature of Kovalyov's films is the incessant horizontal movement across the screen, using tracking shots. Equally, body movements are often nervously quick and gestural, almost reminding us of marionettes, their sudden movements, fixed facial expressions and their inner emptiness pushing out into action as if filling the void of the world. Of course, this is strongly reminiscent of the characteristics of puppets or marionettes located in the nineteenth-century European Romantic movement. The opening credit sequence of *Bird in the Window* shows a bird relentlessly and cruelly chasing down a winged insect, mindless in its action; it represents pure instinct unadulterated by thought or feeling. Rationality or morality has no purchase here, except through our own anthropomorphic projections. It is interesting that Kovalyov cuts from the lovemaking scene to an extract from this sequence of the bird playing with its stricken insect victim, suggesting that the sexual act is as cruel and unloving. One may associate this bird with the stuffed bird standing in the window and stolen by the man as he leaves the house in some disarray at the end, and with which he sits with on the moonlit seashore, accompanied by a haunting Turkish song on the soundtrack. In this final sequence Kovalyov seems to wish to elicit some sympathy for the man's vacuous yearnings, his compulsive urgings for sex, food, drink, and for his inability to connect, his fundamental separation from life, his unsatisfied desires which leave him stranded and alone.

An obvious point is that the bird symbolises the man's urges, and perhaps his cruelty, but it also marks a difference, for if the bird sits, dead and stuffed on the seashore, it is the man *qua* man who has the crisis, experiences the isolation and loneliness. But why did he steal it? Is it an action that expresses an unconscious recognition on his part of what he shares with the bird? We may assume some past attachment to it, so in fleeing the house he takes something that emotionally belongs to him. Or is it simply a spiteful gesture, grabbing anything that is at hand to deprive the woman of what is hers? Perhaps. But whatever may be the case, it feels right and the nexus of explanations here are all plausible enough. It is in this kind of ambiguous but resonant narrative detail that Kovalyov's work excels. But where is sex and desire in this? The bird is the final object coveted by the man to satiate his drives – wine, grapes, the woman, the bird. And in a sense, all these desires are the same – there is barely any difference between his total devouring of the grapes and his desire for the woman. Interestingly, it is the woman who initiates the only sexual act between them, one that leaves her sitting on the edge of the bed, her head bowed while the man chomps away at a bowl of grapes. Implicit here is the woman's post-coital dissatisfaction and sadness and the man's insensitivity, sex being on a continuum with compulsively eating grapes.

There is also a death of a child that lies at the core of this film, even if in narrative terms it is oddly placed, almost treated with an equanimity that implies that more is going on in this moment than the film dares to suggest. At this point the film as fantasy strongly asserts itself. The way Kovalyov cuts the sequence, from the plunge to the man witnessing it as he furtively escapes through the garden, his face covered in guilt as if fleeing the scene of his crime, establishes the 'cause' of the death even if it is not the case in terms of narrative. We can surmise that the boy's desire to see the man leads to his death. The cessation of his desire in this case is tragic but final, like the dead stuffed bird. The man on the other hand lives on, alone, brooding and one imagines desperate in the knowledge of his destructive nature. We do not see the woman's reaction to the boy's death, only a point-of-view shot showing the old gardener standing over the body which we cannot see, looking at her and taking off his cap, the dog mindlessly panting by his side. It is a remarkable example of Kovalyov's symbolic and mythical rendering of his stories, one that only truly belongs in the world created by animation. Such a scene could not occur in a live-action film; its emotional resonance would be too strong using a boy actor.

We are not allowed to linger on this scene as Kovalyov deals with it so quickly. It attests to the predetermined tenor and inevitability of the film's events. We are not dealing with inner states of individual characters, but their expression in action (as with marionettes). The death feels absolutely right in the film's own emotional logic. More pointedly, the film ends immediately after the death with the melancholic image of the man alone on the seashore, not pining for the boy one feels but contemplating his own misery!

Yet it all has to do with desire and sex. The film's most violent scene is the mother's slapping of her son when he exuberantly shows his genitals. Like the man (the father) he too is at the mercy of his sexuality. The knot of desire and sexuality is between the man's animal urges, the woman's own disconnection of sex and feeling and the boy's untrammelled energies marked as sexual. His death marks the death of desire, as the man on the seashore marks its failure – but failure in what way? Perhaps in its unfulfilling nature when disconnected from some more profound contact with the other. In fact, Kovalyov's view seems to be that sexuality and desire are deep obstacles to any emotional connection. *Bird in the Window*'s filmic discourse is quite different to that of *Milch*. The latter is naturalist, unlike the primarily symbolic structure of the former, which is not to say that this film is abstract in any sense. On the contrary, it is brimful with details and observations of life but it is essentially enigmatic, as perhaps are desire and sexuality themselves.

It is the strong rhythms of *Bird in the Window* and *Milch* that provides their compulsive masculine drive, pitched very much at the level of male sexual desire or lust, mirrored by the young boy's rapid movements as he rushes forward unfettered in *Bird in the Window* and in *Milch* by his mas-turbatory rapid pushing back and forth of his toy car, mirroring the father's ever onward movement through the film. In *Bird in the Window* the boy is slapped across the face by his mother for exposing himself at the end of night prayers, witnessed by the man/father who seems astonished by the whole incident. The boy in *Milch* is older, and his touching of himself as he watches his father with the young girl is a furtive action, prompted one feels by the young girl's casual touching of his penis as she waits on the step when deliv-ering the milk.

Milch is a more realist film than *Bird in the Window* with its much more obscure relationships and characters. As I have suggested, the latter operates at a more symbolic level with the death of the boy and the man's retreat to the lighthouse and sea where elegiac music accompanies his morose, sad isola-tion. But what is the matter with him? Why has he retreated from the house?

Images from *Milch* (2000) © Klasky Csupo Inc.

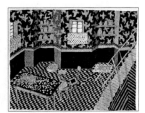

Drawings and design for *Bird in the Window* (1996) and *Milch* (2000)
© Igor Kovalyov

These are questions that do not arise in *Milch* where the turmoils of desire are understood as part of life, albeit of debatable importance. The wife responds to her husband's adultery by placing a milk bottle in front of him after the family drinks and he sighs at the gesture. There is a sense of familiarity here, of a kind of toleration of sexual infidelities. Thus the family survives intact if under strain and the boy finds some solace for his perplexed and confused state on his grandfather's lap, where the groin has become a site of comfort and peace and not excitation.

If *Milch* is about the complexities of sex, it makes no attempt to resolve or explain them. Kovalyov renders sex as activity, as urge to action in these two films, especially *Milch*. Notably, in both films, movement is largely horizontal across the screen. Tracking shots of feet, sometimes in the house, are also part of Kovalyov's stress on what seems an anxious energy, an agitation with morose lulls as the father smokes his morning cigarette or the boy lies and stares at his toy car, his energy expelled in the rapid movement and activities that fills his time. Sex is not depicted through the act, but by way of the desire towards and urge for it. Gratification is a brief temporary state and only old age seems to still it.

Robinson compares the film with Tarkovsky's *The Mirror/Zerkalo* (1975). Like Tarkovsky, Kovalyov deals with a kind of restlessness, similar to that observed in the character of Masha in *The Mirror*. Her anxious state pervades that film but it is not disruptive, or even neurotic, but rather an expression of how she feels both at home and displaced. The tone is set in the encounter, near the beginning of the film, between her and the doctor who flirts with her at the fence. Its ambiguity is precisely sexual. Encounters like that are by their nature so and Kovalyov's understands this too. Sexual attraction and its communication is often ambivalent, vague and at the same time quite clear in the attraction. Or is it? The man in *Bird in the Window* is forever trying to judge the sexual moment with the woman: Is it now? What should I do – offer a gift, go on the attack, seduce? Her own expression is formidable in its directness as her hand stretches out from the bed to draw him in. The milkgirl in *Milch* shares a similar directness as she throws herself forcefully at the husband after being slapped, and as she leaves town running towards an impatient young man on his motorbike in the middle of the night.

Milch is a more fully-achieved film perhaps, solely for the way that the young boy rests his head on his grandfather's lap near the end of the film, offering solace and peace from the world and from his own inner compulsions. The proximity to the old man's groin, the physical site so to speak of the film's central desires and urges (the boy's own masturbating as he watches his father and the milk-girl [vomiting!]), the same girl's touching of the boy on the step, becomes a place of rest when it ceases to be active. Desires are sated in the old man who no longer competes in the sexual jungle (witness the prowling beast crossing the foreground during the man and girl's passionate almost violent meeting). The young boy's daily struggle with his half-recognised own desires also find some peace, tinged with a melancholia that permeates Kovalyov's films.

Interestingly the woman/wife in *Bird in the Window* is hemmed in by desires that are equally defunct, or directed elsewhere, namely, the old gardener and his dog and the mechanical laughing and kissing oriental men. Her own desire is eruptive, like the young girls in her cage-like room, but not compulsive.

In conclusion, it is Kovalyov's loving and sharp observations of the mundane woven into a narrative that uses ellipsis, illogicality and a feeling of unconscious fantasy operating at the level of poetics that place these films far beyond most of what passes for film (and animation) these days. Their refusal to resolve, to compromise on the rich complexity of life itself, while always celebrating its richness and energy, is quite remarkable.

(Thanks to Kamila Kuc for her comments on an earlier draft of this chapter.)

Note

1   I found two other books useful to this discussion, albeit in a more dispersed way – both are by Darian Leader: *Why Do Women Write More Letters Than They Post?* (London: Faber and Faber, 1996) and *Promises Lovers Make When It Gets Late* (London: Faber and Faber, 1997).

References

Pilling, J. (2001) *2D and Beyond*. Crans-Près-Céligny: Rotovision.
Robinson, C. (2005) *Unsung Heroes of Animation*. London: John Libbey.
Stokes, A. (1965) *The Invitation in Art*. London: Tavistock.

On Craig Welch's *How Wings are Attached to the Backs of Angels*

Craig Welch, unlike many of the filmmakers featured in this book, came to animation quite late in life. Although he had trained as a graphic designer, he hated the world of commercial design and advertising, so started working in bookstores and eventually became proprietor of his own. A chance viewing of Caroline Leaf's *The Street* (1976), playing as a short before a commercial feature, prompted him to think about animation as a mode of personal and creative expression. Further 'nudges' came upon expiration of his bookshop lease, when he could not find a suitable location for another, and hearing from animator friends of his wife how much they enjoyed the degree of creative freedom allowed them working on segments of the childrens' series *Sesame Street*. This all led up to a decision to attend an intensive international summer school at Sheridan College, near Toronto, taught by distinguished animation veterans such as Zlatko, Kai Pindal, Zack Schwartz, several of whom had worked at the National Film Board of Canada (NFB). Welch comments that 'although they were in their sixties and seventies, they still had something upstairs, they were open to, and encouraged, new ideas'.[1] His student film attracted the attention of the NFB, which led to him making his first professional film, *No Problem* (1992), a cartoon comedy, clearly influenced by the humour of films by the NFB's Cordell Barker and Richard Condie.

How Wings are Attached to the Backs of Angels (1996) marked a radical change of direction. After attending a number of international festivals he became 'attracted to more experimental films, with a different kind of sensibility'. The idea for the film arose from a long period of virtual immobility due to severe back problems, which led him to research the anatomy of the

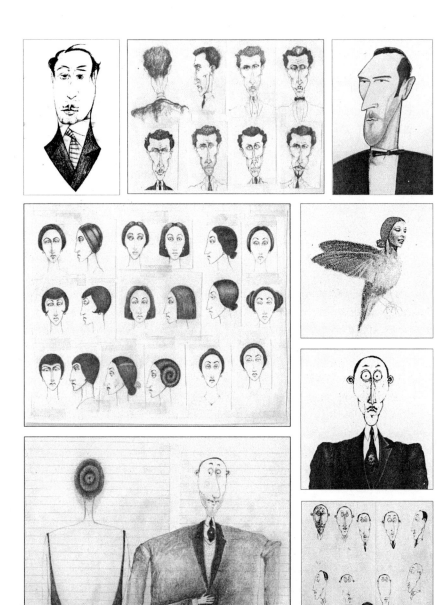

Images and early character designs for *How Wings are Attached to the Backs of Angels* (1996)
© National Film Board of Canada

back. 'Seeing a drawing of a muscle arrangement, called "Wings of Vesuvius", might have triggered something, at one point I thought of it for the film's title'.

The pleasure he takes in precise and detailed draughtmanship is evident throughout the film (as it is from his non-animation related work as a painter), and in the array of intricate mechanical devices it features, imaginative enough but far too sinister to be called Heath Robinson-like. His protagonist's obsessive quest to construct from bird and human skeletons a creature he can make fly, from the controlled and isolated environment in which he lives, is disrupted by the appearance of a mysterious woman, and finally leads to his death by decapitation.

In some respects the film seems almost a text-book example of how the unconscious can drive an artist's vision. As many artists and writers do, Welch remarks on how characters, and a story, can develop a life of their own, and that 'some things I only learned as the film came about'. The final film was very different from the original storyboard. 'I didn't set out to have several different half-narratives going on at the same time but that's what I got... I wanted people to be as bewildered and inquisitive about certain things as I am... With drawing, nothing happens when you sit thinking, it's when you are doing it, applying yourself, that the ideas happen. That's the only way you are going to find what you are looking for, even if you don't know that's what you're looking for. Sometimes things feel they're supposed to happen. Usually producers aren't too happy if you start changing things, but I was lucky: I had a great producer, Marcy Page, who allowed that to happen.'

Of vestigial influences on the film he mentions *memento mori*[2] and Arnold Böcklin's 1880 painting *The Isle of the Dead*, both in itself and as it inspired the Norman McLaren film *A Little Fantasy* (1946). He also cites a love of South American literature, writers such as Gabriel García Marquez and Julio Cortázar, and wanting to suggest something of a savannah feel to the land-scape and sounds of the film. Early designs for both the male and female character have a Latin cast, and it is fascinating to see how these transformed as the film developed.

Whereas the initial, stylised male face suggests a confident Latin lover, it then mutates through more psychologically nuanced versions to the final design, a gaunt visage whose hollowed-out features suggest a desperate, pained attempt to hold all feeling at bay, and something of the skull beneath the skin. The female character's development is even more interesting: early model sketches demonstrate a series of stylised hair-do's; she then transmog-rifies into a creature that is half-bird/half-woman and ultimately escapes the artist's controlling pencil in her final embodiment as an animated/live-action character. Whereas the successive designs for the male character render him an increasingly neurotic figure, the transformation from grotesque, potentially comical bird-woman through incarnations as severe senora to final fleshed figuration suggest her character's increasing strength and empowerment.

Welch explains: 'I considered the male character a case of arrested development, a control freak ordering the universe around him, completely isolated from the natural world. To control something is to kill it. To try to investigate how angels' wings are attached to its back is a folly. It's not answerable. There's an impotency that happens when you can control everything, there is no challenge. So I set him up with a drawn female, but I couldn't get the dynamic I wanted. I couldn't draw realistically enough to satisfy myself, I was more comfortable making little tableaux that she can walk into. I was after the sensation of feeling, of touch, to tap into primal things ... so I shot some scenes with a model, Xeroxed it onto frosted cel, then back-painted it so I could put it on top of the background. This is what gives the extraordinary sense of living flesh to the character, with most of her movements achieved through cross-fades from one frame to another, unlike the jerkiness that would arise from pixellated photos.'

Yet Welch seems genuinely perplexed at the suggestion of some of the implications of the film in terms of its depiction of sexuality and desire. 'I wasn't conscious of putting sex in the film. Although I do remember going out on the studio roof one time for a cigarette, and I was thinking, this thing when he puts his hand between her legs, and it turns into a bird on his finger... What happens between that point having the bird on his finger is for you to fill in. That whole idea of the transition, of how to get from there to there, was tantalising. Then I thought, that's it. I'll just put my hand between her legs and then we'll see who's boss. And now it's a totally different film. And what it afforded was dramatically speaking very interesting. The fact that I use a real woman instead of a drawn one gives it a sensuality that is akin to putting the finger down the back. The moment where you cannot breathe. It was a human thing amidst all this control. Another thing about control: you have to lose control to get the maximum out of the experience. He cannot enjoy it; he's frozen.'

Although Welch emphasises that 'the aesthetic is as important to me as the meaning' adding, in rather self-deprecating manner, 'I don't think I have anything to say',[3] the film itself, however, is deeply resonant. Visually and thematically it seems to have a great deal more to say. The multiplicity of potential interpretations of the film speaks to animation's ability to simultaneously convey contradictory and complementary meanings, particularly through visual transformations, be that through the more stream-of-consciousness mode of metamorphosis or through transitions that play on the similarity of shape and outline.

Of course the woman may be seen simply as the angel of death, as agent of the natural order that asserts itself over human volition and human folly. As Welch points out, towards the end of the film the coat she puts on the male character (as if in preparation for his departure) 'turns into a coat of worms, and one comes round his finger, like a ring, the symbol of mortality'. Her animate(d) presence plays on and alternates between a sense of formal corporeality (the photo-real as against the drawn line) and narrative non-corporeality/ethereality: when she leaves his house she simply passes through the bars of the entry gate, yet in another scene she opens the French windows to enter his living room. At one point she fades from sight; at another is reflected in the mirror, but then on passing it again no reflection appears. Is she his fantasy or is this the way of an angel? An early establishing shot of a stone angel on the bird-bath in the garden foreshadows her entrance. A skull tumbling down the frame introduces and ends the film. A grim joke, then, on man's fantasies of autonomy and control?

Yet the film's visual surfaces and imagery also speak to a highly charged representation of a crippling, ultimately fatal fear of sex and female flesh, the deadly female, and the death of the self in sex. Crisp monochrome intensifies the effect of machine-like precision in the controlled drawn lines. Carefully calibrated camera moves, often horizontal or vertical pans, pause to capture the object of attention, then zoom in to examine a detail. This creates a sense of detached, scientific scrutiny, underpinned by a tension between revealing and withholding information, making (and unmaking) sense of what is shown. The tension established makes the eruption of female flesh and texture into this rigidly determined and repressive universe all the more shocking. The frosted cels used for the woman soften her edges. As the camera moves in on her naked back, the focus seems to blur and fuzz: just as it does when showing clouds in the night-sky into which the man aspires to send out his constructed flying creature. The latter may suggest escape into freedom, but the former conveys both attraction and repulsion; as when the man traces her spine with his finger. Here a sense of yielding flesh betokens sensuality of touch, and a possibility of freedom (from the self?) beckons in these softer textures. Yet as the finger seems to sink into the flesh, there is also fear of engulfment, the messiness of physical intimacy.

Visual motifs with sexual connotations repeat throughout the film. A slit in the curtain parts to reveal the woman, the V-shape of the back of her dress echoing that of the parting curtains. Later, a slit in her back opens up to the man's probing fingers, but as his hand returns to probe again, what is now the exposed skeleton, it closes up again: penetration denied. The two-fingered probe is repeated in the scene where fleshed female and drawn man stand side by side, backs to camera. With one hand he raises her thigh-high skirt, and with the other makes two fingers that clearly thrust towards her crotch. The same V-shape is even apparent in an earlier scene in the (drawn) form of the woodgrain against which we see the pinned fly that is stimulated back to life by tiny, mechanical hands, a series of movements uncannily suggestive of masturbation.

Acts of seeing, and especially touching, signifying a desire to control, are other *leit-motifs* that interweave throughout the film. The mechanical hands, instigated by, but physically separated from, human agency, touch, adjust and control various contraptions. The man's hands perform the operations to combine human and bird skeleton. His blank gaze is constantly searching, directly or through binoculars: tiny pinpoints for pupils, darting in nervous anticipation, and longing. Several scenes involve mirrors, in which he watches himself, and her. A high-angle shot reveals the female character's hands playing classical piano music in his living room. This relatively long sequence, with its soothing musical cadences, is brusquely interrupted when his hand, from top right of the frame, places a bell-jar containing his skeletal part-human/part-bird creation on the piano. Later, when she puts his coat and hat on him, her hands seem almost solicitous, a wifely/maternal 'sending off'.

Following the woman/angel's ethereal disappearance, we see the man sitting, formally dressed, hands clasped in lap, as if awaiting the start of a

Image from *How Wings are Attached to the Backs of Angels*

Image from *How Wings are Attached to the Backs of Angels*

performance. He gazes at the curtain on which a giant close-up of her face emerges, superimposed. Hand-to-body contact now plays out in more ghostly fashion. A shadowy hand appears over her face, as if he is reaching out to her, immediately followed by a reverse-shot, an answering gesture; this time another shadow hand, which we assume is hers, passes over his face.

Of course, such visual repetition is both part of the patterning and symmetry that characterises the whole structure and design of the film. The actions-in-drawn-images to which such detailed sexual connotations were earlier ascribed are also, of course, animation narrative devices, whereby the shape or outline of one object is replaced by another (unlike, say, the metamorphosising, moving line in Lingford's *Pleasures of War* (1998) or Cournoyer's *The Hat* (1999)).

The curiously tender gesture with which she helps him into his coat also suggests another reading. That his casting out a lure to bring her into his domain expresses a desire to escape his self-constructed prison, and that the implied sexual act between them is followed by a fantasy of domestic routine and wifely solicitude. That his subsequent horror at the coat of worms, and that he is next seen crouching, panting in abject terror, represents the return of the fear of such engagement, the terror of loss of control, the vulnerability of yielding to the flesh of another. Such repetition of visual motifs works both with and against the patterning, raising issues but not resolving them, and perhaps speaks to the association of sex with death, both in colloquial French with '*la petite mort*/the little death' as an expression for the sensation of orgasm and its immediate aftermath, and in a wider context, of sex, through its potential for regeneration of the human, implicating its protagonists in mortality by virtue of entering the cyclical nature of life. Sex and love make you mortal.

The male character's self-defeating fantasies of control and possession are underlined by the contrasts in his environment. Uncontrolled proliferation of life, fecundity, in the lush, jungle-like outside, a twisted, stunted, pinned bonsai tree inside. Encroaching tree roots, breaching the gates to his house, are cut off by the same swift guillotine device on the gate that eventually decapitates him: a symbolic castration.

Submission versus control, as a changing dynamic in both sexual relationships and relationships in general, are also played out with teasing ambiguity. After the implied sexual act, the woman-angel (and here she seems more 'woman' than 'angel') bends, her back to camera, in a kneeling position, arms as if pinioned back, trussed for him, a position that transforms (through similarity in shape) into the bird seen flying in earlier to drink at the birdbath. The subsequent shot is of the man holding it/her on his finger, then taking it to a cabinet to be locked in a box. This affirmation of control and possession is, however, undermined in the following sequence: having cut her down to size, as it were, she returns to invade his consciousness, when her face reappears, giant-sized, on the curtains.

This film has often been described as 'surreal', a word all too often used merely as a synonym for 'weird' and/or difficult-to-follow in terms of conventional visual/narrative strategies. It might be, therefore, a legitimate and useful exercise to examine the film's connections with surrealism in its more art-historical context, e.g, tactilism, fear of the female, and sex expressed in simultaneous attraction and repulsion, fantasy, fetishisation of body parts, the interest in inventing controlling contraptions and devices, and so on.

At the risk of labouring an obvious point, the formal devices animation has at its disposal make it a particularly rich medium for exploring and conveying conflicting/conflicted desires and sub-/unconscious states of mind, and it might be productive to explore why this is so. Paul Wells, commenting on the various uses of synecdoche in animation, points up this potential for ambiguity and multiplicity of meaning:

> The use of metaphor simultaneously invites interpretation but insists upon openness. The meanings that may be determined from the use of metaphor resist specificity because they emerge from a second-order notion of representation. Metaphors make the literal interpretation of images ambiguous and sometimes

contradictory because they invite an engagement with the symbolic over and above the self-evident. This second order of construction offers a parallel narrative to the specific one which merely deals with the construction of logically determined and contextualised events. Whilst the symbol invests an object with a specific, if historically flexible, meaning, the metaphor offers the possibility of a number of discourses within its over-arching framework. (1998: 84)

Or, in Craig Welch's words, 'when you put one and one together and it makes three, you get something else coming through, it's not defined, it's exactly where the narrative should be; if you closed it off, if you said it summed up everything, then you don't think anything, when you leave the theatre you don't think any more about it. Things are open, never in life do you close things off and when you do, you run away from it because it might explode. I like that, toying narratively, it suggests emotional things, it is not purely intellectual'.

Notes

1 This and other remarks are quoted from an interview with the editor in 2008.
2 An expression from the Latin, meaning 'remember you shall die', and a term that is used to describe a long tradition in art history of works that are designed to illustrate this reminder.
3 In fairness to Welch, it should be noted that this was said in the particular context of his recent attendance at French-language classes, where he had come to hear the stories of his classmates, many of whom were recent immigrants who had suffered appalling experiences in their native countries, prompting a digression on the realisation that as a white, privileged middle-class male, he felt that anything he might have to say seemed to be relatively unimportant.

Reference

Wells, P. (1998) *Understanding Animation*. London and New York: Routledge.

The Embodied Voice: In Confessional Mode
by Jayne Pilling

Sound, music and voice

> The soundtrack of any film, whether animated or live-action, tends to condition
> an audience's response to it. Sound principally creates the mood and atmosphere
> of a film, and its pace and emphasis, but most importantly also creates a vocabu-
> lary by which the visual codes of the films are understood ... the pitch, tone,
> volume and onomatopoeic accuracy of spoken delivery carries with it a particu-
> lar guiding meta-narrative that supports the overall narrative of the animation
> itself. In the same way as music, the voice, in regards to how it sounds, as much
> as what it is saying, suggests a narrative agenda. (Wells 1998: 97–8)

Whereas, as Paul Wells points out above, there are aspects of sound that
apply to both live-action and animation, it may also be the case that, in part
due to the differences in when and how sound is added to picture in some
forms of animation, it may operate differently. The following remarks are
brief thoughts on the extent to which Michel Chion's observations on sound
in film might indicate useful avenues to pursue, in relation to the films under
discussion, with reference to both music and in particular the effects of using
the human voice, and as introduction to the articles in this section.
  Chion has observed that

> visual and auditory perception are of much more disparate natures than one
> might think... The reason we are only dimly aware of this is that these two per-
> ceptions mutually influence each other in the audiovisual contract, lending each
> other their respective properties by contamination and projection. (1994: 9–10)

He has also explained the different speeds at which we process sound and image:

> Sound perception and visual perception have their own average pace by their very nature; basically the ear analyses, processes and synthesises faster than the eye... There are several reasons for this. First, for hearing individuals, sound is the vehicle of language, and a spoken sentence makes the ear work very quickly; by comparison reading with the eyes is notably slower. The eye perceives more slowly because it has more to do all at once; it must explore in space as well as follow along in time. The ear isolates a detail of its auditory field and it follows this point or line in time. So in a first contact with an audiovisual message, the eye is more spatially adept, the ear more temporally adept. (1994: 10–11)

It is likely that this effect is even more marked in the case of non-traditional animation that challenges conventional narrative modes and characterisation in its depiction of the human, and employs highly individualised and unusual visual styles. Here the eyes indeed have a great deal more to process.

Pedro Serrazina exploits this process of 'contamination and projection', in conjunction with a play on audience familiarity with a particular cinematic genre, in his short film *Tale About the Cat and the Moon/Estória do Gato e da Lua* (1995). The film also demonstrates how the sound/image relationship in animation can operate in ways that live-action cannot.

Visually and aurally seductive, the film uses its soundtrack, and the almost automatic nature of the viewer's response to its voice-over narration, to duplicitous effect. A relatively long title sequence, whose animation simulates camera moves swooping over city rooftops, then down through winding narrow streets, tracking a bunch of alley-cats as they roam, to finally rest on one of them sitting on a roof, looking up at the film's title spelling out on the screen. A deeply seductive male voice speaks over plucked cello notes and nostalgic-sounding accordion music that underscores the melancholic passion of the tale he promises to tell, one of romantic obsession and pursuit. Starkly contrasting black and white imagery, the narrator's vocal timbre and intonation, and the story prefigured, all recall the tropes of classic (live-action) *film noir*: a male protagonist hopelessly ensnared by a *femme fatale*. The voice, sounding weary yet still hopeful, tells us that 'she' will come to him 'when she can, or wants to... I know one day she will come to me, otherwise why would she spend all those hours, all those nights, just staring at me? Nothing else matters. I'll wait.'

The tempo quickens, both musically and visually – rapid bowing on the cello to images of a cat on a boat tossed in a turbulent, moon-lit sea – as he details his search for 'her'. Drawing ever closer to capture and possession,

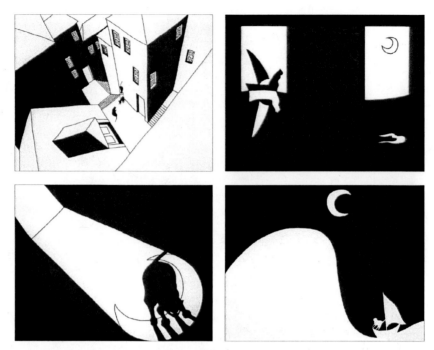

Images from *Tale About the Cat and the Moon* (1997) © Pedro Serrazina

he is constantly frustrated, the object of desire remaining forever just out of reach. He tells of finally 'settling down', as if in acknowledgement of defeat, acceptance of his entirely dependent position, but perhaps in fact yet another strategy – the waiting game. Another *film noir* convention, that of starting from the end, moving back and forth in time, is evoked here.

At first view the alley cats seem there simply to establish an urban land-scape. Because we 'recognise' a familiar narrative in the words heard, it seems natural to assume that this is a story about a man and a woman, the 'I' being the (unseen) male protagonist, and to read the cat as gendered female. A reading reinforced by a long-standing association of feline with female – seductive, mysterious, unpredictable, untameable.

The flow of images, so pleasurable in their sophisticated simplicity of design, serve to distract attention from the fact that what we are watching both is and is not the story we think we are hearing. Gradually we come to realise that the speaking 'I' may well be male, but that the object of his obses-sive desire is fact the moon, and that this is, as the title told us all along, a simple story of a cat and the moon, although it also speaks more generally to the irrationality and obsessiveness of passion. The cat's blind obsession is played out, literally, as the cat is enveloped in darkness, and by the ocean, with the white of the moon reappearing to tease and fuel his desire. Their

union seems denied by the binary opposition of black and white. The transforming drawn lines emphasise this separation, as the cat moves through white frames-within-the-frame, leaps from outlined buildings that fracture into abstract geometric shapes, setting up a visual tension throughout that is only resolved in the film's final shot.

Misdirection, or an 'unreliable narrator' are also devices found in live-action cinema (as they are in literature) but here the play on how what we hear will condition how we interpret what we see is only possible through its animated form (in conjunction with the play on established film genre conventions) to confuse the viewer's sense of gender identity.

Just as interesting, and pertinent to the general discussion of this book, is the extent to which the combination of voice, music and image can so powerfully evoke the human emotions of longing and desire, in a film within which no human characters whatsoever appear.

Images from *Un jour* (1997)
© Marie Paccou

First-person voice-over in Marie Paccou's *Un jour* (1997) is used to rather different effect. The opening words here, 'Un jour un homme est entré dans mon ventre' translates, literally, as 'One day a man entered my belly'. The film originated, in part, from Paccou's remembering her childhood puzzlement at the meaning of an expression that, however odd it might sound in English, in French is clearly a description, or rather circumlocution, of the sexual act; one that is just as likely to perplex a child not yet familiar with the term as the phrase 'a man spilling his seed' might be for an English-speaking child.

The female voice is quite calm, contained. A very measured classical cello accompanies the words, echoing this restraint yet also lending it an undertone of poignant sadness, reiterated in the film's conclusion. The matter-of-fact tone of voice also works to render somewhat less grotesque the image of a woman whose body is horizontally bisected by a little man sticking out of her body. Similarly with the subsequent scenes of domestic routine, and touches of humour in depicting the logistics of accommodating this new situation: she cutting out holes in her clothes, he using a snorkel at bath-time. Yet at the same time, the image is so 'unreal' it is likely to prompt the viewer to a more metaphorical reading, albeit one that allows for multiple interpretations. The film may be read as a simple account of a first relationship; the getting used to, and enjoyment of, developing shared intimacies, everyday routines, and the emotional void left when a couple separates (here, depicted quite literally, as the woman is left with a gaping hole in her body). It may also be seen as a depiction of pregnancy, the presence in the female body of a being that is simultaneously alien and a part of herself, the pleasures of nurturing a new being, alongside the disruption of her autonomy. Or, perhaps, more literally, as about the experience of penetration. Then again, as Don Perro wonders:

> Are boyfriends just 'little men' trying to remain in the womb? Or does our lady of the perpendicular man see her neighbour with a more boisterous womb-mate, a guy who drinks too much and has a terrible temper, and think that perhaps her relationship is not so bad? Is this a case of someone learning to live with her less-than-perfect partner? (1997)

Chion distinguishes between three different modes of speech in (live-action) film: textual (voice-over), theatrical (dialogue between characters) and emanation speech (unintelligible and/or overlapping). Theatrical speech is clearly the norm in most live-action films, (and in most animated features and TV series), and Chion points out that when it is used, textual speech tends to be of relatively short duration, and soon returns the viewer to the theatrical mode (i.e. a voice might introduce a memory, which is then dramatised in theatrical speech). In total contrast, in most art/auteur animation (with the obvious exception of animated documentaries), when voice is used at all, it is textual speech that predominates.

This suggests something of the different ways the voice can operate in such animated shorts, because textual speech,

> unlike theatrical speech, acts upon the images. Textual speech has the power to make visible the images that it evokes through sound – that is, to change the setting, to call up a thing, moment, place or characters at will. If textual speech can control a film's narration, of course, there no longer remains an autonomous audiovisual scene, no notion whatever of spatial and temporal continuity. The images and realistic sounds are at its mercy. (1994: 172)

Such considerations might also be useful in thinking about how the sound-track operates in *The Stain* (1991), a complex film by Marjut Rimmenin and Christine Roche, whose interplay of visual, thematic and temporal elements is discussed in detail in Ruth Hayes' and Karen Beckman's chapters in this book. Textual speech is used to interrogate, undermine and re-interrogate the story as is it told from varying perspectives. The female narrator's archness of tone suggests, right from the start, that the 'Once upon a time...' fairy-tale fantasy of the happy family hides darker secrets. Some scenes are shown via superimpositions of action, through corridors and half-open doors, doors then slammed shut on the barely glimpsed secrets held within. Conccalment is a recurrent visual, verbal and thematic motif; in the voice-over, we hear that 'What mother got best at was hiding' and 'Mother hid so well no one was able to reach her'; even the games played in the house acquire sinister, sexual connotations: 'Hide and seek, doctors and nurses.'

Very different visual styles and animation techniques, often very rapidly intercut in the film's later sections, are matched by an equally heterogeneous range of music cuts. Nursery-style piano music (Schumann's 'Children's Corner suite') plays over the spoken introductory first section; subsequently there are snatches of jaunty sax, that modulate to the melancholic, and hurdy-gurdy fairground organ music, for the wheelchair-bound younger sister as she fantasises disembodied locomotion. There is only a little diegetic sound, the tinny echoes from the younger sister's Walkman, radio shipping forecasts, which also underscores the characters' retreat from the confines and reality of what has happened and is happening in her home.

Chion describes empathetic and anempathetic effects as

> two ways for music in film to create a specific emotion in relation to the situa-
> tion depicted on the screen... [to] directly express its participation in the feeling
> of the scene, by taking on the scene's rhythm, tone, and phrasing ... [that is the]
> empathetic, from the word empathy, the ability to feel the feelings of others.
> [...] On the other hand, music can also exhibit conspicuous indifference to the
> situation, by progressing in a steady, undaunted and ineluctable manner: the
> scenes taking place against this very backdrop of 'indifference'. I call this anem-
> pathetic. The anempathetic impulse produces those countless musical bits from
> player pianos, celestas, music boxes and dance bands, whose studied frivolity
> and naievity reinforce the individual emotion of the character and of the specta-
> tor, even as the music pretends not to notice them. (1994: 8; 10)

Interestingly, he links this 'effect of cosmic indifference' to that of opera: 'This juxtaposition of scene with indifferent music has the effect not of freezing emotion but rather of intensifying it' (1994: 10) which seems apposite in relation to the use of an extract from a Verdi opera in the climactic scenes of *The Stain*.

Considering Chion's distinctions of sound's operating modes on viewer perception, it is notable how often the modes most often employed in live-action tend to be the least often used in the kind of animation discussed here, and vice-versa.

In Confessional Mode

Whilst in both *Un jour* and *Tale About the Cat and the Moon* the first-person voice-over narration speaks eloquently to dimensions of human desire, both are clearly located in the realm of imagined story. Their appeal and interest derives, to some extent, from the viewer's enjoyment of the dichotomy, on the one hand, the 'anything can be imagined therefore depicted' aspects of animation, and on the other, a recognition of the experience portrayed.

The status of the speaking 'I' is clearly signalled at the start of Jonas Odell's *Never Like the First Time!* (2006) in an on-screen caption giving the dates between which 'the following interviews were recorded'. It immediately becomes clear that this is an animated documentary about the loss of virginity via four individual accounts of the 'first time', differentiated by age and gender. First up is a male voice whose tone suggests amused awareness of his callow younger self, and an excited sense of performing this rite of passage as part of an essentially public process of peer-group competition. Equally expressive of a self-conscious ritual, but ironically much more prosaic, the second episode's female voice charts a slow, step-by-step approach over a period of time, as at each encounter with her partner they venture a little further into sexual intimacy. Here, however, amused retrospection conveys a sense of anti-climax, laughingly shrugged off, at the final outcome, as she recounts that the day following the final act, the pair break up: 'we'd completed our mission'. Is the film commenting on differing gender-related differences in reaction? Or reflecting on how peer-pressure can make loss of virginity something of a duty, a mission to be accomplished simply to avoid becoming the odd one out?

More disturbing is the flat, alienated delivery of the third interviewee, whose account suggests an alcohol-induced submission to rape, or an inability or unwillingness to face what might actually have happened. Of the four episodes, this is only one where music is used, quite insistently and dramatically, in contrast to her flatness of voice, and is perhaps an indication of the filmmaker's response to her story, both appalling in its potential effect on the girl, and horribly banal in the frequency of how often such things happen. Trembling excitement and an enduring sense of wondrous discovery is palpable in the fourth and final interview with a 92-year-old man. His sense of triumph seems less to do with 'scoring', more a sense of liberation and relief at discovering the falsity of religious warnings and old wives tales about the dangers of (pre-marital) sex, illustrated by comically literal animations: such as getting pregnant through letter-writing, or that taking a girl's virginity may lead to massive and continuous blood loss requiring stitches at hospital. Instead, he celebrates mutual pleasure.

Although these interviews might in one sense be seen as 'confessional', awareness of the filmmaker's representational strategies enables the viewer to relate to the subjective experiences – to 'feel the pain', as well as the pleasure, as it were – yet to do so from a safe, mediated, almost sociological distance. The documentary format allows for identification in a relatively straightforward way and to resonate because most viewers will also have experienced a 'first time'.

Ian Gouldstone's *guy101* (2006), Alys Hawkins' *Crying and Wanking*, (2002) or Ruth Hayes' *Wanda* (1981), however, all play with a first-person 'confessional' framework as a narrative device in ways that confront the viewer with more uncomfortable, rawer and problematic emotions. The stories told are more unsettling, and for some viewers, even shocking. We are no longer in the relatively safer realm of 'documentary'. Does the voice-over 'I', telling us of even more intimate, troubling because less socially sanctioned, experiences, imply they are autobiographical? If so, does this make a difference to the viewer's response, and may it therefore prompt a more judgmental reaction? It is not so much a matter of establishing the 'fact' of autobiography – these are constructed films, after all – more of thinking about how the 'I' affects readings of the film.

Images from *guy101* (2006)
© Royal College of Art

In *Wanda* the female narrator reads from a journal, extracts of which are also seen on-screen. She tells of how, having broken up with a lover, and taken in a stray tomcat, she becomes progressively more aware and jealous of its sexual activities, in marked contrast to her own celibate state. The film draws on associations of the feline with sexuality; Hayes has pointed out that 'The cat is the wildest domestic animal, yet fluffy, soft, sensual, teeth and claws – comforting soft, yet scary, bite, scratch; and is so often associated with femaleness, a sense of mystery.'[1] The film alternates video live-action footage with drawing, collaged objects and printed illustrations, and this kaleidoscopic stream of images is held together by the voice-over, and a background purring noise that builds up into a steady heartbeat, building tension as the film goes on until the final wry and startling admission of jealousy. The literary quality of the script, and the emotionally charged vocal performance in *Wanda* is very different from the use of voice and sound in *guy101*.

Here the male voice is very deadpan, as it introduces his chatroom buddy Keith, who, via their on-screen dialogue, using chat-speak and internet icons, describes a violent sexual encounter. Some of what we read and see deviates from what we hear. This play on such discrepancies raises interesting issues around credibility on the viewer's part, and more generally the intimacy and anonymity of virtual relationships where people can invent new identities through the stories they tell about themselves, and explore sexual fantasies. For some viewers, it raises the question as to whether they are more disturbed by the robbery and rape or the pleasure its narrator lays claims to. For others, it undermines the veracity they initially assumed through a sense of connection with the use of first-person narration. The low-key tone of voice used by Hawkins' *Crying and Wanking*, her account of a relationship destroyed by the male partner's inability to deal with the woman's honesty about past sexual encounters, reflects the emotional numbness and withdrawal into shame, confusion and solitude of its female protagonist. The attention to sound and voice, and how they play with the confessional format to explore issues of desire and sexuality, is discussed by Hawkins and Gouldstone in the pages that follow.

Note

1   Author's telephone interview with the filmmaker, April 2009.

References

Chion, M. (1994) *Audio-Vision: Sound on Screen*, trans. C. Gorbman. New York: Columbia University Press.

Perro, D. (1997) '*Un jour*: A Woman's Metaphorical Narrative', in *Animation World Magazine*, 2, 9; online: http://www.awn.com/articles/reviews/un-jour-womans-metaphorical-narrative

Wells, P. (1998) *Understanding Animation*. London and New York: Routledge.

Whose Body is It? *by Alys Hawkins*

Crying and Wanking (2002) continued themes from my previous films which explored the relationship between the medical, physical, mental and the emotional, particularly in terms of how the female body is presented, contextualised and understood. For example, in *Bun in the Oven* (1999) my goal was to subvert the presentation of pregnancy and childbirth as a purely medical experience. From the perspective of someone who has never been pregnant, anticipating it, I imagined it as a much more visceral, emotional and bewildering experience than wholesome sex education and TV science shows choose to present it. The film was based on detailed interviews with a number of women about their experiences, but also on my own imagining in terms of my experience of my own body.

I used animation to allow the camera to travel inside the body as well as to view it from the outside, and it was important to me that, in rejecting this medical view of the pregnant body, that I should use the camera to show the body from a point-of-view. We all experience our own bodies from a very different angle of view than that which is commonly presented to us, that of the spectator. This is something I wanted to develop further in *Crying and Wanking*.

In *Hysteria* (2001) I wanted to explore attitudes to medicalised female sexuality, specifically in terms of mental health care in Victorian Britain. My research led me to a huge amount of material from which many fascinating films could made, and I hope one day to be able to return to this. The condition of hysteria, which underwent a series of vogues for different symptoms and treatments, is itself a physical manifestation of emotional distress. I was intrigued by this relationship between the emotional, sexual and physical in medical history. It was, I believe, at a General Medical Council meeting that the concept of female sexual pleasure, of the clitoris having a function in

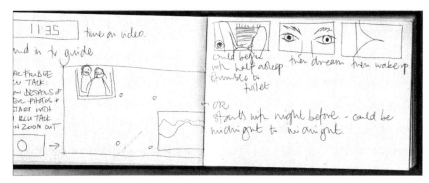

Extracts from sketchbooks for *Crying and Wanking* (2002) © Alys Hawkins

giving pleasure rather like the penis, was first openly discussed, when a doctor practising clitoridectomy as a treatment for hysteria gave a paper.

Initially I planned to make another animated documentary, about premenstrual syndrome, and began a lot of research. What became obvious to me was that a character was probably necessary in order to engage the audience, and at that stage the film started to lean towards a fictional narrative. I knew there were various oppositions which I wanted to explore: private and public, interior and exterior space, light and dark, warm and cool colours.

So *Crying and Wanking* is about a woman's experience of her own body: how she sees and perceives it; shame and guilt associated with female sexuality.

Going back through my sketchbooks now, I realise I wrote and drew a huge amount of ideas as the film started to develop from a rational and informative documentary idea into a much more emotional narrative. I was enormously confused about the direction of the film for a long time, and I am not sure that there was ever a fully coherent storyboard. Parts of it developed as others were being animated – a much less structured process than I'd used before, or since.

In terms of other filmmakers, there were plenty of influences on form (Jane Campion, Wong Kar-Wai, Lynne Ramsay), less so on content. The latter are all live-action feature filmmakers; although I watch a lot of animated shorts I always find it hard to cite those which influence my films. Perhaps that is related to my trying to extend what is acceptable to show within the films I make.

The one animated short which did influence me in the making of this film was Emily Hubley's *Emergence of Eunice* (1980). It struck me with its confessional voice, simple drawings and frankness. Its story, told in the simplest and least dramatic terms, had an honesty I really appreciated: life goes on, you deal with it. It also felt very female in its authorship, and not just because of the subject matter.

The script for my film was essentially a poem, which came out of a lot of creative writing practice combined with the end of an unhappy relationship.

Visually, the film was developed through a series of vignettes: pictures and text, which were starting points for the story. It was the first film I made digitally (unlike my previous films, which were shot on a film rostrum camera) and I wanted to develop a technique of drawing directly into the computer, and working with stacks of drawings rather like traditional animation.

At first I found working with a Wacom tablet and pen frustrating, but as the ideas for the film developed, so did a looseness and simplicity of drawing with a very pixellated line. It was important to me that the film was, clearly, drawn, but also overtly digitally-made.

The vignettes also informed the static, close-up shots, inside the protagonist's cramped domestic space, which make up the film. They do not really explore the space inside the flat, but compress it into locked off point-of-view shots. I wanted to use the camera to give this feeling of being locked inside one's own mind and body, to be inside one's own point-of-view both literally and metaphorically.

The claustrophobia of her isolation in this interior space contrasts with the exterior space of the outside world. Inside her world the familiarity of

I felt worshipped, adored. I felt like he loved me.

I didn't want to wash it off.

I felt beautiful when he drew pictures all over my body in biro, pictures of anything: a man's face, a horse and cart, rude words, my arms and my belly like a school desk, but I loved it.

I don't know what to do

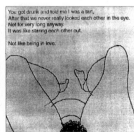

You got drunk and told me I was a tart. After that we never really looked each other in the eye. Not for very long anyway. It was like staring each other out.

Not like being in love.

Extracts from an early storyboard for *Crying and Wanking*

objects and of her body is manipulated by changes in scale and focus.

We only see the character inside the space but are aware that she has a life outside the flat. Jumps in time and from one day to the next provide structure for the subjective experience with which the audience becomes involved, as layers of information are revealed. The television is a constant source of distraction from her solitude, and allows some engagement with the world outside. The telephone provides opportunities for her to interact (or not) with other characters.

I was aware that the story might well be seen as autobiographical, but for me the process of animation filmmaking distances me from any of my own experiences which have become part of the film. Sitting in the dark cinema with an audience watching what you have made exposes you as a filmmaker, but for me it is also a liberating space in which ideas and emotions can be presented and explored. I was not afraid of that, because the filter of communicating through a film allows for sufficient ambiguity. The film is not going to stand or fall by whether it is 'true' or not. The experiences of the character could have happened to any young woman, as far as I'm concerned – though she is a specific character, she is not a 'certain kind' of woman.

Without doubt there were influences and experiences from my own life which informed the film, but I was trying to make a comment on sexual politics, on what is and is not acceptable in a seemingly permissive society, and the differences in acceptability between private and public life. About the relationship between self-image and self-esteem and that contrast between interior and intimate life and public life, with and without 'the mask'; private moments, how behaviour changes when there's no one else around.

Sound is particularly important for creating the atmosphere within the physical and psychological space of this film and is a part of the filmmaking process which I find very creative.

Working with actors was something new which I really wanted to try, especially to produce an emotional response in the audience. I auditioned ten actresses, but struggled to direct any of the actors to read the script without 'acting' it. At a work-in-progress screening of the film, on which I had used my own voice for the working soundtrack, the filmmaker Suzie Templeton told me she thought that my voice worked well, something I had not previously considered.

My own voice is authentic only in terms of being more easily controlled than that of an actor's. It was a confessional, private, 'internal monologue' character of the voice that I could not manage to elicit from the actors I auditioned. I recorded it sitting on my sofa, in three or four takes which I then edited together. The fact that the poem/script was so concise was essential. I do not think I would have been able to improvise on something looser. It was just a case of trying to get the right emotional quality in the voice. It probably helped that I was in the same sort of location as the character – alone in a cramped flat – rather than in a formal sound booth with other people around me.

The live-action was conceived for the dream/fantasy sequences, i.e. if animation is depicting the reality, then an alternate form is required to depict another reality. I was also keen to explore a relationship between drawing and the body, words and flesh, and those sequences were an attempt to move the story forward through that relationship: the intimacy of being drawn upon by her lover, and then the betrayal of being labelled or condemned behind her back.

The other live-action sequences come in the end credits. Initially this simply came from a wish to close the film with an original and visually appropriate credit sequence, but in fact I think that something of the feeling of documentary footage it has helps to release us from the film's claustrophobia, as does the point towards the end of the film where the phone rings. Life goes on. You put on your public face once more and deal with the world. These introspective, navel-gazing hours are interludes which punctuate life, not life itself.

The film's title was never popular, neither with my mum nor the teaching staff at the Royal College of Art! But it was always my feeling that if you could not stomach the title then the content of the film probably was not for you either. In fact, in my mind, the title acknowledges the navel-gazing nature of the film, and I often describe it as 'a film about sex, loss and spending too much time indoors'. The awards the film has won are perhaps the most surprising response, since I never expected it to be 'popular'.

I was certainly trying to move the audience, to create an emotional tension, and to tell a story of loss. But I also wanted to provoke, in terms of questioning what it is acceptable to show, what is acceptable to talk about in terms of female sexuality.

Viewers have presented me with many other readings of the story than that which I intended: that at the end of the film when she says 'I ended it', the woman commits suicide; that the end credits show her dead body in the bath. In fact I wanted to encourage a level of ambiguity throughout the film; the right level being enough for viewers to produce their own readings of the character and the story, but not so much that there is no narrative to follow.

Sound and Emotional Narrative:
Annabelle Pangborn on Scoring *The Secret Joy of Falling Angels*

Annabelle Pangborn is a composer, sound designer and supervising effects editor, and also currently Head of Editing, Sound and Music at the National Film and Television School in the UK. She originally trained as an opera singer, but soon turned to composing and recording her own more experimental work. She had known filmmaker Simon Pummell for some time when she was commissioned to score and create vocal performance for his film *The Secret Joy of Falling Angels* (1991). The genesis of this extraordinarily powerful score is charted below, via an edited transcription of an interview with Pangborn,[1] and followed by an illustrated reproduction of her working notes.

Initially Pummell wanted to ask John Zorn to write the music for the film, with the idea that Annabelle would sing on the soundtrack. The film's producer, Keith Griffiths, worried this might give the film a music video feel, so to give him an idea of how it might work Annabelle produced a demo, using just piano and layered vocals to accompany a relatively detailed animatic of one sequence from the film. When Zorn proved to be unavailable, Griffiths then suggested that she herself score the whole film, with Larry Sider (who had previously worked extensively with the Quay Brothers, amongst others) as sound editor. Sider created the sound effects, 'ranging from pigeon wing flaps to the rustling of shaken silk scarves',[2] and worked with material supplied by Pangborn.

Voice & Cello

Pangborn recounts that through discussion she and Simon settled on the score being two instruments, voice 'as very much linked to the woman', and cello, 'because I could layer it, it could play chords, and as a stringed instrument it could provide a lot of very different textures, not necessarily only classical'.

A rigorous classical conservatory training, subsequently 'unlearned' to explore more experimental singing, had left her confident as a singer and vocalist, 'with no hang ups about the different languages. Whereas, never having written for cello before, I was anxious about the enormous disparity in my own knowledge about these two instruments. In the couple of months before I got the finished film, I borrowed a cello and noodled around on it everyday, and, since I couldn't play, I'd just make sounds I'd record.

'A violinist friend suggested trying to learn to play the opening to Bach's Solo Cellist Suite, and over a six week period I found I could play it quite expressively. Although in the end, I still couldn't play the cello, I *was* left with an emotional residue of what it would feel like if I did play, and *that's* what made the difference, because, particularly when you're using acoustic instruments in a score, it's all about performance.

'The film's opening soundtrack is based all on single notes and it's the performance that counts, not the note and not the instrument as such. It's the texture and a feeling that are important. With the two notes, as the film title goes across the screen, what's interesting is that the first cello thing we hear feels much more part of the soundtrack even though it is a note, an instrument playing a note. The cello also allowed for some very literal associations, because of Simon's use of bird skeletons in the film, and the way their aesthetic differs strongly from the drawn animation. They're brittle, and though softened through the shadow, the gestural movement articulates across the frame in a very different way to the drawn animation. And because the cello can play pizzicato and has plucking strings, there are many ways to play that, you can hit the strings as hard as you want, like a percussion instrument, so I felt that could be exciting material.'

On the vocal score, and her performance, Pangborn comments: 'Whilst key points were notated, integrated into the score, so I'd know what note I was going to start on, a lot of the vocal was improvised in the recording session, and I think that was really key to making it work with the cello. If the vocal had been scored when I scored the cello, I think the music would have been too heavy-handed for the film. It is the improvisation that makes the music so fluid. The vocal becomes something else ... at the end it is singing, but the first vocal entry, when the woman, and then her face, almost comes into focus and then recedes, the vocals are doing the same thing. The synergy between the two things is so organic, I don't see it as music; clearly, it's musical, but also it's just someone's voice. It has a very human presence.

'Obviously the audience gets used to a certain kind of language you are using or a narrative flow, so even by the end of it, in the final sequence, it's quite melancholic, the music is quite fluid, and you haven't seen the woman for a long time, you have just been concentrating on the bird. She comes into and crosses the frame, and she is huge, very dominant, and there is a vocal entry there which is like an 'ah', and that was a very literal interpretation of the picture where she is soothing, as though she's going 'there, there, calm down'. But at that point even though it's absolutely singing, I think we have all gotten used to the rule of the voice in the film, so it doesn't sound like a song. If you had to pin point what kind of presence it does have, it's a very abstracted interior voice for the woman.'

As *Secret Joy...* was her very first film score, on starting work she kept in mind producer Griffiths' advice, which was 'to pay attention to where you think you should hit sync, where the music should literally synchronise with something happening on screen, so the gestures become absolutely united, music and image'. Working with a time-coded VHS tape, she began making notes, and wrote 'a reasonably spontaneous but quite detailed, not exactly analysis, more a kind of notation of what I thought the film was about and what I should pay attention to. There were the two characters, obviously, and I knew that part of Simon's inspiration was pictures of the Annunciation; so you could see this very loaded sexual myth was at the centre of the film.

'Writing these notes, and sometimes logging specific points within a shot, I realised the issue of 'in control versus out of control' had become central to the architecture to what I was doing. This process enabled a quite coherent emotional narrative and a very coherent direction to emerge, mapped out literally on this log, with something very solid to follow, although I did not actually write the score in sequence... When I got the finished picture, I felt the most obvious sequence to do, or what I felt the music had to do, was the bird skeleton sequence I called "The Struggle for Flight": the bird fighting to get out of the cage and taking off. Once I'd scored that, I went back to what became known as the "Alice sequence" that almost directly precedes it, in which the woman undergoes a rather grotesque morphing. This I scored purely for voice, whereas the demo had been tested for voice and piano.

'These two sequences done, musically I could see what the line was, and do the rest. It made narrative sense that the score starts off very fragmented and that whether it's a cello note or the first vocal entry, they are almost like sound layers in the soundtrack, they are do not feel like music cues as such. Then gradually the music becomes more articulated as the narrative gets stronger, and you end up with absolute structured music in the finale.'

Scene by scene commentary

On the opening of the film: 'With Larry and Simon directing the soundtrack at that point in the mix, there was detailed focus on perspective, so although the opening contains rather abstract images, the soundtrack is extremely defined because it has a very cinematic quality of distance and closeness, which even though you don't know what it means, makes you feel like there is a narrative going on. There is a physical sense of space, because he is using that effect of looking through something all the time, and then of course we do get to the cage. Over the word 'Joy', I had done these choral sets and thought that would work over the title and Larry layered them up which I hadn't instructed him to do but it worked quite well.

'The first vocal sounds we hear do sound like I am literally voicing the character. It starts with a humming but then moves onto something much more like an utterance or breathing, so at this stage there is no sense of

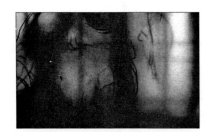

singing. The first time it sounds like singing, it has a quite ethereal quality, strangely, because we have heard her humming in this rather nervous way to start with, so it doesn't seem to be her, even though it is actually her! It seems to be something she cannot quite get a hold of.

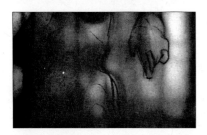

'For me, the key was anxiety, and as it goes on, the idea of being in control and out of control, with the voice literally moving between these parameters. So all of those utterances, those noises, are the 'out of control', but are contained; as if suggesting, 'I am out of control but no one must know that'. And the sung bits are the controlled bits, quite literally.

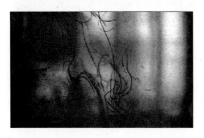

'I'm responding here to the imagery of the woman's naked body, which is constantly morphing and is really quite anxious. Some people who have seen it, as it moves into the "Alice sequence", describe it as almost obscene, they find the movement overwhelming; whereas when it moves to the close-up of the face in the mirror, it's a very controlled image. This is absolutely Simon territory, a Bacon-esque, grotesque distortion, where he is giving something which is aesthetically very beautiful and then moving into a completely grotesque rendering of that imagery and that, more than anything, is what the voice is responding to for the woman.

Images from *The Secret Joy of Falling Angels* (1991) © Channel Four Television

'The voice is following, sliding around the distortion in the drawn line, but again the cello is very controlled. And also quite romantic, which was important to me because I thought there was a romantic undercurrent to everything. Which was beautiful but strangely perverse, especially with those images. There's a kind of feeling of attraction-repulsion.

'These anxious sequences are actually quite confrontational; but, although I didn't really think about it at the time, the music in a way seduces you into watching it. Then the cello goes through a morphing distortion, which the voice was doing previously. Further on, the cello's plucking sound and her moaning really makes people very anxious. Music and image actually swap roles there, because the image is quite stable in that sequence, whereas the music is all over the place. And again we have the very controlled choral stack and the out of control utterances.

'The "Alice sequence" was about creating a sense of intense anxiety. I am using two languages, referencing a classical music language, which is quite familiar, and then using improvised lyrics on top, which really comes out as jazz and an avant-garde type of vocals. The sequence uses both vocals at the same time, so it's layers of my voice, like a mini-choir, with these jazzy vocals on top. As the voice rises, the fact that it is quite vulnerable even though it is controlled, gives it a strange quality. In fact it was originally intended to be quite full voice, but because the recording session was running late, and I was tired and stressed, my voice has got a lot of tremor in it, as when you are very tired, you become short of breath to sustain the vocals. There's a vulnerability and brittle quality, particularly in the higher notes, so the recording literally shows the weakness in the physicality of the voice.

'In the "Alice sequence", the scat singing follows the bird, now quite tiny, and the woman is controlling: even her scream is controlled. Larry layered these vocals, the scream, and kept repeating that, which again I hadn't intended but it also worked very well. And then the score repeats, intentionally, but with the cello thing, which we've previously heard using the bow, now accompanying the images of the skeleton, using the plucked string, the pizzicato, to lead us into a sort of bridge. Here I was very deliberately hitting cuts at certain points.

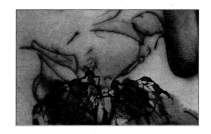

Images from
The Secret Joy of Falling Angels

'At this point, the tension ratchets up yet again, with the main cello line, up and up and up, using a chromatic scale, which is every single white and black note on an inevitable rising scale, and the playing had to get louder, to give it a sense of welling up ever more intensely. Tony Hinnegan, the cellist, had to play it all in one go, and record all of the lines, which was surprisingly demanding. You can hear it has a laboured quality to it; the effort of playing really worked.

'And then we go into the bird sequence ("The Struggle for Flight" in my working notes), which is all about rage, and the final sequence where suddenly the bird is flying, a very important moment. Simon always described that as a moment of release, which it is, although the intensity had to increase. In musical terms and film terms that's a hard cut. The bird is trying to get out of the cage and it gets more and more intense, but you never see the bird take off, or get out. The bird is just suddenly flying, in filmic terms that's a time jump, a jump-cut, so I just started on a new music cue, and the music does something else: the music is not one piece of music that's scored through.

'The idea was to make it very intense and emotionally intense too. There is no sign of the music coming to rest yet, so then when the vocal comes in, it changes everything. And it's a surprising feel at this point, because it really is sung, that really we are back in control again. And I think it's surprising for the woman as well since she hasn't really manifested herself in this way before. And then we go through to a much more melancholic piece and by that time the final sequence is the most structured piece of music in the whole film. We get through this kind of anger through to despair, and acceptance, then it's resolution.'

Visual rhythm

With a great deal more scoring experience behind her now, Pangborn notes how aspects of the film itself facilitated the process of composing: 'Rhythmically the film was solid, coherent, whatever pace it was going at. The skeleton sequence is a good example of that: the bird moving across the screen, whether it's arching its back or spreading its wings, just feels absolutely right. That meant I could write with it, around it, I could change texture quite dramatically, which is what happens in that sequence, because it keeps cutting to those close-ups of wing texture. Larry told me that even though he didn't know what the film was about, he felt that there was clearly a really strong emotional narrative and also it was very rhythmic, so there were two key things to work with.

'The dynamic between the shadow skeletons and the drawn stuff also had quite an effect on Larry and I. Even though Simon's using black and white, graphite pencil, there is something incredibly fluid in a painterly way about the imagery. Also, the different movements, and the textures of movement, were so solidly rhythmical whether it was moving as one fluid gesture or moving in stop frames, which is what the skeleton does a lot of the time. It was always coherent and actually consistent in the most dynamic way. I don't think there was any point where you felt it stopped and I think that made the soundtrack very easy. Well, easier for me in the beginning, where it's very fragmented: I never felt it was awkward, because it's moving between the sound and the music fragments in the picture, so it's always moving forward.'

Recording

The actual recording and mixing process also enhanced the final score, sometimes in unexpected ways. 'It's always a surprise when the musicians play your music because they bring it to life. It's like giving an actor lines to say, suddenly something happens with them. It sounded like I imagined, but different as well, much more intense, but in a good way. In the cello score, its presence is very physical, which is why it works more with the sound than the music, and then some of the pizzicato plucking of the strings is also very abrasive, which again feels more sonic than musical. In particular, when the bird at the climax of the skeleton sequence struggles to get out of the cage, it's quite difficult to tell exactly what are the musical lines and what are Larry's sound effects, because in a way everything is inhabiting the same texture and defining each other. That was a very new thing for me: even though I had been a musician I had never thought about the physicality of the instrument in that way. It wasn't until I started working with sound a lot in film that I became very focused on different sonic qualities.

'Although the score had four cellos playing at the same time, a single celloist was used and each track overdubbed which makes it a very angular recording. This stripped out a lot of the classical feel, and made it much more hard-edged. I was very happy with the cello recording, but I was eager to hear the voice with it, because I knew it was the voice that defined it and the point of the cello accompaniment at times was that it is familiar, and that anchors the audience... Also, we had the picture in the recording session and mixed some of it to picture, and that relationship changes everything, because the music and image are constantly reinventing each other.

'After only seeing the picture on VHS tape on a small TV monitor, seeing it projected during the mix was just astonishing. What was interesting about those close ups of the textured stuff, was that in the skeleton sequence when they come in, there is abrasive cello, and the movement is an incredibly hard-edged fluctuation in the image, but in the conclusion I don't use the cello like that on it, so a lot of those images are just floating with just either the lyrical cello backing or just a vocal on top. And even though they are exactly the same images, the movement in them is totally different. Obviously sound does change the image, but I remember seeing that in the mix and being completely astonished by it. One time I even thought the picture had changed.'

Emotional resonance and meanings

'I think the film is very, very layered. Because obviously there's this strong thing about sex going on, sexual tension and literally what it is to have sex. Then there is the other side of the coin, which is about a very sort of genuine connection, or communion, with someone, a sort of impossible possession...

'In some ways you could say it's quite simple, two people who are obviously attracted to, but scared to death of, each other. Then they come together, and it's an intense union and communion, but also there's that other side of sex, where actually the other person is not present because at the point of abandonment that's the ultimate release, which is the paradox of it. This idea of being a part of someone and not being a part of them which is not simply to do with the act of having sex, is actually part of the human state.

'Even though I don't feel the ending of the film is really sad, I think there is an enormous amount of loss in the film. That's what I think the loss is connected to. There is a thread running through it, which is not about sex, it's like, this is life, this is how it is. But there's also the element ... when you are feeling emotional you are really living. And that's important; and we all go about our domestic business, but to actually connect with something or someone in an emotional way, might not be all plain sailing, or completely enjoyable, but that is living, that means you are alive. And I think that is also an important part of the film as well, just that feeling of connection of feeling to yourself and then transmitting that to another person.

'I think there's a lot of fear in the film, on the part of both characters. In a way the woman is very, very anxious, although at the end you could say the woman is the one who finds herself and the bird who is flailing around. It's the bird who is out of control. Once, when I did a lecture at a School of Sound symposium about the film, someone who saw it could not believe a man had made the film. Whereas I feel it's a completely male film, I don't see how a woman would write this. Because it's so completely a man's point-of-view of the dilemmas of sex and love, you know, the intellectual side of sex and death, the notion of the sublime.'

Notes

1 Interview with Annabelle Pangborn by the editor, July 2008
2 See Kitson, C. (2009) *British Animation: The Channel 4 Factor*, Parliament Hill Publishing, 120–1.

A Composer at Work:
Notebooks on *The Secret Joy of Falling Angels*

SECRET   JOY

Directed by Simon Pummel

Produced by Koninck Studios Ltd

Multitrack with sync pulse
to sub new card ?

Sample cello sounds?

Transfer to 35mm?

25 frames.

Timecode	Shot description
01:33:13	CU more distinct woman.
01:38:09	CU space inside cage.
01:40:01	CU woman's profile - holding mirror.
01:41:06	Profile dissolves into head looking down.
01:42:05	CU profile moving off right.
01:44:13	CU head and shoulders. Moving through layers - face looking into mirror.
01:53:20	CU hand.
02:13:07	CU head - pan down to mirror between legs.
02:20:15	Slow motion opticals: 1) Vaginal Texture. 2) Wing in mirror. 3) Angel with wing.
03:26:09	CU head and shoulders of woman with mirror in cage.
03:31:09	Pan right to CU angel.
03:32:09	CU wing flapping.
03:33:10	Texture.
03:38:15	MS woman in cage and angel flapping - wing.
03:43:20	BCU wing flapping behind bars of cage.
03:46:19	Lead into Alice sequence. UBCU woman's body behind cage bars - pan up body.
03:46:22	BCU woman's "cat" head. Optical?
03:52:00	Texture.

Handwritten annotations:

Woman's voice more distinct

Fade cello (into high, pure sound)

Woman's voice in foreground - pure

Register notches down.
Intense (anxious) cello fragments in background = wisp

Cello Arpeggio - plucked?
Romantic/classic sound in Bach

Low register. Cello begins to move further forward

Cello + vocal fragments builds + moves to rich Baroque sacred sound to form overture into Alice sequence

Slow sad distorted cello (samples?)

Change of registration. Brutal/exit to

Sharp vibration vocal

Feel soprano voice?

Establishment of woman + Angel sequence.
Backlight.
Woman = voice
Angel = cello
MUSIC
Fragmented.
Voice - pure.
Cello - classical } Baroque association

Sound Effects
Stick running across cage
Water.
Wings flapping

Instrumental effects
Pizzicato
Plucked clouds
Organ/Strummed clouds
Arpeggiated chords (Bach prelude)

NB
Woman + mirror.
Texture.
Vaginal + feathers.
Does woman see herself in mirror? but does she fully acknowledge Angel presence?
Carry out subtly mirror and sound effects.

Time	Description	Notes
00:00:00	Texture.	Cello single notes, bowed. Low (Texture refers to depth). Alternate with sound effect. Cracking?
00:06:13	Cage through vignette.	
00:12:09	Texture.	Looking out of cage. Hear soft + brittle after trying to get in it.
00:15:15	Cage through vignette.	Harmonic association between cello + sound. Rising MID, HIGH. and resolution. Use later as glissando
00:20:04	Texture.	
00:22:10	Cage through vignette.	
00:30:23	Texture.	
00:36:04	Title begins. "Secret" pans left. — Cello, single note, bowed. HIGH	
00:38:12	Purple S. — CELLO, resolution MID	
00:39:09	Mix to texture. — CELLO, single note, bowed. LOW	
00:41:18	Ariel pan of cage.	Sound effect + voice - Sigh, mutter? Metal running. Cage is big (resonant) but claustrophobic. } BREATHING?
00:48:06	CU of cage.	
00:54:17	Mix to "Joy".	Voices to punctuate only. Switch to more organic sound qualities. Release moment. } Breathing easing + moving towards long surge, SIGH?
00:55:04	Joy - pan right.	
01:03:13	Mix to "O".	
01:06:16	"O".	
01:08:08	"O".	
01:09:17	"O".	
01:11:00	"O".	
01:13:04	Ariel shot "golden" cage. — Sound effect + voice - utterance - BREATHING.	
01:15:21	CU of cage bars - blurred woman behind bars. Pand down bars.	Stick running down bars. Cello - pizzicato, pregnant.
01:26:23	Mix to woman moving behind bars.	Hear woman's voice in background. Cello - foreground.

Opening sequence.
No continuous music.
Sound alternates between fragmented cello + interrupted sounds with sound effect.

Sound Effect
Stick running across cage.
Scratches.
Wet squeaking, endless?
Wind through feathers?

Instrumental sound effect.
Pizzicato.
Muckled chords.
Open sonorous chords.

Worried bowing on up strings.
Rapid pizzicato.

Squealing + creaking (as) hair on strings.

PART 2

PART 3

04:28:2?	Above continued- mix to colour flash and back to figure rising.
04:35:12	Stubby angel.
04:39:09	Alice head - open mouthed, moving down.
04:44:06	Stubby angel comes into picture.
04:46:20	CU woman's body - legs opening.
04:49:15	Repeat.
04:52:15	CU stubby angel.
04:57:10	Woman's legs opening leading into body collapse.
04:58:16	Body collapse. *Rising glissand - operatic scream*
05:02:21	Scream.
05:04:00	Scream - BCU on shoulders and bottom half of mouth. *opera/chest*
05:05:08	Grotesque angel. *High pure single note bowed on cello/wing flapping.*
05:09:04	BCU woman's breasts. *Chest*
05:13:00	Scream - BCU on shoulders and bottom half of mouth. *chest/opera*
05:14:07	Grotesque angel with wing flapping. *cello/wing flapping*
05:16:18	CU angel torso and wing flapping. *wing flapping /cello (decay?)*
05:21:01	CU woman's breasts - pan up to mouth open in scream. *chest/opera*
05:22:12	Scream. *opera*
05:24:07	Lead into bird sequence. Bird foetus. *Water* *Skeleton in Grotesque Angel*

VOCAL SECTION

PART 1 : SACRED/BAROQUE SOUND
PART 2 : JAZZ SOUND
PART 3 : OPERATIC SCREAM. CHEST GLISSANDO

SACRED SOUND

Choral but slightly distorted implying anxiety lead the Grotesque.
Scat vocal over the top

JAZZ SOUND

Improvised jazz vocal backed by cello imitating double bass/ guitar/ piano.

PART 1

20 secs approx

Timecode	Description
03:54:13	Alice sequence Woman with cat head.
03:56:19	Woman with Alice head - open mouth.
03:58:14	CU woman and cat head.
04:00:13	CU woman and Alice head - opens out.
04:01:23	MS woman and cat head.
04:02:12	MS woman and cat head - body arching, rising and swinging round to CU of cat head.
04:05:01	CU cat head tilting to left, Moves full on into picture - UBCU.
04:07:10	Shorter repeat.
04:10:12	Mix to CU Alice head screaming.
04:12:05	CU cat head.
04:13:04	CU Alice head screaming.
04:14:18	CU cat head.
04:15:17	CU Alice head screaming.
04:17:10	CU cat head.
04:18:09	BCU Alice head screaming.
04:20:00	BCU cat head.
04:21:00	UBCU Alice head screaming.
04:22:15	BCU cat head.
04:23:0 D	Mix to woman with Alice head arching back and rising.

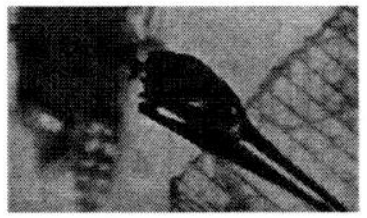

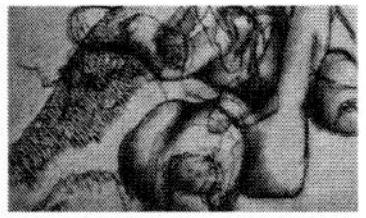

Timecode	Description
07:26:19	Pan round cage only. Sound effect.?
07:29:09	BCU bird flying- BCU bird's head.
07:43:17	Rapid pixolation - bird trying to get sound effect into cage.
07:48:11	Pan round cage only.
07:49:23	CU feathered wing.
08:00:07	Open out to bird and feathered wing flapping.
08:03:14	Slow motion optical. CU head and torso of bird flying in water.
08:10:14	MS bird with feathered wing, flying.
08:15:23	CU feathered wing (charcoal). Pan across to "fleshed out" bird skeleton with feathered wing flapping.
08:27:01	Start of devouring sequence. Woman and angel roll over and down.
08:32:23	Texture.
08:34:23	Woman kneeling over angel.
08:39:18	CU angel
08:43:04	CU woman's head comes into picture with angel.
08:45:18	Woman and angel share picture.
08:48:10	Woman dominates picture.
08:53:19	Woman and angel (pink?), sexual rocking motion.
08:54:23	Mix to woman and angel - picture opens out (blue?).

Handwritten annotations:

Was flying Released print

sound effect

Was flying. Keep add flesh sound.

Feathered wing → more diatonic harmony.

26 secs. at 62 mm
- 8.22.17
32 ÷ 16
8.21.18.

Angel hovering throughout

FINAL SEQUENCE

Running

46mm = 78.25 beats tympanic

156.5 beats
157 beats / 7 mins.

4 = 4 or 39.125
40 beats.

2 mins 11 secs

46mm = 78.27 beats/min.
170.65
171 beats/2 min 11 secs
3/4 = 57 BARS EXACTLY.

BIRD SEQUENCE

CELLO SEQUENCE
Wormed bowing on open strings with pickup.
Climactic dissonant melodic line.
Coned glissandos (tremure).

Sound Effect
Skeleton beating against cage.
Wings flapping water.

Instrumental Sound Effect.
Wopped bowing building to frenzied cello rattle cello creak.

Plucked arpeggio - fragments begin to cohere.

Timecode	Description	Note
05:29:05	Slow motion opticals in water. 1) Profile of bird head. 2) Vignette of above. 3) CU bird head. 4) Bird sitting.	
05:58:00	CU sitting bird - looks around, L to R, R to L.	
06:06:07	MS bird into bird moving "front legs" and arching neck anxiously - animaloid.	
06:14:18	CU above.	
06:20:05	Skeleton wings beating. Sound effect?	
06:27:17	Texture.	
06:31:23	MS bird from back moving neck and head R to L.	
06:35:20	CU head coming into picture. Distorted CU bird moving across picture.	
06:47:19	MS bird getting up - about to take-off.	
06:49:13	Repeat.	
06:51:03	MS bird flapping skeleton wings. Hollow, erupting wing flapping?	
07:01:11	Opens out to MS bird flying.	
07:05:00	BCU bird's head moving into left of picture. BCU bird moving across picture.	
07:06:24	Bird trying ot get into cage. Sound effect.	
07:08:20	Texture.	
07:14:10	CU bird's head beating against cage. Sound effect.	
07:23:17	Bird flying around cage (no frenzied head beating).	

63:10
54:17

08:47:06 Release Point - Angel finishes hovering + — RELEASE POINT
(enters woman)   Woman on A6.

08:57:12 Woman and angel - more claustrophobic.
(red?)

08:59:13 Texture.

09:04:15 Woman and angel. (red?)

09:06:0? CU woman, angel face and wing merging.
Pan across bodies.

09:10:03 Texture.

09:12:19 Woman and angel. (blue?)

09:15:13 Texture.

09:21:21 Woman and angel. (red?) — Release point

09:31:18 Bird feotus in woman.

09:32:17 Bird feotus dissolves.

09:35:00 Just woman head bent back.   Pure woman's voice in foreground.

09:35:14 Woman and angel.   Pure voice.

09:36:05 Just woman.   Pure voice.

09:37:00 Woman and angel.

09:38:15 Bird feotus in woman.   ] cello-worried bowing

09:39:12 Bird feotus dissolves.   ]

09:41:12 Just woman.   Pure voice.

09:42:06 Woman and angel.

09:42:13 Texture.   ↓ superimposed Pure C.

09:55:06 Mix into woman and angel (blue?)

09:57:08 Bird feotus in woman.   ] cello-worried bowing

09:58:16 Bird feotus dissolves.   ]

10:00:14	Just woman.	Pure voice
10:01:09	Woman and angel.	
10:02:02	Just woman.	Pure voice
10:02:23	Woman and angel.	
10:03:18	BCU woman and angel (red?)	
10:04:03	BCU bird feotus in stomach.	Cello-borned bassus
10:05:02	Feotus dissolves.	
10:11:00	UBCU bird feotus in woman.	→ Classical vibrato.
10:11:06	Bird feotus suspended in water.	Pure voice.
-10:13:17 — Titles?		
10:26:05 Titles		

Ian Gouldstone on *guy101*

The story is true insomuch as *guy101* is the story of Keith, who I met in a chat room back in 2000. We chatted on and off for years about all sorts of nonsense - bowling, camping, cars, sex, politics... After we'd known each other for a while, he opened up about the stuff he was into. The story in *guy101* has a few details stripped out which I felt complicated things too much. When the guy came back, there were·more men, and I know that there was a dog involved in one instance. Ack!

I will never really know if Keith told me porky pies. But from what I know about the guy, the pictures he sent me of his other sessions, it all adds up to me. Plus, I have a profound trust of Keith. I really see him as a remarkable, creative and fundamentally good person.

My 'research' for the film was interviewing Keith about specifics of the story, while also trawling Google for what I could about the demographics and landscape of Akron, Ohio, Keith's make of car, his breed of dog, his bowling league. There is a huge part to this film which, for me at least, deals with how much information you can find out about the surface of a person with the help of modern technology. Yet when it comes down to using that technology to help try to make sense of what makes people tick, what's going on inside, it's rather useless. The film builds up to this super-saturation of information and statistics in the early stages so that I can juxtapose it with the complete lack of information in the latter stages of the film.

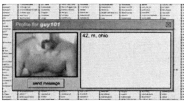

Image from *guy101* (2006)
© Royal College of Art

Captured from Animatic software

Over the years, as I researched the facts of Keith's story, I actually became less and less interested in the actual events, and more and more intrigued by his (and everyone else's) attraction to 'edge-play' (sexual play at the edge of personal limits). So by the time I started writing the film, it was not really a story I was telling, but an exploration of edge-play that I was leading. That's why I think the really important story within the film is not actually Keith's, but the narrator's. He is the one who is slowly discovering what edge-play is really about.

Ultimately, though, I wanted the audience to discover what edge-play is about. Of course, I couldn't physically tie the audience in their seats, blindfold them, and whip out my implements, so I figured the film had to do this on my behalf in its own way – with an extremely compelling story, increasingly stripped down visual and aural cues, and a profound reliance on people's imaginations.

Just as great edge-play turns horrible when you lose control, film becomes intolerable when it is happening to you instead of happening with you. That's why *guy101* needed to have a rock-solid narrative foundation. I knew that if anyone lost the thread of the story, all of the visual and aural experimentation on top of that would be pointless. I like to think the film was an animation edge-play session where the safe word was my voice-over. To that end, I wrote the film as a radio play first. I probably wrote a dozen drafts before I even started thinking about the visuals.

One of my main goals for the film was to present the audience with a cold, factual scenario and let their own experiences and attitudes really shape the drama. I gave them the statistical skeleton of a story, and asked them to fill in the emotional bits. For that to happen, I figured the voice needed to be as non-assuming as possible yet still be captivating. And I wanted a simple narrative voice-over to safeguard against all the risks I wanted to take with the rest of the film (animation edge-play).

I did try to involve some actors in the process, but it didn't work out for many reasons. It proved very challenging, and time consuming, to communicate what I wanted to the actors. And since none of the actors I found were willing to put in the time necessary for practically no money, I was forced to do the voice-over myself. For days, I was constantly rehearsing the voice-over in my head with different timings and different characters (camp teenage girls, indifferent regionally-accented labourers, political statisticians, etc). I remember reading out the script to my flatmates in my best super-enthusiastic, bubble-gum chewing, teenage girl voice. The look of absolute horror on their faces suggested this was going in slightly the wrong direction. Eventually, I found the voice that just felt right – it was engaging, it didn't give too much away, and it wasn't trying too hard to be something it was not. So I recorded my first draft with my computer's built-in microphone. In hindsight, I think the uncomplicated voice-over works because it makes mental room for audience to concentrate on all the stuff happening on screen and in their heads.

The final voice-over is actually a giant mishmash of dozens of takes with loads of filters on top. As an indication of how picky I was, there are words within the film that consist of individual syllables spliced together. Also, I'm ashamed to say, my voice is not really that low. I pitch shifted it down by a semi-tone in order to give it a bit more presence. Heck, maybe the scary, unknown nature of this process helped me relate to Keith's edge-play experiences a little better, too.

Once the voice was roughly timed to where I wanted it, from there the film naturally segmented itself into scenes which led me straight into the extremely long animatic process which was continuously evolving throughout production.

For every scene, I had at least three or four completely unique ideas to choose from, so in the end I disposed of mountains of material. For example, the attack scene at the end was going to be a red and black plaid monitor test pattern where the colours gradually went outside the PAL/NTSC display range, causing the display to buzz and create new colours. I justified this as technological edge-play. But, like many of the other ideas that didn't make it through, it was just trying too hard to be clever. It would have completely disrupted the story that's meant to be happening in the audience's imagination.

Captured from Animatic software

Indeed, trying too hard was something that I was constantly struggling with. In animation, I see so many filmmakers trying to illustrate what is happening in their own heads. That approach is fine by me, but since the film was supposed to happen in the audience's heads, I had to fight my own impulses to over-illustrate the scenes.

Those discrepancies [editor's note: between what you hear on soundtrack and what you see on screen] were deliberate. As the film goes on, the link between the voice and the images deteriorates – the images become less explicit and more implicit of what's going on in the story. That 'sir' part is just a very early stage of that process of disconnecting the two streams. I did have lots of ideas of how to first do

Images from *guy101*

that, but the 'sir' seemed to be the most engaging to me without being too outspoken.

When I first showed the film, I had no idea what to expect of the audience, so I suppose all their reactions were unexpected. I've had a few people come up to me and say, 'Nice, but I've heard that joke before.' After explaining that the story is true, they're never really sure what to say.

From the start, I was aware that this story could be construed as fairly stereotypical. And I didn't want to ignore that and pretend that this one singular story was earth-shattering for everyone. Hence wanting to go with such a sterile approach. It purposefully refrains from judging Keith, and lets the audience do it instead (if they so choose). Even though I never think of the film as gay cinema, I imagined some people would identify it was such and use it to confirm their stereotypes of gay people. One man wrote to me and said that he was offended because of this and that I was exploiting gay men. I wrote back and explained that, for me, while the story is true, the film was more an experiment in storytelling that needed a sturdy story to support it. By his gratuitous use of exclamation marks and capital letters, I got the impression he didn't really want to discuss the issue, though.

So to give you an actual answer to the question of homophobia/gay stereotypes, yes it does bother me. But that's because I feel like I failed those people – I didn't succeed in getting those people to see how the film is about them as much as it is about Keith. Scratch the surface of the film and it becomes less about a singular encounter between two men and more a big study on things like human sexuality, our online lives and storytelling in film.

I've had a few teachers and parents come up to me at festivals and ask to use this film to start a discussion with their students and children about sexuality and online safety, etc. This was definitely my favourite reaction. All I ever wanted *guy101* to do was to get people thinking and talking after they left the cinema. I don't even mind what their conclusions are, just as long as the film encouraged them to use their imaginations and their brains.

And I suppose I should mention there have been a few times when people have emailed me out of the blue and said, 'That was hot. Can we have sex pls?'

Script development on *guy101*

This was an early draft of the script for the film *guy 101*. The 'information' it presents is sometimes absolutely based on fact, sometimes drawn purely from my imagination, and throughout reflects a process of shaping the original material as a story for a film, and exploring issues as discussed in the previous interview. – *Ian Gouldstone*

42/M/Akron

3 tasks

    i)   Voiceover about Keith's life (5 lines)
    ii)   Voiceover about Keith's adventure. Complete with great details and ending expressing his pleasure with the situation.
    iii)   Storyboard / list of his everyday activities

THOUGHTS are in **BOLD**

POTENTIAL CUTS are in *ITALICS*

i)

Keith Knight is 42. He lives at 235 Twain Road, Akron, Ohio, 2 blocks west of Summit Lake and 4.7 miles southwest of the Goodyear Blimp airdock. He works as a professional hairdresser at the Clearview Salon where the wives of middle-class professionals from nearby communities go. *A trim costs 24 dollars and 99 cents.*
Keith enjoys camping, hot air ballooning, classic cars, and bowling. He is president of his bowling league, and has an average score of 248. *He schedules the bowling meets every week and wears size 10.5 shoes.*[1]

ii)

At 4:17 pm on August 25th, it was 80 degrees outside with 33% humidity. Visibility was 24.6 miles. Keith took out his black 1978 Mercury Cougar for a drive. It had been waxed 2 weeks prior. At the beginning of the journey there were 37,463 miles on the car. The fuel gauge needle was 7/8 of the way to full. Keith buckled his seatbelt and pulled it tight.

----

[1] **<note... could things like machines and people in first part be more submissive to keith? He commands. They respond.>**

43 minutes after departure, the car was traveling along Interstate 76 from Youngstown. A Leonard Cohen song was playing on the radio station that would fade out of hearing in 10 miles. Keith saw a man standing on the side of the road with his thumb out. The man measured 5 feet 11 and one half inches tall and was approximately 19 % body fat. Keith signaled right and stopped next to the man. The odometer read 37, 488 and the fuel gauge needle was 2 degrees from where it was previously. Keith thought this hitchhiker was 37 years old. In fact, he was 39.[2]

The man opened the car door, sat down in the passenger seat, and closed the door again. He did not buckle his seat belt. Keith lowered his foot by 30 degrees and the car accelerated to 72 miles per hour, 7 miles per hours over the legal speed limit for interstates in Ohio. It was 18,937 seconds from sunset.[3]

…

The hitchhiker said he was horny.

…

He spoke with a southwestern accent.

…

The hitchhiker asked Keith if he knew any women.

…

Keith knew several women…

…

But Keith said no.

…

The hitchhiker asked Keith if he was gay.

…

Keith said yes.

…

"Suck my cock."

…

Keith said yes.

…

The car burned 3 gallons of gasoline returning to the double garage of 235 Ira Avenue. Keith and the stranger entered the house through the back door.

Keith offered him a drink.
12.5 fluid ounces of beer.
Anything else? [4]

…

---

[2] **Get rid of internal state?? Or is it ok to shape expectations here?**

[3] **<They crossed over the county line between Portage and Summit counties. Visuals, to show a change in mood>**

[4] **<I see this as a very loaded question.. is it sufficient to show Keith's submissiveness?>**

The stranger took off his belt…

…and tied Keith's arms together. He pulled Keith towards the stairs and tied him to the banister. He kicked him in the stomach twice and left Keith on the floor. The bruise would take 8 days to disappear.

The stranger left through the back door of the house and entered the double garage. He opened the door of the 1978 Black Mercury Cougar, sat in the driver's seat, and closed the door again. He did not adjust the mirrors.

<PAUSE… 3 hours later>

The stranger returned with 3 other men. They had an average of 21.3% body fat. Two of them were bald headed and one grew up in Memphis, Tennessee. He wore a camouflage cap and hunted deer at the grounds of a local nuclear power station. The last man had a dog named Harley that had never had sex with a man before. They both had large ears. The stranger smoked a cigar.

The four men and the dog entered the house and saw Keith naked and tied to the banister. Harley walked up and sniffed his leg. His owner pushed him aside with his left foot. He kicked Keith in the back of the knee with his right foot. He unzipped his jeans and urinated 8.2 fluid ounces on Keith as he lay on the floor coughing.

<One bald man sorted through Keith's plates. He threw them at the wall in a pattern. Yes. No. Yes. Yes. No. 55% percent of Keith's plates were smashed into 20 fragments or more. 5% were in 15 to 19 fragments. >

Harley barked.
The stranger blew a smoke ring.

The man in the hat spat on Keith. He took 33 fragments of the plates and forced 16 of them into Keith's mouth. Those remaining were thrown at Keith's torso and bounced into the urine on the carpet.

The second bald man withdrew a Colt .357 Magnum from his belt. It contained 5 bullets. He cocked the pistol and pointed it at Keith from 6 feet away. He advanced 4 paces and ran the barrel of the gun along Keith's wet forehead. *<He had inherited the gun from his father, who had fired it once.>*
Urine contains 16 times as much urea as sweat does. Smokeless gunpowder and urea both contain significant amounts of nitrogen.[5]

The stranger held the end of his cigar against Keith's neck for 7 seconds. His chest for 5. His testicles for 12 and a half. They would result in 2 first degree burns and 1 second degree burn.

---

[5] **Maybe this could be a more visual comparison here?**[5]

The .357 Magnum pushed 3 inches into Keith's mouth. It clicked against the ceramic, probed, and withdrew covered in blood and saliva. It entered Keith's anus covered in the same material. The handle was decorated with imitation maple. *The maple leaf is a prominent Canadian national symbol.*

The four men battered and raped Keith for the next 2,134 seconds. They untied Keith and left in 1 green sedan and 1 red pick up truck that drove 19 miles on a gallon of gasoline.

Keith had gained 18 bruises, 8 burns and 6 cuts on his face, torso, and limbs. There were 37,751 miles on his car and the fuel tank was 63% empty. The temperature outside was 74 Farenheit. There were 324 seconds until sunset.

Lying on the floor, untied, Keith blinked twice and lifted his head 10 degrees to watch it… perfectly contented.[6]

iii) Typical day in the life of Keith

Wakes up to radio.
Jogs.
Showers.

---

[6] **Thoughts so far:**

Perhaps the beginning is a bit too numerical.
This script is too long. It takes 6 minutes to read it.
The second part has to concentrate on the role reversal…
In the beginning, things need to be more subservient to Keith.
Maybe there could be more references to the time until sunset.
Does the rape part need to be extended?
In the next section, the writing could be more flowing, more poetic. More enjoyable and less constrained. Also, Keith needs to be submissive in second half. Try to avoid using Keith as the subject of the sentence in the second half.
Could this be written in such a way that it recounts the process through an internet conversation?
Could there be a shift towards the present tense in this?

Visuals?
Abstract imagery
Portraits of Keith
Live Action
Dogs and Guns, plates and belts.
Cameraless animation?
What makes sense for the story? Desensitizing the situation. Reported story, reported images. A tour through Keith's house. Build a big CG version of his house and just tour it?

Drives to work—the salon.

Colors some hair. Trims.

Picks up the groceries. Doesn't like to cook that much. Buys a lot of frozen food.

Takes some groceries to his mother's house.

He goes home and changes into his bowling clothes.

He goes bowling.

He smokes a cigar in celebration and wins a trophy.

Final Thoughts:

Visuals?

Could these visuals be JUST about bowling: a sport about precision, control, but then certain moments of chaos when the pins start rattling around, flying, uncontrollably. Could I concentrate solely on the wrist restraints, the heavy bowling balls, the slick and polish of the lane, the precision machinery... all this machinery and preparation that is dedicated to these short moments of total chaos? It could reflect all the control in Keith's life... and that one feeling of release. I can see a long shot of a pin-crash.

Also all the math of bowling would prove to be an interesting link with all the statistics told in the story.

Finally, I am thinking about HOW I position my statistics within this film. Currently, I think that they are too spread throughout the film and not used effectively. My current thoughts are to have them used very sparingly at the beginning of the film if at all. When the hitchhiker arrives, the statistics start. Kind of interrupting the flow of the story. They shoot off at tangents and unsettle you because what you really want to hear about is the hitchhiker story.

As the hitchhiker part of the story progresses, more statistics are introduced. But it is when Keith is tied up that there is a burst of statistics. So many it is almost unintelligible.

Then a pause when the hitchhiker leaves.

The hitchhiker returns with the other men. You get a very fast build up to totally intense overlapping statistics about the scene. About the number of bruises on Keith's body. His number of broken bones. The number of cuts. Lesions, burns. The temperature of the cigar. The weight of the dog. The number of hairs ripped off of Keith's head in the process of the rape.

If this were paired with the bowling imagery described before, I think it could be quite potent.

Final Script: *guy101*

I met this guy.

On the internet.

In a chat room.

His screen name was…

"Guy101".

And his profile was pretty empty.
Just
"42. Male. Ohio."

There was a small picture of him
with a large handlebar moustache.

And no shirt.

His name was Keith.

And over time,
we talked about all sorts of stuff:
cars, sports, politics, whatever.

I learned factoids like: "Keith bowls an average of 185 and wears a size 10 ½ shoe."
"He enjoys camping." "Collects classic cars." "Volunteers at a battered women's shelter."
"And alphabetizes his spice rack. Labels front."

Anyways, he lives in Akron, Ohio
in this three-storey house
on a street called Twain Road.
It's about two blocks from this big lake
that has lots of different fish in it. Dace, grouper, and Sunfish…

It's all about 5 miles from the Goodyear Blimp airdock.

From what Keith tells me,
the first 2 floors of his house are … fetching. Antique furniture, original fittings,
rescued trinkets. Everything in place.
Everything with a story.

But his computer is up on the third floor,
what Keith calls his junk space.
And when he sends me pictures,
you can't see anything. Not really.

And Keith lives alone in this big house, so I ask him, "Why you live alone in that big
house?" and he tells me, "My partner died 8 years ago…"

Anyways. Once, he told me about the time
he picked up a hitchhiker
on Interstate 76.

The road was empty.
Keith was driving his 1978 black Mercury Cougar with 37,000 miles on it. Cruising at
55, he sees this guy on the side of the road in a wrinkled plaid shirt and a hunter's cap.

The man's holding out his thumb.
Keith stops … and picks him up.

They drive off … and they're both pretty quiet … then the hitchhiker, he does this thing:

He says, "I'm horny."
And Keith says, "O!"
Then he asks, "Do you know any women?"
And Keith says "No."
Then he asks "Are you straight?"
And Keith says, "No."
So he goes, "Suck my dick."
And Keith says, "Yes."

So they drive back towards Keith's house,
passing the Goodyear Blimp airdock and the lake.

Inside…
Keith offers the man a drink.
He wants a beer.
And then Keith asks, "Anything else?"

They're now up on that third floor.

And they get real close to each other.
Keith takes off his clothes.
The man takes off his belt.
He runs his hand up Keith's back…
Right up his spine…
Past his neck…
And grabs him by the skull. Knees him in the gut. Throws him to the floor. Ties him up.
Blindfolds him. And steals his car.

Three hours later
the man comes back. With a cigar. A hunting knife. And a .357 magnum.
He kicks Keith in the gut. Burns him with the cigar. Cuts him. Pushes the gun
in Keith's mouth and tells him to suck it while he fucks him.

And then
he unties him.
And leaves.

Keith ends up with seventeen bruises, seven cuts, three sprains,
and five third-degree burns all over his head, torso and limbs.

And the thing he tells me he really regrets?
And the thing he tells me he regrets?
Not getting the guy's phone number…

Modes of Reality

Mixing Memory and Desire:
Animation, Documentary and the Sexual Event
by Karen Beckman

In her essay, 'What's Wrong with this Picture?' feminist filmmaker Michelle Citron explores the role of home movies in forging family memories, asking from whose point-of-view such collectively shared memories are crafted, what kinds of behaviour are typical in these amateur films, how we understand the relationship between home movies and documentary, and what kinds of memories and events are foregrounded or suppressed. She notes that these films, which 'teeter at the edge of both documentary and fiction' (1999: 19) offer a memory of childhood from the parents' – and usually the father's – point-of-view. These acts of constructing the nuclear family unit, Citron argues, continuously omit 'the dark side of life', such as the anger and betrayals that occur in family units. Dancing girls, baby baths and family vacations – such is the substance of the home movie, a form in which 'the child never grows up, gets drunk, sleeps around, or breaks your heart' (1999: 11). Yet having noted the ideological work of concealment and construction that home movies enact, we need to consider in what alternative ways the medium of film might be used to document, construct and narrate those key moments of and perspectives on lived experience that fail to find a place in family albums and reels. In her own practice, Citron responds to this question in a film like *Daughter Rite* (1979) by combining her own real home movies with 'fake' documentary footage that has been scripted, directed and acted. The DVD collection *Desire and Sexuality: Animating the Unconscious* (2007) includes a number of films that reveal the affinities between animation and mockumentary as two forms well suited for supplementing and critiquing the home movie's sanctioned visual records of childhood, adolescence and family life. These include: *The Stain* (Marjut Rimminen and Christine Roche, UK, 1991), *Forever and Forever* (Michaela Pavlátová, Czech Republic, 1998) and *Never Like the First Time!* (Jonas Odell, Sweden, 2006). Each of these films explores distinct aspects of what animation has to offer the practice of giving visual and narrative form to sexual experience and desire. In spite of their differences, they all challenge us to think about a series of interrelated questions: 1) How do these animated films attempt to document real experiences of sex and desire? 2) What understanding of sex and desire do the films leave viewers with? 3) How does the mixing of memory and desire impact our sense of temporality? 4) What kind of interaction between sound and image occurs as these films attempt to give form to past sexual encounters and elusive or taboo models of desire?

In this chapter, I want to concentrate on the first of these shorts, *The Stain*, exploring it as an example of an animation film that hovers in the space between fact and fiction, and that simultaneously evokes and responds to the spectre of the home movie and its aforementioned limits. *The Stain* opens with a live-action close-up shot of a newspaper column in which personal announcements seem to be mixed up with national news reports. Sandwiched between one announcement that declares 'Life-long campaigner for women's rights, Vera Havel, was killed at the age of 78 while climbing the twin peaks of Mount Charlotte' and another that offers the banal fact that 'Official government figures show a sharp rise in unemployment figures', we find the following notice under the heading, 'The Stain': 'Two eighty-year-old twins committed suicide after a violent family feud over a gravy stain on the tablecloth. Lance and Clive Brown-Smith of Slough-on-Sea shot themselves in the head.' After the camera has zoomed in on this central item, this short then moves into the realm of drawn, model and puppet animation, never to return to the black and white print of the news. Yet as we consider the film that follows in the wake of this shot, we might usefully remember that Rimminen and Roche choose to sandwich their narrative between the story of a feminist who dies trying on the one hand, and a report of depressed national economic conditions on the other. This frame poses questions to keep in mind as we consider the main body of the film and its claustrophobic representation of desire and sexuality: what does feminism have to say about private family narratives? What is the relationship between the public realm of work, nation and economics and the private realm of family, feuds and desire?

As the opening piano music fades, the newspaper cutting gives way to a drawn image of a higgledy-piggledy castle poised precariously on a rock in the middle of the ocean with a washing line hung with tablecloths blowing in the wind in front of the castle. As the camera zooms in on the castle's front door, the classically British female voice of (actress) Chrissie Roberts' narration shifts the temporal frame of the film from the daily specificity of the newspaper report to the mythical time of the fairy-tale: 'Once upon a time there was a beautiful lady and a rich gentleman who lived in a house by the sea.' When the camera reaches the front door, the screen fades to black, underscoring the difficulty of crossing the boundary between public and private space. The narrator continues: 'The husband went out to the office, but he always returned to the house by the sea, where he taught the wife games.' As the front door cracks open, the husband enters the house and take off his gloves, but this time, the spectator is positioned within the interior space of the couple, getting an insider's view of the family's incestuous desires and sexual 'games'. But exactly whose desire is represented here? What form does the representation of taboo sexuality take here? And what is the relationship between the narrative bound within the walls of the house by the sea and the world outside the door through which the father enters?

On one level, *The Stain*, in the feminist tradition of Angela Carter and Jeanette Winterson, uses the suspended and ahistorical time of the fairy-tale to take the narrative beyond the experience of an individual subject in order to explore the ubiquity rather than the uniqueness of the 'dark side of life' that Citron sees as excluded from the sanctioned images of the home movie genre. While the opening news cutting may imply that the film depicts the aberrant desires of one exceptional family in which a range of incestuous bonds in additional to spousal rape are implied (including the father's games with his daughter, and the twin brothers' games with their sister, resulting in a baby of uncertain descent), this exceptionalism is countered by a single inter-title early in the film that states: 'In my opinion, the family is probably the most criminal cell. – Jean Genet.' This movement beyond the desires of the specific protagonists with which we begin – Lance and Clive Brown-Smith – prevents the film from being merely a finger-pointing exposé of a particularly dysfunctional family. Instead, through both the filmmakers' own gesture of fantasising the sexual back-stories of others, and the universality that the fairy-tale frame imposes, *The Stain* reinforces an understanding of desire that psychoanalyst Jean Laplanche (1999) has articulated in terms of a force that *always* exceeds the individual subject, making the task of documenting the 'truth' of an individual's desire almost impossible. As Judith Butler writes, 'Laplanche thus posits a foreign desire as a precondition of "one's own" desire. Who desires when "I" desire? There seems to be another at work in my desire, and this *étrangèreté* disrupts any effort to make sense of myself as a bounded and separate being. I may try to tell the story of myself, but another story is already at work in me.' (2005: 74). But if the incestuous desires of the father and the twin brothers cannot be located in them alone, how does animation allow the film to represent the difficulty of maintaining the 'bounded' self?

On one level, the film certainly functions as a condemnation of the way sexual desire has been used by male members of the nuclear family to oppress female family members as when Rimminen and Roche, recalling Charlotte Perkins Gilman's short story from 1891, 'The Yellow Wallpaper', show the mother disappearing into the home's wallpaper upon the arrival of the baby that is presumably the offspring of her daughter and one of her sons, or in the many scenes that depict the father or the sons chasing mother or daughters through the gothically-distorted architecture of the home. Yet if the film uses animation and the fairy-tale structure to supplement, expose and condemn the lacunae of the home movie – the criminality that Genet sees at the heart of the family – it also does more than this. Indeed what saves the film from becoming an overly simplified and binarized view of illicit familial desire in which men emerge as perpetrators and women as victims is its visual, narrative and psychological complexity through which even the darkest moments of this alternative to the home movie resist reductive moral judgements.

While the mother disappears into nothingness, the sister emerges as a complex character who is both victim and agent in the family violence, pushing her baby down the stairs, and dancing fierce tarantella-like steps as she plays her own strange game of house while her brothers are at work. In a series of shots that move among drawn, model/puppet animation and live-action, we see the sister manically enter her brothers' room with a feather-duster, exploring their fetish objects (gold stilettos, breast lamps and deranged Barbie dolls), moving through the house wearing white cotton gloves that align her more closely with the figure of the magician than with the vanishing woman that was her mother. The film cuts between live-action images of filthy sinks and dirty milk bottles and drawn animation shots of sparkling surfaces; yet, in another Carter-like spin on the fairy-tale motif, the live-action shots show the sister less as a victimised Cinderella than as a white-gloved witch who effortlessly sweeps the soiled traces of everyday life, such as dirty plates and tablecloths, into the home's many drawers and cupboards. Reinforcing this sense that the sister is something more than a victim, we see her gleefully reach into a framed image of 'the baby' at the top of the stairs, her touch magically animating the image and allowing her to 'push' the baby down the stairs a second time (we see her push the baby down the stairs in an earlier scene, but here the act seems to repeat itself, this time as a self-reflexive animated image).

While the sister's violence toward 'the baby' – a character who appears in the model animation sequences as a grown woman in a wheelchair who constantly fiddles with her radio, making messes for her older sister-mother to clean up – might threaten to render 'the baby' into a helpless female victim in her own right, Rimminen and Roche also prevent the audience from adopting this perspective through the complexity of their character development, a complexity which at times became difficult for even the filmmakers to stomach. As Roche notes: 'I started resenting this child as being totally manipulative, awful and then I started identifying with the older sister who originally I didn't like very much.'

After showing the film's drawn image being pushed down the stairs by the baby's older sister, the film cuts to a model animation sequence of the baby wheeling her wheelchair across the room to gaze out of the window, as the narrator, to the tune of a fairground organ playing Strauss waltzes, tells us: 'The baby saw things a tiny bit differently; in fact she sometimes wondered whether anyone saw things like she did at all.' As we cut to the baby's point-of-view, we return to drawn animation images of the ocean that surrounds the family home. While most of the film's ocean views signal the presence of historical time outside the house – one ship hits an iceberg and sinks, while another is bombed by warplanes flying overhead – the baby's view of the world introduces a distinctly surrealist and feminised alternative to either the masculine world of war and business outside the home or the home's incestuous landscape. As a ship sails along a frozen ocean in the background of the image, a severed pair of women's legs wearing red ice-skating boots cuts swiftly to and fro across the frame. While these torso-less legs may recall the baby's own confinement to a wheelchair, the twin brothers' fetish objects, the fatal red shoes of Hans Christian Andersen's fairy-tale which ends with the brutal amputation of a pleasure-seeking girl's feet, or the misogyny that underlies the surrealists' fascination with the fragmented female form, they simultaneously represent the ability of the baby to visualise life and mobility outside of the family structure, and to use her own physical and psychic wounds as well as the family's destructive patterns of desire as the starting point for creative acts of imagination. In effect, the baby here doubles the gestures made by Rimminen and Roche themselves.

This possibility of a distinctly female surrealist vision is again suggested toward the end of the film when, as the narrator tells us that someone is going to 'give the game away', the magician-sister picks up a knife from the white tablecloth, directly evoking images from Maya Deren's *Meshes of the Afternoon* (1943), another film in which the architectural structure of the home combines with film's transformative effect on space and time to convey an audio-visual sense of the strangeness of subjective experience. If the animated familial desires that find no place in live-action home movie footage emerge initially as forces that deform *The Stain*'s female protagonists – decorporealising the mother, maddening the sister, and crippling the baby

– Rimminen and Roche draw on animation's capacity to exceed live-action's depiction of the world as it is to depict the possibility that deformation might mutate into transformation through acts of imagination. Though the film ends with the death of the twin brothers and the collapsing of the sister's house of cards, as a naked female body crashes through the window of the oppressive dining room and flies out over the open sea, we recall again the film's opening shot, which memorialises the efforts of women's rights campaigner Vera Havel to conquer the twin peaks of Mount Charlotte at the age of 78.

References

Butler, J. (2005) *Giving an Account of Oneself.* New York: Fordham University Press.

Citron, M. (1999) 'What's Wrong with this Picture?', in *Home Movies and Other Necessary Fictions.* Minneapolis: University of Minnesota Press.

Laplanche, J. (1999) 'The Drive and Its Source-Object: Its Fate in the Transference', in *Essays on Otherness.* New York: Routledge, 117–32.

The Stain: Interviews with Marjut Rimminen and Christine Roche

Fairy-tales frequently explore the horrors inside the domestic cupboard, often crammed full of evil mothers, traitorous fathers and twisted siblings. In the old days, the apparatus of magical settings and props helped to distance the reader from seeing how close the stories were to everyday life, as did later glosses which scapegoated step-parents and step-siblings. *The Stain* (1991), based loosely on a real domestic tragedy, returns to the primal scene of the fairy-tale, inside the nuclear family, where the happy ending is a fantasy as impossible as the wheelchair-using sister's dream of skating.

A woman's voice, comfy as cocoa at bedtime, narrates the events for us, while several animation techniques illustrate the actions. The first part, in drawn images, shows Mummy and Daddy who play games in a house by the sea, games which we never see, but which involve pursuit and capture, and clothes being scattered. A girl and then twin boys are born, and the games continue. Eventually, another girl is born, the parents disappear, and the baby takes a fall down the stairs, which leaves her crippled for life. In the second part, rendered mainly with animated puppets, barely dormant tensions and resentments begin to crack the claustrophobic domestic peace of the children. The youngest child, petulant and messy, retreats into a fantasy world (expressed as drawn animation). The older sister obsessively cleans the house, always vainly striving to wash out a stain made by the 'baby', which will never come out, a 'stain' whose full meaning is elucidated only at the end. Meanwhile, the twins work in the City, and indulge their secret perversions on the sly. As the musical soundtrack swells to an operatic crescendo, everyone finally snaps and someone 'gives the game away', revealing the incestuous secret which has crippled all their lives.

Images from *The Stain* (1991)
© Smoothcloud Films

Like Greek tragedy, even though the outcome is already known from the newspaper clipping which opens the film, nothing prepares the audience for the inevitable climax which ensues, the sense of terror augmented by the sudden jump cuts between the drawn and the three-dimensional, which the score underpins beautifully. Its visceral impact is like an excellent production of Oedipus Rex, which itself was, after all, just another family drama. (Felperin 1992: 57)

The Stain came about because illustrator/cartoonist Christine Roche and animation filmmaker Marjut Rimminen had wanted for some time to make a film together about the family as an institution.[1] They spent many hours in conversation working through various ideas, and their own personal histories. Then, almost simultaneously they came across a news item – about a pair of octogenarian twins in Slough-on-Sea, near Eastbourne, committing suicide following a row about a gravy stain on the table-cloth – that sparked their imaginations, one hearing it on the radio, the other seeing it in a newspaper, and from this they developed a story that became the film.

Their initial treatment for the film argued 'With animation one can give presence and meaning to concepts like: unconscious; id/ego/superego; reality/phantasy; what is the relationship between between the inside and the outside; as well as express feelings, and illustrate the dynamics of relationships.' Some of this can be seen in the extracts from the notebook Christine Roche kept during the development of the film, presented in the next chapter. The following comments by Rimminen and Roche on their creative process are drawn from separate interviews with each filmmaker conducted at different time periods.[2]

Research and development

CR: What was interesting in the pre-production stage was that we let each other be completely free to talk, a lot of which did appear in the final film, but some didn't. In terms of deciding what was to be portrayed, what neither of us ever did was to question ourselves as to why, so it was able to grow organically. It was only at the editing stage, some two, three years later, sitting behind the editor, we'd look at each other and say 'this means X'. It was during the edit, as we were watching, that the violence of the feelings really came through, but during that preparatory period, it was just about letting ourselves be led by the subconscious.

MR: Christine and I decided to go to Eastbourne and play sleuth. We talked to journalists and people in the town, but nobody knew or would speculate on the suicide. We went to the house, peering in from outside. This gave us a lot of insight: the detached house, the high walls with broken glass on them to keep intruders out, indicated wealth and isolation. Everything was immaculately kept, even the greenhouse windows were clean. The curtains were drawn, letting in only a little daylight. It all indicated control freakery, and these became the big sister's qualities.

There were things we observed that we used: an older man mowing the lawn, whose looks and dress were like those of the twins in the film, and some things we didn't. Going there made it somehow very real to us.

MR: As part of our research, we had weekly meetings with Julia Vellacott, a psychotherapist specialising in suicide. At the beginning it was not so much about the story; her first question to us was 'why does this story interest you?' So it became *our* story. We had to think: why were *we* interested? All this generated so much energy, and prompted such realisations. The first thing we changed was the victim – the sibling had to become a girl because we needed to identify with her, we don't necessarily understand the men. Julia gave us reading lists, books about dysfunctional families and family secrets, which gave us more confidence to tackle the issues. Often the problem with personal films is that they are too personal, they lose universality.

But research can go on forever, you need to know when to stop and leave something to be discovered. Since animation takes such a long time it needs to have some discoveries along the way. The scene in which the photo of the daughter/sister as a baby is scribbled on, defaced – that wasn't something that was planned, it just happened as the picture was there, and it worked.

CR: All the research is something you do, digest, then spit it out but without reference, instead of trying to grab onto things to illustrate a concept. It's important not to get stuck in a concept from the beginning, be frozen to it. The baby was originally a boy but became a girl, because that's what we knew. The storyboard was played with, allowing for a process of 'what would happen if...?', and seeing what felt right. It tells you, as writers often say, the puppet master becomes the puppet.

MR: A storyboard is never finished, it's constantly changing, which is very

Production still from *The Stain* © Marjut Rimminen (right) & Christine Roche (left)

exciting, because it means you're evaluating as you go along. Clearly, however, 2D animation needs to follow a storyboard. So every morning I'd redraw the sequence that was to be shot that day. Working on such a small scale, as we were, can make things more flexible. For example, we did the house as a model, but it didn't look right, it felt too table-top, so we changed it to drawn.

CR: The film was mainly edited at the storyboard stage, although some sequences had to be cut or shortened later, for example, some of the twins' fantasies, and where to put the sequences of the boy's room with the Virgin Mary icon, or the shoes.

MR: The edit was a long and hard process – even though the structure is there, it can be improved and clarified by good editing. An editor brings a fresh eye – at the end of two years' animation you become rather blind. The mere cutting of thirty seconds can hurt but then makes it so much sharper.

Structure and style

MR: I've always had an interest in different techniques and styles, from working in commercials. Each offers its own qualities for storytelling, and mixing them can expose layers of perception and psychology. Originally we intended to use the fact that Christine and I had such different drawing styles to explore the characters' different subjectivities. But because Christine was designing the characters, I found myself blocked.

The solution was to use puppet animation for the 'reality' sequences, with drawings as the subjective or fantasies of individual characters. Even though I had never done stop-frame animation before.

Image from *The Stain*

CR: I was interested in the challenge and the potential of a collage effect. As a visual artist that gives you more leeway, to add extra things, emphasise certain objects. We wanted it to be quite theatrical, and structured it around the three sittings at table ... at the shooting stage we decided to make it morning, noon and evening, so there could be more play with the lighting.

The first part is the history, the mother realising that the father has raped the daughter, burying her head in the sand; the second part is the moment of now, and time passing, living an apparently 'normal', but really a fantasy of, family life. No sounds intrude from the outside world; the third part is the sequence at the dinner table. Everyone is mad. The mother who had refused to acknowledge what was happening; the fantasy of men going to work, her fantasy of perfect order, being the angel of the house, all this is boiling under the surface, but the family still sit down to the meal. For the young sister, madness is her freedom, her escape. And now we hear the sounds of the outside world.

A consistent illustration style is used for the history. Other drawing styles are the fantasies of the brothers, the baby, the mother.

The 'cartoony style' sequences (e.g. the men as judges, Hitler) were always seen from child's point-of-view; another example is the mother with the apple (I always remember her as transforming into a witch, although in fact she doesn't!). The girl sees things in cartoon terms, not quite grotesque, but clichéd; very black and white in meaning, although we also see that she's the only one who has imagination. The puppet animation is the reality, and the live-action shows what she does i.e. hiding things away, whereas her fantasy of order lies in the drawn.

Process

MR: I like working with perspective, so I did the layouts, Christine did the design, backgrounds and characters. Because it was the first time I had animated puppets, our plans didn't always work out. Because puppets can only do what puppets can do. The big sister sequence was modelled from Christine's drawn designs. Christine likes small feet, so there was a problem with her tiny shoes; it was impossible to animate them walking, so to cheat, we have her go to lean on the wall.

CR: The wheelchair for the girl was originally there because it was easier to animate, but then it needed the backstory of how she came to be disabled. Retrospectively it can be seen as symbolic – sexually falling from grace.

MR: The music was there from the beginning, the

Images from *The Stain*

Production stills from *The Stain*

rhythms trod into memory as we were shooting. The operatic music fits with the fact of having fixed expressions on the puppet faces.

CR: Because of the way Marjut felt towards the younger sister and the way she animated her, she began to assume a persona which I didn't think of in the same way as Marjut did. So I started resenting this child as being totally manipulative, awful and then I started identifying with the older sister who originally I didn't like very much. Then I thought, hang on, there's something behind this woman who goes round hating the cleaning and things she's doing. And she ends up alone in the house, totally mad. I felt warmer towards her, and that was a surprise.

MR: It's not so much a case of manipulation as of survival. It was survival in my mind. The only way for her.

Notes

1 They had previously collaborated on a film based on Roche's cartoon strips, *I'm Not a Feminist But...* (1986).
2 Interviews with the author: Marjut Rimminen in September 1991 and June 2008; Christine Roche in October 1991 and June 14, 2008.

Reference

Felperin, L. (1992) 'The Stain (review)', in *Sight and Sound*, 2, 7, 57.

the BABY:

is at the center of
things:

of the plot
of attention.

it is the stain

it needs / demands
sucks dry
provokes / controls.

sister
it is the child (illegitimate?
incest?)

Sister / Mother   Women = mothers
always.

it is at the center of the web.
the power of the powerless. Finally,
it pulls strings – it gets
away with MURDER

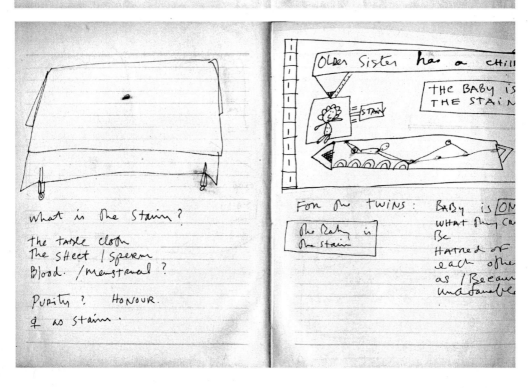

in spite of the most obvious
evidence that a great deal
more must constantly be
going on in your mind that
can be known to your
consciousness. Come, let
yourself be taught something
on this point! What is in
your mind does not coincide
with what you are conscious
of; whether something is
going on in your mind
and whether you hear of
it are two different
things.
Freud.

Uses of Enchantment
B. Bettleheim.

The father can never satisfy the
void of the child. The desire
that
can not be resolved.

The props of real Family
(House / Walls / Victoriana)
serving as devices to

deny sexuality.
the
victimisation: no Breeding.

Denial of Sexuality

what is the Stain?

The table cloth
The sheet / sperm
Blood. / Menstrual ?

Purity ?   Honour.
+ as Stain.

Older Sister has a child

THE BABY IS
THE STAIN

= STAIN

For the TWINS: BABY is ONe
The Baby is   what they can
the stain   be
                              Hatred of
                              each other
                              as / Because
                              unatainable

3 way power

3 as victims.

Death of Mother when Baby
is Born?
Do they Symbolically kill
Mother when Baby is Born?
Mother / Sister (the same?)
cat & mice game in the
House.
Fantasy or Reality — same: its
their perceptions that Cont.

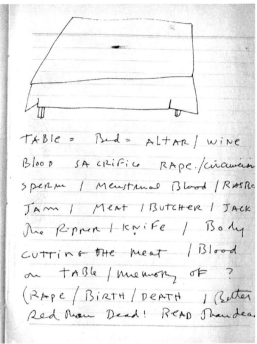

TABLE = Bed = ALTAR / WINE
BLOOD SACRIFICE RAPE. / Circumcion
sperm / Menstrual Blood / RASBe
JAM / MEAT / BUTCHER / JACK
the Ripper / KNIFE / BODY
CUTTING the MEAT / Blood
on TABLE / memory of ?
(RAPE / BIRTH / DEATH / Better
Red than Dead! READ than dea

Ⓐ The Sister:

She's the stain. SHe is stained.

The BABy is hers. 'out out DAmm spot'

She serves / cleans / protects the Baby.

Keeps it [glass jar drawing] under a glass jar.

Stops it from leaving.

is the Baby illegitimate / Fathers Baby - Incest.

The BABy is a Girl? SHe protects the girl. against men. testors of the girl.

Women as Stain.

Women as victims.

women colluding with existing order / ideology.

women as castractors - Does she castrate her son ? turns him into a girl -

use

The Baby is is their BABY?

TWINS + older sister.

Live together in a Big House.

ONce upon a time lived ..... (The Fairytale) in a Big House by the sea.

I Ncest

a BaBy is Born.

Whore the Father? UNSPoken.

HATred For the CHILD WHO SPLits them up.

They live together as BROthers/sisters/Fathers/Husbands

the STAIN is the Guilt.

They finally kill it,

They murder each ot

FOR the twins: THE BABY is [THE STAIN]

CAUSE FOR DISHARMONY.

the order of the house is out of [ORDER.] when [Child] is BORN

The 3rd one, the odd one. disrupts the symmetry.

[twins / twin set / Things in two's - [the ARK: [PAIRS]

[the House is the ark.]

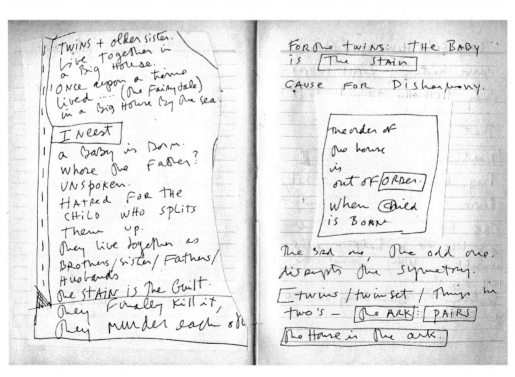

Wheel chair / her extraordin
energy. Seductress - Provokes
manipulates.
Reality / Fantasy dosn't
matter — its her perception

oF self

provoke
twins.

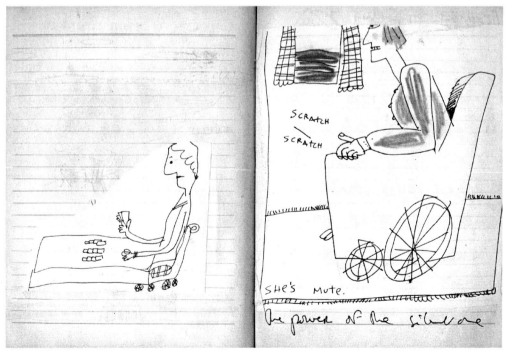

SCRATCH

SCRATCH

SHe's Mute.

the power of the silent one

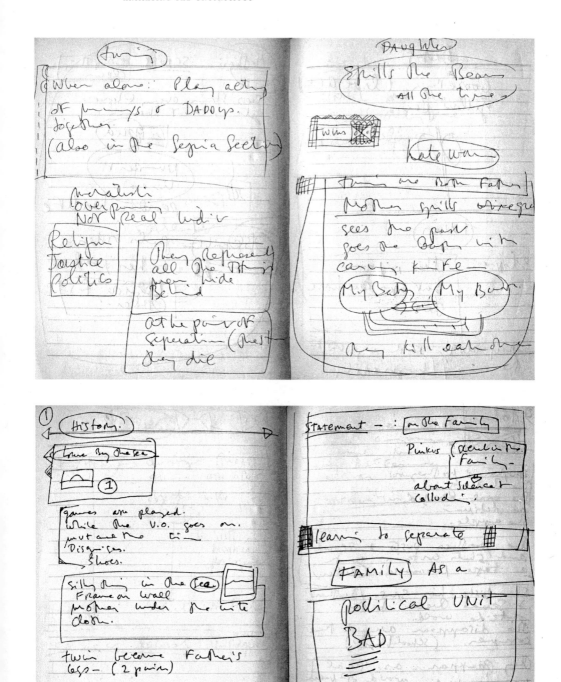

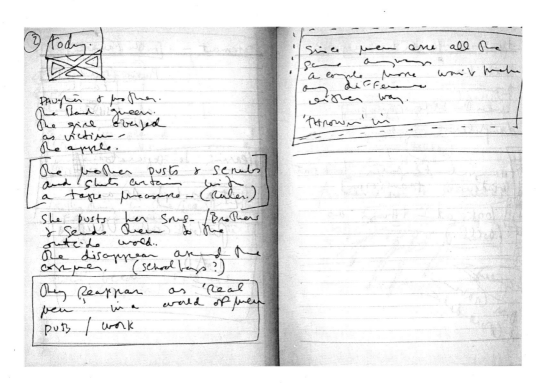

(2) Today.

DAUGHTER & brother.
The Bad queen.
The girl overlaid
as victim —
The apple.

The mother dusts & scrubs
and shuts curtain with
a tape measure — (Ruler.)

She dusts her sons/Brothers
& sends them to the
outside world..
The disappear around the
corner. (schoolboys?)

They Reappear as 'Real
men' in a world of men
pub / work

Since men are all the
same anyway
a couple more won't make
any difference
either way.

'Thrown' in

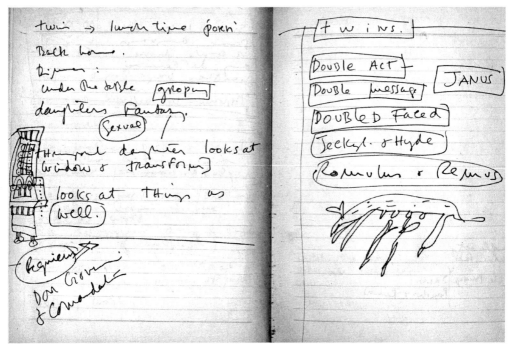

twins → lunch time porn.
Back home.
Dinner:
under the table groping
daughters Fantasy.
Sexual /
Husband/daughter looks at
window & transform
looks at Things as
well.

Requiem
Don Giovanni
& Commadale

twins.

Double Act
Double message   JANUS
Doubled Faced
Jeckyl. & Hyde
Romulus & Remus

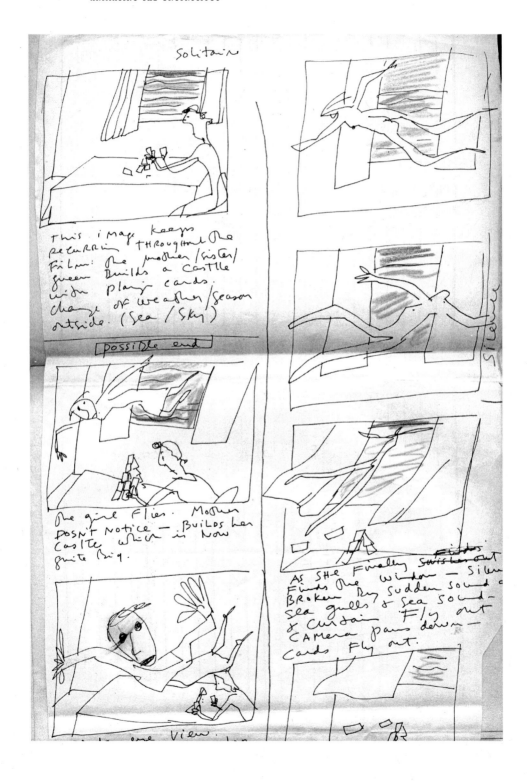

Extracts from Christine Roche's sketchbooks for *The Stain* © Christine Roche

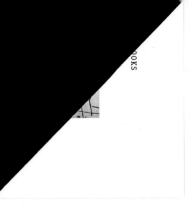

The Animated Body and Its Material Nature
by Ruth Hayes

We interface with the world and others through our bodies. While we may like to believe that our conscious selves perceive and process all that we are exposed to, the raw data of experience comes first to our senses, unmediated. Especially with intimate experiences, we construct an understanding of reality only after we've woven together the disparate threads of sensory input to form a whole. Many of the films in the *Animating the Unconscious: Desire and Sexuality* DVD collection (2007) work at constructing a subjective sense of reality from fragmented first-person experience. Others are commentaries on sexual and relational phenomena that the filmmakers have observed. In several, the material qualities of the hand-drawn line, the juxtaposition of digital simulations of line, collage, space and light or the mix of art media in one work play on viewers' senses to give them perceptual experiences that echo physical and emotional ones.[1]

The films discussed below attempt to communicate individuals' subjective, lived experiences. In his writing on the animated film, documentary and realism, Paul Ward introduces Bill Nichols' idea of 'magnitude' to discuss how animation can portray the reality of subjective experiences:

> 'Magnitude' ... constitutes that which cannot (easily) be represented in a representation. It lies in the realm of the affective, the emotional, and as such appears to have little to do with the 'rational' and 'empirical' realities so often seen as the foundation of good documentary practice [...] 'Magnitude' refers not only to how accurately, or for what purpose, a documentary represents a recognisable anterior reality, but also how this makes us feel. (2008: 20)

The feelings triggered by the use of different materials may be subtle, but they play an important role in how these animations make us feel. They are as vital to the work as the content of specific images, the action, or sounds and words heard on the audio-track. The animator invests physical and emotional energy in the deliberate designing and crafting of each frame, as he or she builds the temporal structure of the work. The artefacts of this process flicker in front of viewers continuously, reminding them of the work's constructed nature and the conscious effort and subjective intent underlying it. This evidence of the hand at work, indexical traces of the animator's efforts, can communicate states of mind and evoke similar states and emotions in viewers.

Traditional cartoon animation, emphasising the personalities of characters, seeks to efface and make seamless the fact that each successive drawing is made of lines that are different from those in the preceding one. Calling attention to the line itself distracts from the believability of the character as an independent agent in its own world. In non-traditional drawn animation, the artist may want to foreground visible differences between frames, using it to amplify mood or announce his or her subjectivity and/or the desire to engage viewers in a similar subjective state. Distinctive line quality emphasises the animation's constructed nature, and puts viewers on notice that the image is unstable. It might metamorphose at any moment.

In *The Hat* (1999), Michèle Cournoyer uses a coarse brush and ink line to collapse the time between a young girls' sexual abuse and her adult persona as an exotic dancer and sex worker. Cournoyer's images are iconic, but the broad gestures that created them are indexical. They are evidence of the passion with which she approaches her subject. The simplicity of their forms allow them to metamorphose rapidly from one to another, creating a confusion in the viewer that evokes the destruction of personal boundaries as a result of the violation of sexual abuse. The man's hat becomes the woman's breasts with very little alteration in shape. In one long metamorphosis sequence the figures of the girl/woman and the penis constantly merge and reform themselves. The woman's figure loses its proportions and the line becomes rougher. The singular focus required to generate a long sequence of hand-drawn animation is intensified by repetition. Repetition of forms mirrors repetition of abuse and repetition of trauma. The unstable imagery and the coarse brushwork convey an unfiltered directness that is urgently drawn, as if the artist is rushing to exorcise the experience.

In *Repete* (1995), Michaela Pavlátová uses a similarly coarse, quickly drawn line to construct three couples' interpersonal routines and show the collapse of their relationships. But Pavlátová's line is not an urgent exorcism. Instead it communicates the haste of an idea arising from closely observed behaviours, and impatience with the roles that women assume. These cartoons of relationships set in a contextual scenario of a man walking his dog, drawn in black, show stereotypical gendered behaviours. One woman feeds, one rescues, and the third offers sexual satisfaction but never delivers. Each interaction is a cycle that repeats several times in tight sync with the musical soundtrack. The gestural lines that Pavlátová uses to draw the interactions become predictable and rhythmic through repetition, much as an individual's idiosyncratic behaviours might become over-familiar to their partner.

Pavlátová draws the three couples in different combinations of colour and media. Red crayon, blue paint and teal crayon identify each one's repetitious and predictable exchange. The frames within the frame that contain these scenarios distance the viewer. When the dog disrupts this order, he violates the frames of the established relationships, running through everything, scattering and fragmenting the lines themselves. The crayon and paint strokes dissolve into chaos and then resolve into new relationships.

One casualty of the increased use of digital tools in animation is the direct connection to the animator's gesture that comes from a hand-drawn line. In vector-based animation software, the line can be made smooth, distancing it from its origins in the hand. This may parallel the emotional distance of promotional animations or cartoons. Alys Hawkins resists the impulse to process her digital lines in *Crying and Wanking* (2002). She keeps the traces of her strokes on the Wacom tablet raw, communicating isolation and the grief that results from the betrayal of intimacy. Hawkins contrasts her line drawings with photographic and video elements. The juxtapositions of these different materials evoke the protagonist's sense of self at different stages: one of brooding and grief, one of restoration and healing and one of reconnection to the world, and in the latter, self-reflexively piecing together images as she recovers balance after the event.

The film begins with low resolution black and white video images of an eye, a hand making ink doodles, a twisting phone cord and animated sketches of forms that reveal themselves to be point-of-view images of the protagonist's own naked body. Low-resolution video references home movies and the confessional approaches of other independent filmmakers such as Sadie Benning. Wavering lines portray her breasts, belly and crotch. These loom large in the foreground while her small feet recede towards a vanishing point. After the title, an animated face appears and says: 'You asked about my past and I told you.' This female voice seems to speak to the viewer, however it soon becomes clear that the 'you' is her lover. In subsequent live-action shots, a male hand draws animated images onto the woman's belly, as if using it as his canvas. The doodles are charming and playful. A small bird disappears into her navel and the words 'You made me feel beautiful' encircle it. But the drawings are actually superimposed on the footage of the woman, not drawn on her skin, and the footage was not shot from her point-of-view. This sequence represents a remembered intimacy. It is reconstructed, not an indexical record of it.

The live-action imagery has immediacy, juxtaposed as it is with drawn sequences of the woman brushing her teeth, rubbing her hands and wiping a coffee mug. The sight of real flesh after drawn representations of the body is arresting. However, the drawn sequences have other emotional reality effects. The subjective point-of-view framing, unexaggerated motion and lack of both polish and detail express direct, first person observation.

The woman reconnects with herself in a long drawn sequence, again using point-of-view framing, in which she steps into a tub and soaks. The first point-of-view animated sequences began with fractured, disconnected shots that build to recognisable images of the body. The continuous nature of this sequence reaffirms the links between the body and the self. The lines anchor themselves in space, so that the body moves naturalistically in the water and tub. Again, the lack of detail and polish in these lines communicate direct experience, but this is a restorative and contemplative scene, in which Hawkins recuperates the lover's gaze for herself and emerges whole.

The end credits of the film are written directly on the wet skin of the woman's body, shot in live-action in the bathtub. The wet ink runs down the skin proving that it's not superimposed as in the earlier shot with the lover. This is an indexical record of the woman's use of her own body as her canvas, as well as her presentation of her experience as a creative work to an audience of outsiders. As such, it completes the act of re-appropriation that she needs to resolve the crisis.

In discussing the 'materiality' of digital imagery, one can distinguish between the use of tools that directly capture a physical object or movement, via digital photography, scanning or drawing on a tablet, and those that simulate dimension, lighting effects. The physical presence of the artist is more evident in the former, and less so in the latter. In *Never Like the First Time!* (2006), Jonas Odell uses both types of digital animation techniques to interpret the stories of four people asked to recount how each lost his or her virginity. In all four, the voice-over interview audio occupies the viewer's conscious mind, while visual elements comment on the action and feed the senses. Each experience is qualitatively different, and that difference is visible in the material characteristics that this digital work synthesises. Yet the synthetic nature of these material effects also evoke an emotional absence, whether it be a distance from the narrator's youth, nostalgia or numbness resulting from violence.

In his design for the first story, in which a man recalls his sexual initiation as a teenager, Odell contrasts hand-drawn and digital techniques in

Images from *Never Like the First Time!* (2006) © Filmtecknarna F. Animation AB

three ways to communicate a light, comedic and upbeat tone. He combines two-dimensional representation with computer-generated camera movement and depth effects that evoke three-dimensional space. He mixes photographic elements of textures, bathroom fixtures, lamps and other furnishings into the drawn outlines of the scenes. Odell's characters are line drawn but he has animated them as articulated two-dimensional puppets. The exaggerated features and linear quality are juxtaposed with movement generated by the software's interpolation between keyframes. Each of these contrasts heightens the sense of a memory that is being recalled and re-enacted. Synthesised camera movements through layers of flat scenic artwork give the environment an aspect of insubstantiality as if seen through memory instead of immediate experience. Photographed elements might anchor the story in non-fiction, however drawn elements and variations in line quality (from the crude to the more refined) suggest the inevitable unreliability of all memory. The characters' gestures lack the subtlety of 'real' human motion but instead operate somewhat mechanically as dolls or automata might. This makes them engaging and comical, but also suggests the narrator's distance from a younger version of himself. By his overt construction of characters and environment and his avoidance of cohesive realism Odell mirrors the work of construction that takes place when we convert our lived experience first to memory, and then to story.

In the second narrative, Odell uses rotoscoping to emphasise the deliberate and matter-of-fact approach that a 14-year-old girl and her partner take to the process of shedding their innocence. The voice-over recollection is illustrated by the white outlines of two empty figures rotoscoped from live-action. The outlines suggest both the absence of deep connection between the girl and the boy and the narrator's amused distance from herself as a 14-year-old. Here there is little sense of the hand-drawn line. Odell's outlines are simple and clean with a minimum of variation in width or solidity. He superimposes the figures over realistic, detailed backgrounds apparently composited from photographic elements. The camera moves that follow the figures emphasise the realism of these conventional middle-class settings. The lack of evidence of a distinctive human hand creates a space for projection. How does each viewer fill that void?

The third subject in the series tells how she lost her virginity through rape. As with the second story, Odell's visualisation of this episode uses live-action filmmaking conventions to structure the shots; however, his processing of the footage (re)creates a cold, threatening and fractured world through which the protagonist and her two friends navigate blindly. High contrast black and white imagery buries in darkness details that might provide familiar anchors

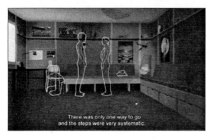 

Images from *Never Like the First Time!*

or navigational tools for viewers. Extreme camera angles distort objects. References to consumerism and alienation pepper the shots. A bar code occupies the left of the frame in the first shot. One background has a graph paper pattern. Some drawn elements have the generic feel of clip-art. In other shots, frenetic lines sketched around characters' heads evoke the anger and impulsiveness of graffiti. In this story, there is no subtlety to the young woman's experience of violation and loss of control over her body. Everything is in stark contrast.

Odell provides a sense of transcendence in the fourth and final episode. An older man recalls his first sexual experience with warmth and nostalgia. Odell returns to the use of articulated 2D puppets in 3D space that he features in the first episode, but here he composes artwork almost entirely from photographic elements and appropriated advertising imagery from the early twentieth century. These contribute to his portrayal not only of an innocent youth, but a pre-World War II milieu of gentility and ease. Ornate elements of lace, foliage and wallpaper patterns create visual richness. Clothing advertisements torn from old magazines slide to the floor when the two characters undress. These material artefacts of another age make the scene tangible and also carry historically determined meanings and evocations of social mores and attitudes. The flat aesthetic of this narrative has no hand-drawing, unlike the first and third stories. Its complex artwork and saturated palette are richer and warmer than in the second story. The collage artwork composes a cohesive world. Just as the two characters seem to retain their innocence even after their sexual experience, no impulsive sketches or other extraneous

Images from *Never Like the First Time!*

Images from *Never Like the First Time!*

visual elements reveal irony, cynicism or self-consciousness. Here, it is a non-material element that communicates the 'magnitude' of this particular story. Odell simulates atmospheric effects through light and colour that reflect the joy and sense of the sublime invoked by the interviewee. At the beginning, the light is neutral and scenic elements are nearly monochrome. Later, saturated red, green and yellow-orange hues flood the man's small apartment while the deep blue of the night sky fills the window. At the end of the story, scenic elements are vibrantly coloured, communicating the man's sense of wonder at the magical qualities of the newly perceived city.

Ian Gouldstone also matches first-person voice-over narration of an apparently actual experience with digitally constructed images to represent an intense, violent sexual encounter. However, in his film *guy101* (2006) he uses them to focus attention on emotional distance itself. As the narrator recounts making the acquaintance of 'Keith' in a chat room, Gouldstone recreates the experience of entering and browsing through it by using computer-generated icons, text and other elements appropriated from the operating system interface. He constructs a screen-based virtual environment onto which viewers may project their own vision of the events they are told about. The narrator describes his knowledge of Keith in terms of his house, car and collectibles. These are surface details gleaned from posted photos and cursory exchanges of text messages. But even as these various material aspects of Keith's life are described, the immaterial digital screen reconstructed in the animation itself keeps us at a distance. Apart from one re-enacted shot of a figure masked by darkness at the climax of the film, we only see superficial iconographic representations of Keith's world. The 'chat room' is virtual. Text messages tell us who is in it, but their physicality is completely veiled. In this world, language, as text or icon, communicates everything. Gouldstone uses this lack of materiality to keep us removed from Keith and any understanding of his actions, emotions or desires; *guy101* leaves viewers disoriented, shocked and uncomfortable, feelings that the narrator might have experienced as a remote witness to Keith's story.

Of the films discussed here, Marjut Rimminen and Christine Roche's *The Stain* (1991) has the most tenuous connection to a lived experience. As with Hawkins', Odell's and Gouldstone's works, voice carries the weight of the narrative in *The Stain*. However, filmmakers Rimminen and Roche actively use art media and animation techniques to split viewers' perceptions among the characters' and the narrator's different subjective realities, and in the process construct a critique of bourgeois family dynamics. Using the newspaper story of a double suicide as a jumping-off point, they develop a narrative about incest that depends on the contrasting materials and reality effects of drawn and puppet animation as well as several short live-action sequences.

The language of the story's prologue has fairy-tale elements but the sarcastic tone of the narrator's voice sets up a conflict between the ideology of family unity and lived experience. The imagery mirrors this divide. The action is animated using cel techniques with flat characters and more detailed backgrounds. But a grainy texture overlays the imagery, as if dust and dirt have accumulated on the artwork, casting a grimy shadow over the story that hints at the family's corruption. Dust and dirt are anathema to traditional cel animation so for animators this effect may cause some discomfort. For other viewers it may trigger and frustrate unconscious impulses to clean things up. In any case, they announce the shadowy side of this domestic narrative.

Rimmenen and Roche animate the 'present' of the story with puppet animation, using the reality effects of three-dimensional space and lighting to emphasise the tension and animosity amongst the characters. Shots of the sisters and brothers staged around a dinner table suggest the hierarchy of their relationships and routines. The wheelchair-bound younger sister (the 'baby') and her tall, domineering sister oppose each other at either end of the long table. The brothers, represented as Siamese twins, sit in the middle. The puppets' motions are stiff and mechanical. Their movements and mask-like faces communicate the rigidity required to maintain a state of denial.

The filmmakers use two-dimensional collage and under-the-camera drawn animation to represent the wider world outside the house. Appropriated photographic elements of ships and airplanes reference the real world and the rapid passage of historical time from which the family seems completely divorced. Sequences of non-cel drawn animation express the two sisters' different points-of-view and desires. Juxtaposed with the puppet scenes, they provide commentary on the roles they play in the larger scheme of things. The younger sister's reveries are brightly painted and use loose lines. The older sister's dedication to her brothers as the men of the family is portrayed in simpler sequences of iconographic imagery. In one, the strong rhythms of the music and the narrator's sarcasm accompany simple lines that diagram bourgeois ideology and how it operates as a system. In another, the film-makers inter-cut drawn animation that shows the older sister cleaning with puppet sequences that show a real stain highly visible on the tablecloth. These are drawn in ink and brush using minimal colour and sketched with the same sense of urgency we see in Cournoyer's and Pavlátová's films.

Finally, a series of highly edited live-action shots portray the older sis-ter's obsessive cover-up as we see her white-gloved hands clean and tidy the house. Threadbare carpets, a filthy sink and silver service stuffed into linen drawers echo the corruption at the foundation of the household. The live-action has the reality effects of 3D space and lighting, but the rapid montage of the hands' movements disrupt these to further emphasise dysfunction and delusion.

The live-action and puppet-animated sequences of *The Stain* present fractured versions of the family's objective existence, while the physical qualities of line and the art media of the several 2D drawn sequences add layers of their subjective realities. The juxtaposition of different materials and techniques in *The Stain* puts viewers to work identifying their own responses, 'reading' these different realities and constructing meaning from the whole.

Animators can use an infinite variety of materials to tell stories, comment on social and psychological realities or explore their own personal experi-ences. Voice and image may carry literal content, but the physical qualities of the materials from which the imagery is made, processed by the animator's frame-by-frame construction of a separate temporal reality, can help viewers access a sense of the original experience and/or story that inspired the work. Viewers can appreciate new subjective positions through close observation and consideration of the material properties of an animated work as well as the emotional and visceral reactions they have to those properties. We engage in similar practices as we respond to and make meaning of our own experi-ences in the world.

Note

1 These are aspects of the works that may not be recognised in the first viewing. Really 'seeing' them and re-constructing them takes an effort that usually means multiple viewings. As audio

can so easily overpower image, turning off the sound during the second or third viewing helps one detach from the narrative and focus on the image and its materiality.

One of the unfortunate side effects of the ubiquity of media on the web, in sites such as YouTube for example, is that image details that reveal the material qualities of the artwork are lost through bad quality compression. Blocky compression artefacts blur line strokes and limit viewers' perception to main action, sound and colour. To really see the details of the animated image, one needs to locate high-quality digital reproductions of films, if it is not possible to access to them in their original formats.

Reference

Ward, P. (2008) 'Animated Realities: The Animated Film, Documentary, Realism', in *Reconstruction: Studies in Contemporary Culture*, 8, 2, XXX?

Index